P9-EDE-743

COMMUNITY
MENTAL
HEALTH

WITHDRAWN
UTSA LIBRARIES

Nashville • Abingdon Press • New York

Rx tsa

COMMUNITY MENTAL HEALTH:
the role of church & temple

HOWARD J. CLINEBELL, Jr.
editor

Copyright © 1970 by Abingdon Press

All rights in this book are reserved.
No part of the book may be reproduced in any
manner whatsoever without written permission of
the publishers except brief quotations embodied in
critical articles or reviews. For information address
Abingdon Press, Nashville, Tennessee.

ISBN 0-687-09221-3

Library of Congress Catalog Card Number: 71-124752

Scripture quotations noted RSV are from the Revised
Standard Version of the Bible, copyrighted 1946
and 1952 by the Division of Christian Education,
National Council of Churches, and are used by
permission.

Scripture quotations noted NEB are from *The New
English Bible, New Testament,* Second Edition, ©
the Delegates of the Oxford University Press and the
Syndics of the Cambridge University Press, 1961,
1970. Reprinted by permission.

The quotation from *The Angel That Troubled
the Waters* and other plays copyright 1928 by
Thornton Wilder; copyright renewed 1956 by
Thornton Wilder.

John B. Oman's chapter "One Parish's Educational
Counseling Plan" is reprinted from the May, 1968,
issue of *Pastoral Psychology.* Copyright 1968 by
Meredith Corporation.

SET UP, PRINTED, AND BOUND BY THE
PARTHENON PRESS, AT NASHVILLE,
TENNESSEE, UNITED STATES OF AMERICA

FOREWORD

When the Community Mental Health Centers Act was adopted in 1963, it provided Federal support for the development of a national program of comprehensive mental health services based in local communities.

The statute was adopted in response to public demand for adequate treatment of the mentally ill. Additionally, for the first time, it established as a matter of public policy the need to provide a wide range of mental health services to *prevent* mental illness and to improve the mental health of the American people.

From its inception, the community mental health services program has recognized the importance of the churches and members of the clergy in meeting the mental health needs of the people.

In 1961, when the Joint Commission on Mental Illness and Health published their final report *Action for Mental Health,* the survey indicated that 42 percent of the persons who encounter mental or emotional distress seek out the assistance of a clergyman as the first person to whom they turn for help.

Since that time, community mental health centers have been organized in each of the fifty states, and their staffs have learned that members of each community come to them for help and guidance in a wide variety of living situations in addition to requests for treatment of mental illness.

Mental health professionals and other supporting personnel are learning to extend their helping abilities through consultation with all manner of persons who shape community attitudes and events. As a matter of fact, the use of techniques of consultation has become a major concern of all community mental health services personnel, as communities search for effective means to collaborate in meeting their problems.

COMMUNITY MENTAL HEALTH

In itself, consultation is not a new profession, but a means of communication. Consultation may well become the most effective avenue through which the gatekeepers of the community can help to reverse the procedures of confrontation and violent dissent.

In the belief that the clergy, with mental health professionals can make a significant contribution toward solving the special mental health problems of communities, the National Institute of Mental Health is cooperating with the National Council of Churches in an effort to discuss collaborative roles in the area of community mental health.

A work such as this volume, edited by Dr. Clinebell, provides information and opinion on the development of the community mental health program, expressed by men and women who have been closely associated with that development. In so doing, this book may provide an impetus to those community residents who are concerned with the improvement of modern community life.

STANLEY F. YOLLES, *M.D., Director*
National Institute of Mental Health,
1964-1970

CONTENTS

CONTENTS

INTRODUCTION
The Community Mental Health Revolution—Challenge to Churches and Temples

The phrase "community mental health movement" describes an exciting social revolution which is occurring in this period of history. It is a movement of profound human significance. Indeed, it is one of the most important social revolutions in the history of our country, perhaps of the world. Its influence will eventually be felt by every person in our land as a revolution of healing and/or of human fulfillment.

The revolution has two fronts. The first is a massive effort to win a battle that mankind has been losing through the centuries —the provision of humane, effective treatment for the mentally and emotionally disturbed. A dramatic new strategy has brought the battle to the setting where it belongs and can be won— the community. The movement is away from the futile pattern of warehouse care in isolated institutions and toward a broad continuum of early, intensive, and varied treatment in the local community.

The second front is to develop more effective ways of fostering positive mental health in all persons, to stimulate their growth and to help them release their unique potentialities for creative living and relating. Thus, the mental health revolution is good news both for the hundreds of thousands who are acutely burdened, and the millions who live half-lives (or less) of quiet or not-so-quiet desperation. Even the most mature persons among us have ample room to grow; therefore, the positive thrust of the mental health revolution should eventually benefit all persons in our society.

Here is a brief survey of how we got where we are. The whole thing began on a cold March day in 1841 when a remarkable woman, one of the great women of American history, Dorothea Lynn Dix, visited a house of correction in Massachusetts and found mentally ill people chained to the walls. That was a little over a hundred years ago in "enlightened" America.

11

She began the one-woman crusade which led to the establishment of mental hospitals. The gradual progress which was made in the humane treatment of the mentally ill was mostly scuttled by World War I and the great depression. Snakepit-like conditions in mental hospitals were, to a considerable extent, the result of the tragic effects of these two social upheavals.

Since World War II, however, the tide has begun to turn. A surge of citizen and professional interest helped to produce, in 1946, the passage of the national Mental Health Act, establishing the National Institute of Mental Health. The federal government became involved in research and helping to fund training of much-needed personnel.

In 1955, in response to continued public interest, Congress enacted the Mental Health Study Act, under which the historic Joint Commission on Mental Illness and Health was appointed. In December 1960, the final report of this Commission was presented to the President and to Congress. This is now available in a book called *Action for Mental Health*.[1] For the first time in our history, a comprehensive strategy was available on a national level for meeting the gigantic unmet needs in the mental health field.

Then in 1963, under the influence of President Kennedy, Congress authorized grants to permit states to study their mental health needs and resources and prepare a long-range comprehensive plan, state by state, by which the Grand Canyon–like chasm between *needs* and *resources* could gradually be bridged. The deadline for completing these state plans was September, 1965. It behooves each of us to learn what are the major provisions of the mental health plan in one's own state.

February 5, 1963, was a great day for mental health in this country. On that date, President Kennedy sent to Congress the first presidential message dealing exclusively with mental health and mental retardation. In it he called for a bold new approach. He said there was no use putting new money into the outmoded approach based on the old concept of giant

[1] (New York: Basic Books, 1961.)

mental hospitals out in the country. Never before had the forgotten people of our society—the mentally ill—had a champion at this level. Congress began to move. The message included a challenge to develop a fundamentally new concept. That new concept, perhaps the most exciting in the field of psychiatry since Freud, is the *comprehensive community mental health center or service*. This is the image which is guiding what is happening in our local communities. Within a few years there will be hundreds of these centers in the United States.

The community mental health service is not a new name for an outpatient clinic or even for a regional unit of a state mental health program. It is not necessarily a new complex of buildings. Basically, a community mental health service is a program and a nerve center. Its goal is to coordinate and provide mental health services to meet the total mental health needs of the community.

What services are required? First, mental health education, to teach people the principles of mental hygiene and growth, and thus prevent mental illness. Second, special education to reach community leaders. Third, early help for persons with life crises and emotional disturbances to keep them from moving into major problems. Fourth, evaluation and research; this means continual looking at the needs of communities as they change in order to keep the program geared to these needs. Fifth, consultation for ministers and other helping professionals to enhance their ability to assist persons in crises. Sixth, a wide continuum of coordinated treatment programs, including day hospitals, night hospitals, foster care homes, halfway houses, alcoholism treatment programs, treatment for the chronically mentally crippled, and programs for the mentally retarded. There will be inpatient, outpatient, and emergency services, as well as partial hospitalization in the community. General hospitals will be encouraged to include psychiatric services to make them readily available for those in crises.

Crucial in all this is the concept of *community organization*. Those responsible for mental health planning in a region seek to identify the needs of the area, plan strategy, and then develop and coordinate resources for meeting the needs.

The mental health revolution is a major challenge to churches and temples. The challenge is for them to become vigorously and creatively involved for two fundamental reasons: (1) *The mental health revolution needs the churches and temples; it needs them on both major fronts—treatment and prevention.* Without maximum church participation in this remarkable social revolution, the struggle will be slower and less effective. (2) *Churches and temples must be involved to be true to their mission and to be relevant to contemporary human needs!* The revolution needs the churches and temples; the churches and temples need the revolution. Mental health is "an idea whose time has come." If religious groups and leaders miss the boat in this revolution, they cannot stay "where the action is" in ministering to human need and pain. Mental health centers would then become the *de facto* churches in that they would be doing more to meet the growth and healing needs of persons than the churches.

A strategy is needed for motivating rank-and-file churchmen, lay and ministerial, to become involved, committed, and enthused about the mental health potentialities of both their church programs and community programs. The key to motivation is to help religious leaders discover that this is *their* revolution, as well as the mental health leaders' revolution. This discovery can be facilitated by confronting church leaders with these facts:

(1) *Mental health deals with that which is of central importance to churches and temples, the wholeness and fulfillment of people.* Churchmen who take the "ho-hum," "leave it to the psychiatrists," or "let's get back to religion and stop fooling with psychology" attitudes toward community mental health, are ignoring two facts: the basic purpose of the churches and temples is "the increase among men of the love of God and neighbor"[2]; and, as a teacher of psychiatry has stated, "a person is mentally healthy to the degree that he is able to live the two great commandments, to love God and neighbor fully." As churchmen we

[2] H. R. Niebuhr, *et al., The Purpose of the Church and Its Ministry* (New York: Harper, 1956), p. 31.

should rejoice that the mental health movement is a growing, concerted effort by person-serving agencies and professions to give human values greater priority. Churches have the chance to cooperate in this dynamic social movement. Churches and temples major in people. So does the mental health movement! We are natural and complementary allies.

(2) *Mental and spiritual health are inseparable.* The health of one's relationships with self and others (mental health), and with God, the universe, and ultimate values (spiritual health), are deeply interdependent. No understanding of mental health is complete if it ignores spiritual health. (By spiritual health, I mean the adequacy and maturity of one's relationships with the vertical dimension of existence.) No conception of spiritual health is complete if it ignores mental health. Positive mental health is synonymous with the biblical term, "wholeness." Both point to the fulfillment of human potentialities for living a constructive life in mutually satisfying, loving relationships. Mental health is a contemporary label for a century-spanning concern of the Hebrew-Christian tradition. This concern was reflected in the life style of one who said, "I have come that men may have life . . . in all its fullness" (John 10:10 NEB). Every clergyman is deeply involved in mental health concerns whether he knows it or not. As members of one of the oldest counseling, caring professions, clergymen can *affirm their heritage* by increased involvement in mental-spiritual health ministries within both religious and wider communities.

(3) *The enormous load of suffering and wasted creativity produced by an absence of mental health constitutes another reason why churches and temples have an inescapable responsibility.* Behind the cold, familiar (perhaps *too* familiar) statistics of emotional illness are the warm bodies and live souls of human beings suffering the hell of brokenness. By moralism and immature religion, churches and temples have contributed to this suffering. Even where the religion that hurts has been absent, the religion that heals has not been generally available. If churches and temples pass by on the other side of the Jericho Road of mental

illness and health, they do so at the cost of sacrificing their mission to help the troubled and heal the broken.

(4) *Religious communities have unique and essential contributions to make to the mental health revolution.* If the churches and temples don't make them, they won't be made! These contributions can enlarge and enrich the image of positive mental health by bringing an emphasis on values, meanings, and relatedness to the Spirit that permeates all of existence. Congregations can make their unique contribution to mental health best by being responsive to their reason for being. As such, they will "turn people on" to God, life, creativity, relationships, tragedy, loving, being real, and fighting evil in society. This ministry moves far beyond the important goal of helping the mentally ill. Its ultimate aim is life in all its fullness.

Theologically educated persons can help the mental health movement avoid narrow vision-limiting definitions of mental health. They can do so by a continuing emphasis (a) on a "height psychology" (Frankl), which points to the eternal, the transcendent, the *imago dei* in man, which must be fulfilled if he is to be mentally healthy; (b) on a "breadth psychology," which sees man as essentially relational and his wholeness as the aliveness of his relationships with nature, God, his fellows, and himself; (c) on a "depth psychology" including both psychoanalytic awarenesses and a theological emphasis on the Ground of Being at man's deep center.

This volume is one response to the challenge to the churches[3] of the community mental health revolution. It is designed to serve as a practical resource for clergymen, mental health professionals, and lay leaders in churches and temples. It is for those who have a desire to increase the participation of religious leaders and their congregations in community mental health programs. It is hoped that it will be useful both as a stimulus and as a guide to creative involvement in the community mental health movement.

It may be helpful to the reader to know what specific purposes were in the minds of those who formulated the design of this

[3] The words "church" and "churches" are used in this volume to refer to the total religious community, including both churches and temples.

16

book. They desired that it should accomplish these objectives:

Share the insights and experiences of clergymen who are involved in the community mental health movement.

Give guidelines and practical suggestions to churches and temples which wish to increase their involvement in community mental health programs.

Acquaint mental health professionals with the significant roles which clergymen and congregations can and should play in community mental health services.

Delineate some of the unique contributions of clergymen and religious groups to mental health action on both the therapeutic and preventive-educational fronts.

Arouse enthusiasm among laymen, clergymen, and denominational and ecumenical leaders for effective participation in community mental health on local, state, national, and international levels.

Suggest ways of facilitating interprofessional collaboration between clergymen and mental health professionals for the benefit of the parishioner-patient.

Describe some training patterns designed to release the mental health potentialities of clergymen and church laymen.

Provide some guidelines for clergymen who desire to enter specialized ministries in the mental health field, and to mental health program leaders who are considering such appointments.

Describe some of the ways in which clergymen are now involved in community mental health.

Explore the directions which research on the churches and mental health can profitably take in the years immediately ahead.

In retrospect, these objectives seem overly ambitious, even grandiose, so far as their possible accomplishment in any one volume. But each of these objectives reflects an urgent need in the present relationships between religious and mental health organizations. It was believed that the probability of making significant progress toward these objectives would be increased by inviting "mini-chapters" from a considerable number of persons actively involved in community mental health as it relates to the churches. From my perspective as editor, I am impressed with the variety and combined richness of experiences and backgrounds represented among the authors. The interprofessional and ecumenical nature of the authors certainly adds to the chapters' usefulness as resources in our pluralistic society. Clergymen from twelve different denominations are represented. These authors, from a variety of professional settings, are among those who are providing dynamic leadership in the teaching and practice of pastoral care as it relates to community mental health. Those who have contributed from the perspective of psychiatry are persons who are aware of the church's multiple roles in mental health and are helping to build communication bridges between clergymen and mental health professionals. The degree to which the book achieves its objectives is, in my view, a direct result of the caliber and the insights of these knowledgeable authors, both clergymen and mental health professionals.

Following an overview chapter, the book consists of four major sections. The first deals with the crucial matter of the church's role in *prevention,* including the dual thrusts of community outreach and change, on the one hand, and stimulating the growth of persons within the life of the church, on the other. The next section focuses on various facets of the church's role in *treatment* of the emotionally and spiritually disturbed. Following this is a section dealing with the *clergyman's role in community mental health services*. The final section highlights some aspects of training and organizing for mental health action within churches and temples. Included also are chapters dealing with interprofessional cooperation, research, governmental programs, and mental health as it relates to family life around the world.

It will be evident to the perceptive reader that none of the sections is fully comprehensive in covering its subject. The book does not aim at a systematic discussion of the church's roles in community mental health. There are numerous gaps which could not be filled because of limitations of space. The topics which are discussed open windows of interest and understanding into areas which are much wider than those covered in the book. Each chapter aims at being such a window-opener.

I must report that the authors contributed their chapters because of their interest in advancing the effective involvement of churches and temples in mental health. Royalties realized from the project will be divided between the American Association of Pastoral Counselors and the Association of Clinical Pastoral Education, two professional groups which have helped raise the level of training and practice in the pastoral care field.

Howard J. Clinebell, Jr.
Claremont, California

1
AN OVERVIEW OF THE CHURCH'S ROLES IN COMMUNITY MENTAL HEALTH

E. Mansell Pattison, M.D.
Associate Professor-in-Residence, Department of Psychiatry and Human Behavior, University of California at Irvine, California

Following World War II the American public became aware of the long neglected needs of the mentally ill. Among the major studies that ensued from the enactment of the National Mental Health Study Act in 1955 was a comprehensive analysis of the role of clergy and the churches in mental health. The results demonstrated that the clergy were on the front line of contact with people in emotional distress. Further it was noted that the clergy and the churches were in a position to uniquely provide a number of major services relevant to both the care of the mentally ill and the promotion of mental health. Community mental health programs were planned that would be intimately involved in the structure and function of the community, including programs related to the clergy, who are a major professional group in the community, and programs related to the churches, which are major institutions of the community.

Among the key concepts of community mental health programming are those of primary, secondary, and tertiary prevention of mental illness. *Primary prevention* is concerned with the elimination of conditions that produce emotional illness and with the promotion of conditions that will foster mental health. *Secondary prevention* is concerned with the early and effective detection of emotional problems when they do exist, so that such problems can be resolved before producing serious disruption in a person's life. *Tertiary prevention* is concerned with rehabilitation that will prevent the development of chronic disability in persons who sustain severe emotional difficulties. Community mental health programs are concerned not only with providing direct clinical services to the emotionally ill, but also with developing services in the community related to each of the above three levels of prevention. The clergy and the church are in a vital position to contribute to each level of prevention.

The Clergy and the Church in Primary Prevention

A major concern in primary prevention is for the social and cultural attitudes which determine behavior. The church has long been one of the major social institutions that has defined how people should see themselves and direct their behavior. Thus, the teachings of the church regarding human nature and human relationships may foster either mentally healthy attitudes or destructive, neurotic attitudes in its members. Inevitably a church teaches its members, either directly or indirectly, how to deal with aggression, anger, pride, sexuality, competition, social relations, child-rearing, and marital relations. The paramount current challenge to the church today is to re-examine its implicit and explicit teachings in these areas of human concern. The church can be a major constructive force for mental health in the community if its preaching, church school curricula, and formal and informal social gatherings provide a cohesive and coherent sense of healthy human relationships that will guide, sustain, and encourage healthy emotional attitudes in its members.

A second area of primary prevention where the church can participate is in the provision of group activities that offer intimacy, support, and relationship. No person is able to maintain his existence solely by himself. We maintain our integrity as humans through the emotional nurture we receive from family, friends, and associates. The church in its programming can provide opportunities for participation in a number of formal and informal groups that provide this normal and necessary human nurture.

In addition to these groups, the church can also provide group social relations to persons who are exposed to particular life stresses which make them emotionally vulnerable. Through participation in church-sponsored groups a vital contribution can

21

be made to sustaining such persons. Examples would be groups for adolescents, old people, single middle-aged adults, divorcees, and servicemen. Such groups are intended not to be therapy experiences, but rather to provide opportunity for human contact and relationship to people who are relatively isolated and need structured means of participating in human relationships.

Still another area of primary prevention is the provision of both material and human assistance to people in the midst of life crises. It is not unexpected that people will experience emotional distress during times of crisis. That in itself is not psychopathological. Yet people do need help in living through and effectively coping with crisis. Here the pastor and the people of the church can be available to assist in a natural human way. For example, the family that moves to a strange city can find advice and assistance in the church during their relocation; or the family that has suffered a death can find support and comfort in their bereavement; or a family may find itself unemployed; or the house may have burned down. These may seem like simple, common predicaments. However it is in these common life crises that emotional distress may be either generated or averted, depending upon the human resources available to the family in crisis.

A final area of primary prevention has to do with social concerns. Here the church may lend its official public support; supply monies; provide clerical and lay leadership, volunteers, and facilities to programs aimed at redressing social problems in the community which are contributory factors in producing mental illness. For example, churches may participate in interracial dialogue programs, preschool education programs such as Head Start, nursery school programs for children of working mothers, alcoholism education programs, sex education programs, open housing programs, health and education programs for migrant workers.

In summary, all these areas of primary prevention have to do not with those who are mentally ill, but rather with the provision of relationships and assistance in dealing with common crises and stresses of our society. This area of primary prevention is one where the church must take the lead, for mental health services cannot provide this type of normal everyday nurturance which everyone needs and without which people will run into emotional distress.

The Clergy and the Church in Secondary Prevention

In the area of early identification of emotional distress the clergy are in the most strategic position in the community. The National Mental Health Act studies revealed that when people encounter emotional distress they are more likely to turn first to a clergyman for assistance than to a physician or mental health professional.[1] Why do people turn to the clergy? Clergy are the most numerous of professionals (350,000 in the United States), they are widely scattered into the most distant geographic areas where no other professionals may be, they are easy to contact at any time, they are less expensive, their role and function are usually well known so that people know what to expect when they seek help, and they often have had ongoing contacts already established so that in a time of emotional crisis it is natural to turn to them.

The function of the clergy here may be twofold. If a person presents serious emotional problems that require the skills of mental health services, the clergyman is in an advantageous position to help the person obtain needed professional help. However, if the clergy were to refer all such persons to already overburdened mental health facilities it would swamp and capsize our community mental health services. Rather, the clergyman may be the most effective care-giver in many situations of emotional crisis. In the early stages of emotional crisis a modest amount of emotional support and guidance may be sufficient to help a person work out an emotional problem. However the same problem, if unattended, may compound over time and then require prolonged and skilled professional care. Thus this does not suggest that the clergyman should play the role of pre-

[1] See Chapter 16 for a fuller report on this study.

23

liminary psychotherapist, but rather that in his pastoral role of guiding, supporting, and responding, the pastor may afford sufficient help to alleviate many emotional problems brought to him. He can then be selective in referring those persons who require intensive and skilled mental health services.

In summary, the clergy are in a critical position in the community as the first contact for many persons in emotional distress. Appropriate pastoral care at this juncture may prevent the development of serious problems in many persons.

The Clergy and the Church in Tertiary Prevention

A major problem in the care of the mentally ill is that once a person has been defined as deviant (i.e., mentally ill) and to a large extent taken out of the community for treatment, that person will usually experience great difficulty in re-entry into the community. People are often suspicious of those who have received treatment for emotional disorders. The ex-patient may have difficulty finding a job, being received back into social circles, renewing friendships, and feeling comfortable in participating in the activities of his community. The church can assist here by affording an atmosphere of acceptance, receptivity, and interest. Church members can reach out to the ex-patient and draw him back into the human relationships of the church, and assist in vocational and social relocation. Some churches are supporting special ministries designed to provide specific help in social re-entry. Other churches support group activities designed specifically for ex-patients who can meet and share experiences and problems with others in like situations.

Finally, churches can develop liaison with community mental health programs where church people can establish contact with patients who are still in treatment programs, so that the abrupt transition back into the community is bridged by already established human relationships.

In summary, a crucial need exists for a community to which the patient can return after treatment and receive acceptance, support, and assistance. The church is a major institution that can provide just such a community of human relationships. Hence the church is in a position to contribute directly to tertiary prevention.

The Role of Clergymen in the Program of a Community Mental Health Center

Up to this point we have discussed the many instances where the clergy and the churches in the community can collaborate with community mental health programs in providing services related to prevention in mental health. It is assumed that community mental health programs will (and many do so now) actively work with the clergy and their churches in developing such community services. However, to successfully and effectively engage the churches and clergy in such preventive programs it is necessary to have specially trained clergy on the professional staff of community mental health programs. Such clergy will not only have had training in seminary, but will have acquired accredited training in pastoral care and pastoral counseling. Their function will lie not in the area of church-sponsored pastoral counseling programs, but rather in serving a particular professional role in a community mental health program. The *pastoral specialist* in a community mental health program may serve the following four functions:

1. Director of Pastoral Care. In this area the pastoral specialist would provide and coordinate religious activities for patients receiving inpatient or part-time hospital care. This would involve many of the usual religious activities that a pastor provides: religious worship services, administration of the sacraments, individual pastoral calls, religious study, and discussion groups. When patients are hospitalized they often feel estranged from their community life; thus, the provision of religious activities while they are hospitalized may serve to provide continuity, as well as the primary nurturance that persons may receive from their religious participation. Further, many patients may wish to maintain their relationships with their own pastor and congregation. Here the pastoral specialist may serve as a liaison, helping

the patient to maintain such contacts, and helping the parish pastor and people to understand the needs and problems of the patient. Finally, the specialist may coordinate special programs and services in which various churches may jointly participate.

2. Consultant in Treatment. Here the specialist will continue to function in his pastoral role, but now as a consultant with particular knowledge and skills that may assist in the treatment process. The specialist may counsel a patient regarding theological or spiritual questions. Very often during states of emotional distress religious issues may loom large for the patient, or the patient may seek religious answers as a defense against dealing with his human problems, or in cases of profound emotional disorganization may develop distorted and destructive religious ideas. In these circumstances, the pastoral specialist may be in a position to provide guidance and clarification to the patient. He may also offer support in periods of stress or anxiety during treatment, help the patient fit his religious background into his therapeutic experience, and participate in religious rituals that may therapeutically benefit the patient. In recent years more attention has been given to the role of religious values in psychotherapy. Here the specialist may serve as a consultant and interpreter to the professional psychotherapist in regard to the religious concerns and values of the patient.

3. Diagnostic Consultant. As more religious persons seek mental health services it has become apparent that the relevance of religious background, participation, and values requires attention in the diagnostic and evaluative process. Here the specialist may function as a member of the diagnostic team as an expert on religious matters. He may interview the patient and explore the patient's religious life and attitudes as part of the diagnostic evaluation. As an expert on various religious cultures, and with a knowledge of the role of religion in personality structure and function, the specialist is in a position to offer relevant insight for psychodynamic diagnosis, for evaluation of the manner in which religious issues should be dealt with in treatment, and the means by which religious resources may be used in rehabilitation.

4. Liaison to the Religious Community. Here the pastoral spe-

cialist will function in a role which capitalizes upon his clerical identity, religious knowledge, and contact and identification with the religious community. He will carry on mental health education and consultation programs for the clergy and churches in the community. Similarly, he may conduct seminars on religious aspects of mental health for the staff of the community mental health program. In his liaison role, he will be a primary agent in developing and maintaining liaison between the community mental health program and the churches of its community. This will include the development of a referral network, and assisting in the arrangement of after-care and rehabilitation programs in the community in which the clergy and churches will participate.

In summary, to effectively implement the resources of the clergy and the churches in a community mental health program there is need for clinically trained clergymen who can fill a professional role on the staff of community mental health programs. Such a professional clergy specialist will be an expert in both mental health and religion and will be a major link between these two dimensions of community life.

The clergy and the churches can move toward effective involvement in these areas of preventive community mental health through the following:

a. development of committees in the church that will gather information and implement programs and services within the church relevant to mental health.

b. provide representatives from the church to local citizen mental health associations.

c. provide representatives to the boards and advisory committees of the local community mental health program.

d. support the participation of the pastor in mental health in-service training programs designed for parish clergymen.

e. support local and general denomination programs related to mental health, including exploration with leaders for the development of such programs.

f. recommend, encourage, and support the appointment of pastoral specialists to the professional staff of the local community mental health program.

PART I

the church's roles in prevention

Churches and temples, with their long tradition of concern for human wholeness and growth, have a major stake in the preventive mental health thrust. It is here that they can and should make a vital contribution; *this is their most important contribution to the mental health revolution!*

Prevention is a multi-leveled thrust. As was made clear in the first chapter, *primary* prevention consists of reducing the incidence of an illness in the population at large; *secondary* prevention involves reducing the duration of an illness through early diagnosis and treatment; *tertiary* prevention has to do with reducing the permanent damage from the illness by effective rehabilitation.

Primary prevention, as viewed in this volume, involves fostering positive mental health (as distinguished from the mere absence of gross psychopathology) through stimulating the growth and fulfillment of persons. For this to happen, the social conditions which block human actualization must be changed. In terms familiar to clergymen, the *pastoral* function (counseling, nurturing the growth of individuals and families) and the *prophetic* function (social action) are complementary, and equally essential in a church's mental health ministry. Changing the systems of injustice, discrimination, conflict, and exploitation which stultify human development is a crucial part of the mental health role of the churches and temples.

Because prevention covers a wide spectrum, the chapters in this section range over a considerable area. The main emphasis is on primary prevention. The opportunity of churches to utilize their own programs to help persons cope constructively with crises, grow through small sharing groups, and satisfy their interpersonal and spiritual needs is discussed by three of the authors (Clinebell, Jernigan, and Leslie). Two of the authors (Brown and Bockus) look at the overall characteristics and climate of our society as these influence the development of persons. The implication of rapid social change for creating a person-maximizing society are examined. One paper (Bonthius) deals with how clergy and laymen can function effectively in changing community systems and structures. Two papers (Purdy and Snyder) describe ways in which clergymen have participated in the preventive aspects of community mental health programs.

The importance of primary prevention becomes evident when one recognizes that there will not be in the foreseeable future nearly enough professional counselors and psychotherapists to meet the constantly expanding population's need for such services. The only realistic hope lies in more available and efficient preventive programs, in addition to pouring increased efforts into salvaging persons after the damage has been done. Therapies are costly; often they are only partially effective. The mental health movement is properly giving highest priority to providing humane treatment for those suffering most acutely; but it is also devoting increasing energy to prevention. Religious organizations exist as centers of human growth and actualization; primary prevention is therefore the mental health area in which they have a natural and almost unlimited opportunity. There is a spirit of excitement in those churches and temples which are coming alive to this opportunity.

2.
THE CHURCH'S ROLE IN CREATING AN OPEN SOCIETY

Frank M. Bockus, B.D., Ph.D.
Executive Director, Ecumenical Center for Religion and Health, South Texas Medical Center; Adjunct Associate Professor of Human Ecology, University of Texas Medical School, San Antonio, Texas

Our society is faced with a crucial task; right now we are not doing much about it. Futurists tell us that we face a world of ever more rapid and complex change. Moreover, they predict that the mentally healthy individual of tomorrow must be flexible and open-minded. He must be capable of constant adaptation to changing conditions.

Preparation for life in a constantly changing culture will require a new kind of education. Schools and colleges place their stress on cognitive growth, and well they should. Life in our technologically oriented economy demands a person with rational know-how. But if the character ideal for tomorrow is the open self, how are we to train such a personality? Today we leave his development virtually to chance, to informal and almost willy-nilly patterns. We must begin now to construct human development systems that equip persons for openness and flexibility.

As children grow up, families provide most of the basic resources they need. Not the least of these inputs, in addition to material requirements, are the resources of personality and character development. Here it is that individuals internalize the assumptions and attitudes which dig into their minds and shape behavior. Children learn their parents' outlook and way of life not so much by what they say, though that is important, but by what their elders do. Through almost unnoticed, everyday encounters and emotionally charged expectations, parents reveal their deepest beliefs and practices. This is the hothouse environment of character development.

The parent of today feels himself in a double bind. In our complex world, society has placed an even greater burden on parents for their children's emotional and character development. At the same time we have done little in a formal way to support families in the task they are expected to bear. Little wonder that many parents feel as if they are trying to hit a moving target—in parenting they try to socialize their children toward an ever-changing and often confusing character ideal.

Character guidance was once an easier task than now. At least, so it seemed. When we lived in small-town settings, parents could look passively over their shoulders at the behavior norms of the community. Guidelines seemed more perceptible. As the crises of life came along, there was a great deal of security in fixed and accepted patterns for coping with decisions and actions. Of course, this limited environment could and often did become stifling and confining.

For most of us city dwellers, small-town culture is a relic of the past. Urban man experiences diversity, anonymity, and cultural diffusion. We reap the whirlwind of an incredibly fragmented existence. As one social scientist notes, the urban family too often encounters the monotony of sameness and sterility. We live in neighborhoods, both gilded and grimy ghettos, in which our houses, neighbors, incomes, and ways of life are practically homogeneous. Families in the city become isolated from one another. They become separated by race, age, class, and neighborhood.

Thus, families have broken loose from the past. They are set loose on new and uncharted tasks. They try to socialize their young toward a culture whose most stable traits are change and diversity. Can we design character development systems to prepare people for such successive episodes of upheaval and change? Can we educate open selves for an experimental and changing culture?

Our emerging model of community mental health reflects a kind of systems approach. Earlier patterns of remedial and individual therapy, though still important, simply are inadequate to our contemporary task. Today various resources for mental health are being drawn into comprehensive and community-wide networks of care geared to all people. By tailoring services to meet human need as early and as specifically as possible, we hope to prevent undue deterioration. By enabling an individual to remain with his family, on his job, and within his community, we can help him back to his feet in the shortest period of time.

Unfortunately, much of our present-day planning, worthwhile though it is, is not directed to primary prevention in the most positive sense. Our efforts are colored by remedial mindsets. We focus too much on the repair of broken personalities. Our need now is a developmental model. In this, energy is spent on the provision of adequate human development resources. With respect to mental health, this means channeling our efforts toward the education of the open self. In this new model we major in mental health instead of illness.

I believe that the neighborhood congregation is uniquely situated to contribute to emerging human development systems. The church, in this view, becomes a human development center. Of particular importance is its ministry of *family relations development*. Religion is intrinsically identified with values and symbols of human growth. The rituals of religious tradition are clustered around many of life's major moments, such as birth, marriage, and death. In addition, the neighborhood church is often located near the residential sector of the community. It is close to the family circles where character and personality development take place day by day. It is situated, through its ministries of family relations and child development, to share in the creation of an experimental and open style of living.

Many of the critical moments in life are common to us all as human beings. Some of these incidents in the life cycle are primarily biological, such as birth, the onset of puberty, pregnancy, or old age. Some incidents are more socially defined, such as going to a new school, to college, to military service, or to one's first job. Getting married, becoming a parent, encountering death in the family—such occasions provide insight into the thoughts, feelings, values, and conflicts of the life cycle.

Ordinarily, these novel moments in life upset the everyday balance of individuals and families. It is both easy and normal to become confused and disoriented. Our response to these critical incidents can be either creative or harmful. We can approach them in either an open or a closed manner.

Some people face anxiety and uncertainty openly. They express their feelings, most often to people close to them, and through such interaction work their way through the episode. But some people, and all of us to a degree, tend to follow a more closed mode of adapting. We deny the crisis. Our disquieting feelings remain unexpressed. And inevitably, we begin to feel isolated, lonely, and different. We deny much of ourselves, both to ourselves and to others.

Most of the critical episodes of life raise profound questions of value and character. It is here that the great issues of our day impinge upon the ordinary person. Questions of suffering and death, of morality changes, or of social justice and purpose often demand frightfully ambiguous and binding choices.

In relating to their children during these critical moments in life, parents often cease to be open and exploratory. If parents are to equip their children for the coming cultural change, they themselves must be changing. They too, must quest for life's meaning and purpose. What happens too often, unfortunately, is that parents quit listening to their sons and daughters. Out of their own vulnerability, they fake greater certainty and self-confidence than they truly possess. Sometimes their ambiguity gets expressed in a demand for compliance and obedience to their own views. If they are honest with themselves parents begin to realize their own ambivalence and uncertainty about life's pressing dilemmas.

In its parish life the neighborhood congregation can offer growth groups focused around critical stages in life. There can be groups for pre-marrieds and newly marrieds, as well as for couples who have been together for years. Other groups can be organized around parent-child relationships at different ages. One particularly important age in our time is young adulthood. People at this age are faced with many of life's most binding choices—marriage, vocation, and life-style.

Of increasing importance today is the conjoint family growth group. Individuals live in families, and families possess histories, ideologies, role expectations, and unique communication patterns. Learning groups that reach the entire family unit simultaneously have decided advantages over more individualistic approaches.

As the church undertakes a more careful family ministry, resources that heretofore were restricted to counseling settings can be brought into innovative family growth groups. The minister will continue to require skills in counseling, depth communication, and group process. But he will need to shift his energies from counseling, particularly with individuals, to the more efficient model of growth groups. Traditional resources, depth psychology, counseling, and guidance can be brought to bear on normal families through group process.

Moreover audio and video recordings, the exciting new learning tools of today, no longer need to be restricted to counseling and training settings. They can become learning media in human development groups. Quite often they provide emotionally laden experiences that evoke emphatic responses between people. They provide a common frame of reference for all the members of the group. In addition, media are useful in expediting both self-confrontation and empathic encounter between persons.

In one sense, the church is ideally situated for a family ministry. In another sense, it is very ill-equipped. Family relations counseling and development is a professional field. It requires, as was said earlier, training and competency in communication. psychosocial relationships, and group process. Very few ministers have any clinical training whatsoever in these areas. On top of these existing deficiencies we have now added new professional requirements of conjoint family counseling and guidance.

But the contemporary minister can re-tool. Most parish pastors recognize their need for more training in family counseling and guidance. Many would welcome some form of continuing education in the field. What we need today, then, are models of consultation and in-service training geared to the parish setting. Seminaries and clinical training centers can provide the supervisory leadership for these new patterns. Such on-the-job training is becoming an increasingly significant form of education in our time. It is a pattern most appropriate to the ministry. Through it the church can fulfill its manpower requirements for a changing society.

For additional reading

A Chance to Grow (Boston: WGBH Educational Foundation, 1967). This volume interprets crisis theory and conjoint family guidance. It also provides verbatim transcriptions of conjoint family interviews around eleven critical episodes of life.

Fromm, Erich, *Man for Himself.* New York: Rinehart, 1947. Fromm's theory of character development remains one of the best available.

Rieff, Philip. *The Triumph of the Therapeutic: Uses of Faith After Freud*. New York: Harper, 1966. This book affords an analysis and interpretation of our coming experimental culture.

Satir, Virginia. *Conjoint Family Therapy*. Palo Alto: Science and Behavior Books, 1967. This volume offers a theory of family relationships, communication, and therapy. Implications for growth groups are suggested.

3.
RAPID SOCIAL CHANGE, THE CHURCHES, AND MENTAL HEALTH

Bertram S. Brown, M.D.
Director, National Institute of Mental Health, Chevy Chase, Maryland

The basic question is this: Can religion and mental health really work together? In fact, can any two groups with territorial and tradition hangups work together? The soul is our mutual turf. I intend to discuss the general issue of territoriality and boundaries in a time of social change.

One social force or institution influences another, and it is this interaction that is important in any discussion of community mental health, air pollution, education, welfare, or religion.

SOCIAL CHANGE, CHURCHES, AND MENTAL HEALTH

The turbulence of a rapidly changing scene surrounds us, and the same forces that are creating turmoil in the cities, on the campuses, and in the local schools are shaking up this infant movement—community mental health. Like all youngsters, this child is adapting to its turbulent environment and actually incorporating social change as a phenomenon into its way of life and way of thinking. The survival, however, of older institutions, such as the church, depends upon their ability likewise to absorb, integrate, and deal with this phenomenon of accelerating social change.

Predicting social change and creatively rolling with the punches—has been my bread and butter for the past decade. I have come to believe that this turbulent period of great transition will not last and that we will come into smoother sailing sometime in the foreseeable future. This is analogous to the turbulence of airplanes and missiles as they pass through the sound barrier. If they can survive the shock wave and not shatter into bits, if the pilot understands the wild readings on the instruments, they soon pass into the smoothness and serenity of supersonic flight.

This somewhat optimistic prediction of things to come may not seem helpful for the here and now, because we live in an era of fear, anxiety, and worry, and our question and our text is how can we adapt now and in the immediate future to this rapid rate of social change.

One approach is to loosen our thinking, free up and swing. To use current jargon, we must break out of our professional bags. No longer can we deal with the gigantic problems of today by the seeing with one eye and one point of view. And it is not only a matter of seeing, it is a matter of comprehending; and comprehending means taking it in—not part of it but all of it, or at least as much as our hearts and minds can absorb. To do that, we must hear as well as see, feel as well as think. To grasp something, we must not only touch it, it must touch us. To do all this, to do our job, we must do all these things all at once and all the time.

Is this multiple level viewpoint, this super-comprehensive approach, this grandiose goal, a task only for geniuses or something that only fools will attempt? It is a task for all of us as human beings, a task for which religion as an institution and clergy as professionals are uniquely equipped in theory if not in practice.

The professionals leading the field and using this multiple simultaneous approach are those dealing with material and money—the engineers and budgeteers. The current "in" word for this all-encompassing approach is systems: systems analysis, systems engineering, client systems, the health system. Before we become overly impressed with any one approach, no matter how broad it seems, special caution is due if it promises too much.

Scientists and thinkers have developed a variety of conceptual frameworks—ecology, for example—that attempt to intellectually grasp this great need to make sense, to organize complexity; but I think it is a fundamental mistake—be we scientists, ministers, or otherwise—to think that only science and engineering and business are attempting to deal with this problem of complexity, simultaneity, and constant change. Art, as well as science, attempts to make sense out of complexity. Drama and poetry, music and painting, all create new beauty as they distill human experience and inner and outer realities.

In brief, social change—this rapid, turbulent, accelerating scene—is more than a professional challenge; it is a total human challenge, and to deal with it as human beings, be we professionals or nonprofessionals, we must unashamedly call upon the full range of our human capacities and interests—scientific, artistic, and religious. Furthermore, we must realize that our full range of capacities is limited by our own heritage. The way we were taught language in the first few years of life limits our ability to conceptualize what other people think. The heritage we have by age six, thirteen, or twenty limits our way of grasping from other places and other cultures. And we must realize that other cultures, such as those of Africa and Asia, offer possible ways of thinking and feeling not available to us, barely seen at the periphery of our consciousness, and yet perhaps the most critical thing that we must take in if we are going to swing with the current turbulence. More and more people are realizing that they must learn to understand the communication process between peoples of different cultures.

The turbulence of social change is rocking the boat in many areas, including religion. Churches increasingly see missions in the streets of American cities; segments of church membership stirring up controversy; urban congregations moving to the suburbs; such issues as birth control, draft resistance, rebellion.

Each organization, be it the American Medical Association or the church, thinks it is going through its own unique identity crisis. The church is just another organization in the problems of our times. Each of the organizations has within it a militant social action group that feels that the time for justice, for equality, for decency, for concern for black Americans and minority groups has come, and either the parent body recognizes that they are right or they threaten to splinter or leave the organization.

On the other extreme in organizations are the methodologists, who feel that no change is needed or possible—any change is certainly not within the purview of the professional role. They grant the right of concern to citizens and humans but never confuse the issue by considering the possibility that the clergyman or other professional is also a citizen or human being.

In the middle is the large band of apathetic practitioners, who are passive rather than active. But they too feel the buffets of the waves of social change. The majority of mankind has always comfortably sat in the hump of the bell curve, carried along by the extremes as they have their tug-of-war.

Each organization realizes that something must be done—dropouts must be brought back in, youth must be made to want to come in. Look around and see that misery loves company, and the company may have a lot to teach about what to do and what not to do. For example, we have to be cautious about those who advocate social change or organizational shift not as a responsible and responsive thing but only for personal gain. New groups and coalitions must emerge to hammer out these changes, coalitions that encompass the old leadership and the new members, several generations and many points of view. There will be value in consultations from others who are concerned but are not members of a given group or profession.

Perhaps more fundamental in this difficult and troublesome phenomenon—social change and a rapidly shifting scene—is not the social change itself but social change for what? That "what," of course, brings us smack up against the gut issue of values.

No other social institution, with the possible exception of philosophy, concerns itself as deeply with the matter of values as does religion. Religion is based on the respect and dignity of the individual, on self-determination and adequate opportunities for the individual, and it has had as its goal the health of both individuals and society and the improvement of the quality of life.

The concept of quality of life, of course, is one where opinions vary, fashions change, and fads develop. But is there any question that we should strive toward an improved quality of life for ourselves, our families and for all mankind?

Clergymen can offer a dynamism, a commitment to the eradication of misery and the improving of lives. There is no contradiction in helping an individual adjust to a harsh system, and striving at the same time to change that sick system. Too many of us feel that we must be of one extreme or the other. We change the system all or none and have no time for the individual casualties. Or we devote all our time to the individual casualties and pay no attention to the sick system that produces them. Down with these false polarities between the parish minister and community organization, between psychotherapy and community mental health in my own field. These polarities render us asunder.

Our need is to integrate our pieces of the action, to complement our efforts. If we are to deal with social change we must remember that it is a pot in which we are all cooking and that we are going to become the nourishment for the next generation.

4.
TRAINING CLERGYMEN TO CHANGE COMMUNITY STRUCTURES

Robert H. Bonthius, B.D., Ph. D.
Director of Community Action Training Services of Northern Ohio, Cleveland, Ohio

This chapter is addressed to clergymen who wish to improve their ability to engage in social action, not by themselves—a mistake that can be fatal!—but as leaders of men, their congregations, other groups. It is written in the hope that laymen will read it, too. The way that it is set forth must be taken by the clergyman and a group of concerned laity. It is a way of shared concern, shared leadership and above all, shared risk.

The first part has to do with what it takes to initiate and to continue significant social action. The second part tries to answer the question, How can I, a clergyman, get started? Both parts are based on experiments in training at Case Western Reserve University in the Internship Program for Clergy. Both parts draw on other research, including that which is in process at CWRU in Cleveland, the Urban Training Center in Chicago, and the Metropolitan Urban Service Training Facility in New York City.

The Support the Clergyman Needs

Significant social action requires four supporting groups. By "significant social action" I mean that which is aimed at changing the structures of society. Most of the action churches engage in is symptomatic relief, not structural change. Symptomatic relief is any action which relieves suffering without altering the system which produces it. Tutoring in the slums is an example. To be sure, it is significant in that it helps an individual child, and that should not be discounted. But it is relatively insignificant, because it does not alter the system which is producing millions of such needy children. Significant social action works for alteration in the contents, methods, personnel, policies, and tax structures which make that educational system what it is—a ghetto school. Changing the teacher-pupil ratio might prove to be a significant social change.

To initiate and sustain this change the clergyman needs help. He must have sustaining relationships of various sorts inside and outside the religious organization. They can be diagrammed as follows:

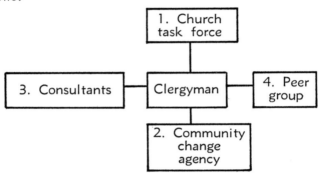

1. *Church Task Force*. The clergyman needs allies in his constituency—congregation, higher judicatory, whatever group he represents as leader. Theologically, in terms of mission, he has no business going it alone. Politically, he cannot. He must be able to know there are those who are with him, those who want action, too, those who will "go" with him. This group need not be the majority of the congregation or other church group. It might only be 2 percent of the constituency. It depends on what 2 percent! They ought to include some articulate, respected people, people with the power to influence others. If the risk is high, the clergyman needs to figure whether or not he and his allies can outmaneuver the opposition. (This is not easy in a congregational type polity. It is easier in a presbyterian type—here the main thing to do is have a majority of the Session on your side! An episcopal polity is still another matter; a great deal depends on whether the bishop is pro, con, or neutral. But here, too, a lay constituency that is with the clergyman is vitally important.) A clergyman who cannot involve some of his people in a task force with himself is probably slated either for ineffectiveness or dismissal.

2. *Community Change Agency.* Next in importance for a clergyman is his connection with a community change agency—reformist or revolutionist in approach, i.e., working within a structure for change or organized outside existing structures to press for change.

A community change agency is any group, organization, or task force that has arisen anywhere in the area to redress a wrong, attack an injustice, heal a hurt, remedy a lack, stop an aggression, protest a practice, demonstrate a need. Be careful that its strategy is not one of symptomatic relief rather than structural change. If it *is* the latter, seriously consider relating to it. A clergyman must have roots or find them in some secular agency that is actively engaged in change action. Otherwise he will know little of what the problem is, what needs to be done, or how. Such an agency gives him perspective, a fellowship outside the church, and a lever with which to get the church task force involved. Except in rare instances, a church body neither initiates nor sustains social action alone. Normally, a church task force has to have a community change agency with which it can link itself, and through which it can channel its energy for social change.

3. *Consultants.* This is a growing group of persons to whom the clergyman needs to be related. They are anyone who is an expert on some aspect of analysis, strategy, or theology. Books can be consultants. More often consultants are "living books" in the community. A consultant on poverty may be an ADC mother, a caseworker, a sociology professor, a Salvation Army officer, a black nationalist. A consultant on strategy may be a union leader, a politician, a specialist in organizational behavior at the university, a corporation executive, or a youth gang leader. No one can be ruled out as a possible consultant. The need of the clergyman is to have a growing group of persons to whom he can turn in crisis or for planning to get facts, find out what is going on, secure judgments, seek advice. Periodically, a clergyman should take time off from parish duties and spend all of his time with consultants, e.g., in an action training program, a group process lab, or an urban studies institute. Ideally, some of his lay allies should do the same.

4. *Peer Group.* A fourth supporting group no clergyman can do without is a peer group—like-minded persons of his profession in or outside his denominatin. He finds comfort and challenge in such a group. On occasion he finds it politically important either for himself or for one of his peers. It does not have to be a large group. It may not meet officially. But it is a "beloved community" nonetheless. In the worst times it is the local version of "the seven thousand men who have not bowed the knee to Baal." In the best times it is "the boys whooping it up after the game." (There are times when the good guys win even in "this naughty world.")

How to Get Started

There is a way to get started in social action that is equally useful for clergy and laity, and equally useful as a start and as a style of continuing involvement. It is the basis of social action in that it provides the sensitivity to social problems that is constantly needed to know where the action is.

The way is this:

> Victims
> Change Agents
> Powers
> Experts

1. *Victims.* These are the people who appear to be the sufferers in the situation or those who are the rank and file. They are the ordinary citizens, the men in the street. It is a matter of first importance in understanding a social problem that you get to the person who is on the receiving end of things. Generally speaking, these are obscure people, although in unusual cases they may emerge as spokesmen, voices of the powerless. The mass media may have given them prominence at one point or another, but this is not usually the case. Victims have to be sought out. They seldom come to you.

2. *Change Agents.* Individuals speaking for the victimized; persons working outside existing organizations or within them to bring about structural change; "natural" leaders of men in the street, who know their problems and feel their concerns; con-

cerned persons in established organizations who see the need for change and are working for it—these are change agents. They are important sources of information and understanding.

3. *Powers.* Powers are people who are decision-makers in the established organizations of society, the organizations which by and large control the systems, determine the policies, provide the money and make it. A particular power may be a "front man" or a man behind the scenes. He may have power, or he may advise those who do, or he may simply represent them to the public.

4. *Experts.* Many other persons need to be taken into consideration. They may be lumped together as experts. They may be thought of as consultants. An expert is anyone with an interest in the problem but not a vested interest, anyone who has accumulated a fund of knowledge through contact with the situation over a period of time. The expert may be a scholar, a reporter, an articulate person without formal education, a business researcher, a government worker, an archivist, a long-term resident of the community in which the problem exists.

In addition to personal sources, there are written sources of information which can get the inquirer further into the scene. These consist of statistics, surveys, news or research reports, monographs, books. They may be obtained from public institutions or private files—with permission, to be sure!

The course of such sensitivity to social issues may be diagrammed as follows. And it can be followed in getting to know *any* social issue.

Written Sources	*Oral Sources*
1. *News media*—papers, radio, TV	2. Agents (in order of importance)
(ALWAYS CROSS CHECK)	a. Victims
	b. Change Agents
	c. Powers
3. *Documents* (other than news media)	d. Experts

Anyone who is willing to risk the time and association with people who are strangers to himself and living in different ways than he is can get where the action is. It is a matter of personal investment in people, especially victims of injustice. The most casual reading of the Bible suggests that the prophets knew social problems because they knew victims, change agents, and the rest. But this cannot be carried out alone, at least not effectively, because support groups are needed. Getting very far into action requires the build-up of allies within the church, in secular change agencies, among peers, and with consultants.

For additional reading

The best reading on this subject has yet to be written. But there are some well-known starters:

Warren, Ronald L. *Studying Your Community*. New York: Free Press, 1965.

Young, Pauline V. *Interviewing in Social Work*. New York: McGraw-Hill, 1935.

Mills, C. Wright *The Sciological Imagination*. New York: Oxford University Press, 1959.

5.
THE LOCAL CHURCH'S CONTRIBUTIONS TO POSITIVE MENTAL HEALTH

Howard J. Clinebell, Jr., B.D., Ph.D.
Professor of Pastoral Counseling, School of Theology at Claremont, California

Mental health is a central and inescapable concern for any church or temple that is alive to its mission with and for people. Churches and temples collectively represent a sleeping giant, a huge potential of barely tapped resources for fostering positive mental health. Specialized ministries such as chaplaincies, pastoral counseling centers, and clergy staff members in community mental health programs make invaluable contributions to the mental health renaissance developing in our nation. But even broader contributions await release in the priests, pastors, rabbis, lay leaders, and grass-roots members of religious communities (i.e., congregations). Approximately 124 million members of 320,000 churches and temples are served by 246,000 clergymen and rabbis. The immense mental health contributions of organized religion will be released only as increasing numbers of churches and temples become *centers of healing and growth*— centers for healing the brokenness of individuals and relationships, and settings where persons find stimulation for lifelong growth toward their fullest humanity.

There should be an increasing reciprocity between churches and community mental health programs. One function of a community mental health center is to help develop the latent mental health resources of all its areas' churches and temples. On the other hand, these congregations have an opportunity and an obligation to give vigorous moral support to comprehensive community mental health programs. The functioning of an ecumenically oriented, clinically trained clergyman on the mental health center staff is essential to the bridge-building process by which such reciprocity grows.

Clergymen counsel more troubled people than any other helping profession. This is a major contribution to the therapeutic dimension of mental health. However, a larger contribution by ministers and churches is in the area of prevention of mental ill health by fostering positive human fulfillment. This growth ministry is at the center of the church's mental health mission.

Unique Contributions of Churches and Temples

Mental health professionals have a right to press the crucial question, What are the *unique* contributions of religious groups to positive mental health? Vigorous churches and temples are instruments for feeding those basic heart hungers which, when starved, result in personality crippling, and, when satisfied, produce strong, creative, loving people. The positive mental health function of religious groups is to perfect their methods for meeting these personality needs:

1. The need for *an opportunity to periodically renew basic*

trust is satisfied by religious groups through corporate worship, symbolic practices, sacraments, and festivals. Erik Erikson declares:

> There can be no question that it is organized religion which systematizes the first conflicts of life . . . . It is religion which by way of ritual methods offers man a periodic collective restitution of basic trust which in adults ripens to a continuation of faith and realism.[1]

Erikson holds that the infant develops a sense of "basic trust" or "basic distrust," depending on the quality of the mother-child relationship. The core feeling that life is trustworthy becomes the foundation for all subsequent need-satisfying relationships. For those whose ability to trust is limited as a result of early experiences (which means all of us to some degree), organized religion offers a way of reestablishing trust. The mental health significance of this is far-reaching, e.g., it is likely that many forms of mental illness are rooted in a massive disintegration of trust.

2. The basic need for *a sense of belonging* is provided by meaningful involvement in religious groups. The sense of solidarity with persons joined by common commitments and similar ideologies increases group cohesion. Satisfaction of this need is particularly crucial in our fragmented, transient, urban society where rootlessness and loneliness are epidemic. Churches and temples often serve as substitutes for the missing "extended family"; this is an invaluable resource when crises strike. Having or lacking support of a network of relationships can be the difference between coping or collapsing under pressure.

Alongside Freud's will-to-pleasure, Adler's will-to-power, and Frankl's will-to-meaning, is another, more basic human striving and need—the *will-to-relate*. Man *is* his relationships; the quality of his relationships determines the quality of his mental-spiritual health. Only through relationships can he satisfy his will to pleasure, power, or meaning. When one is blocked in the ability

---

[1] "On the Sense of Inner Identity," in *Psychoanalytic Psychiatry and Psychology,* Robert Knight and C. Friedman, eds. (New York: International Universities Press, 1954), I, 353.

to relate in mutually satisfying ways, alienation, loneliness, rage, and sickness (mental and physical) follow. The "distanced" person is cut off from both the potential riches within himself and those in relationships. (This understanding of man illuminates the importance of *relationship-centered* approaches to pastoral care and counseling.) A creative church, through its small groups, offers many opportunities for families and individuals to satisfy their will-to-relate.

Because of their vertical frame of reference, religious groups can help satisfy the will-to-relate to the ultimate dimension, the dimension of Spirit. The longing to belong in some ultimate sense, to feel an at-homeness in the universe is satisfied for many in worship which reawakens the awareness of "the mystical unity which underlies all human life" (Cyril Richardson). This experience is energizing, feeding, and healing; it overcomes the sense of cosmic loneliness, the feeling expressed by a mental hospital patient: "I'm an orphan in the universe." One may relate such experiences to Jung's collective unconscious or to findings in parapsychology. However understood, they change one's existence from a "world of walls without windows" to a connectedness with life.

3. Religious groups also provide *an opportunity and resources for meeting the crucial need for a viable philosophy of life.* The religious community's tradition and belief-system offer ethical guidelines within which (or even against which) individuals can develop their own functional value hierarchies. Erikson points to the crucial role of values in ego strength. One of the major mental-social health functions of organized religion is to stimulate persons to discover authentic values to which they can commit themselves. The proliferation of character disorders in our society underlines the imperative nature of this function. The frequent presence of a "value vacuum" (Frankl) in the personality and relationship problems brought to counselors emphasizes Erich Fromm's conviction that every human being needs a "system of thought and action shared by a group which gives the individual a frame of orientation and an object of devo-tion

tion." [2] Organized religions provide the most accessible and most traveled (though not the only) route to this goal. In the search for the unique contributions of the religiously and philosophically oriented counselor, Gordon Allport's question provides a clue: "May not (at least sometimes) an acquired world outlook constitute the central motive of life, and if disordered, the ultimate therapeutic problem?" [3] Religious groups satisfy the need for "an object of devotion," or what Tillich calls "the dimension of ultimate concern." The need to find a worthy, non-narcissistic focus of self-commitment is compelling; only by such a self-transcending commitment rooted in a vital philosophy of life can one cope creatively with existential anxiety. By existential anxiety I mean the non-neurotic anxiety which is inescapable (and incurable psychotherapeutically) and which results from man's awareness of the abyss of death, including the living death of meaninglessness. This anxiety is a stifling, paralyzing force unless one has developed a functional philosophy of life; a life style of "generativity" (Erikson), i.e., self-investment in the ongoing human race; and relationships of trust with at least one other person and with the Ground of Being. If one has these, existential anxiety becomes a stimulus to creativity. For many persons, coping with this anxiety is facilitated by devotion to the God of justice, love, and truth, and to the realization of his kingdom. For many others, traditional theological symbols are blocks to the discovery of their own object of devotion and workable philosophy of life. Relevant religion seeks not to defend old orthodoxies but rather to aid persons in spiritual discovery, encouraging them to be as true to their own light as the prophets and Jesus were to theirs.

The uniqueness of *pastoral* counseling is derived in part from the minister training as an expert in spiritual growth. As the only helping professional with systematic training in philosophy and theology, he should be particularly helpful in facilitating growth

[2] *Psychoanalysis and Religion* (New Haven: Yale University Press, 1950), p. 21.

[3] Rollo May, ed., *Existential Psychology* (New York: Random House, 1961), p. 98.

in the area of meanings, values, and relatedness to God. As a theological counselor (or counseling theologian) he can integrate theology and psychology in the spiritual growth-stimulating process. Counseling methods can be useful in working through blocks to growth in the spiritual life.

4. A related need is for a *humanized view of man,* i.e., a doctrine of man which emphasizes his capacity for decision, inner freedom, creativity, awareness and self-transcendence. The existentialist perspective in psychotherapy provides us with a fresh spring of resources for meeting this need.[4] The man who asked, "Am I only an organic computer?" reflects the impact of dehumanizing social forces and reductionistic (and mechanistic) views of man which are among the causes of psychopathology. The Hebrew-Christian view that man is formed in the image of God and has a basic uniqueness in the animal kingdom is, therefore, much needed in our situation.

5. Religious groups can help satisfy *the universal need for experiences of transcendence,* providing vacations from the burden of finitude (the sense of being caught in nature with its sickness and death), and the tyranny of time. Attempts to escape from a flat, two-dimensional spiritual universe are involved in the widespread search for instant transcendence through drugs, particularly the hallucinogenic drugs. Religion is a sounder path to moments of transcendence. It can restore the sense of wonder which, in our worship of the golden calf of technological cleverness, often gets trampled underfoot like a delicate flower. In the rites, myths, and dramas of religious groups, the symbolic and the artistic are regularly renewed. Thus contact with the depths in man which Freud plumbed, and the heights which he did not, is restored helping to strengthen one's relationship with the whole self and the world. Mental health values in religious practices are realized as by-products of participating as the spontaneous celebration of life and of experiences of depth relating to God, other persons, and self.

6. *Support of individuals and families in both the develop-*

---

[4] See H. J. Clinebell, Jr., *Basic Types of Pastoral Counseling* (Nashville: Abingdon Press, 1966), pp. 263-64.

mental and accidental crises of living is another need-satisfying function of religious groups. At the various growth stages churches have rites of passage, for example, confirmation. These are group-supported and symbolic ways of coping with the anxiety resulting inevitably from loss of old securities and the threat of the unknown stage ahead. Natural subgroups within healthy churches spontaneously provide emotional support of those in accidental crises such as hospitalization. Group nurturance allows persons to use the crisis as an opportunity for growth. Thus, their coping muscles are strengthened for meeting the next crisis.

7. Religious groups can meet the need *to move from guilt to reconciliation* utilizing the time-tested pathway to forgiveness—confrontation, confession, forgiveness, restitution, and reconciliation (restoration of the broken relationships). Organized religion has centuries of experience in this area. When integrated with recent confrontational counseling approaches, e.g., Glasser's "reality therapy," this heritage can make a unique contribution to mental health. The pervasive pall of guilt in much psychopathology underlines the importance of this resource. Appropriate, reality-based guilt responds to the traditional forgiveness process. Neurotic guilt often calls for counseling skills to resolve the hidden conflict at its roots.

8. *Religious groups can help meet the need of persons to be instruments of personal growth and social change.* They do so by providing motivation, training, and opportunities to be change agents. When all of existence is discovered to be sacred and one's life is viewed as a trust to be invested in enhancing human values, motive-power for significant involvement is created. There are two styles of change agent ministries, the *prophetic* and the *pastoral care–educational*. The former focuses on changing the structures of injustice in society through social action; the latter on changing individuals through counseling, nurturing, and educative relationships. Both are shared responsibilities of laymen and clergymen. Mental health is a useful bridge concept for a much needed wedding of prophetic and pastoral. By pastoral care and counseling, blocked, self-absorbed persons can be "set free to minister." A person is mentally healthy to the degree that

he is free enough from his own hang-ups to be able to be responsive and responsible in his relationships. If he is this, he *will* be a growth agent in others' lives and he *will* continue to grow.

Implications for the Church's and Temple's Programs

There are many implications of this perspective for developing church and temple programs. These needs of people could be met *much* more fully than they are now in most churches.[5] Some innovative religious groups are learning to release their mental health resources. Here are some of the thrusts of such creative churches and temples.

There is a kind of *research and development* climate produced by continuing to seek better answers to, How can *this* church meet the growth-healing needs of its congregation? and of its community? Regular evaluation of existing groups and programs and continuing experimentation with new approaches are present. Both inreach and an outreach (fellowship and mission) are major thrusts in the programs of such churches. Furthermore, there is systematic reflection on how *each* aspect of the program can become more productive of healing, growth, and social change.

Several church program areas are particularly rich in minable mental health ore. One is the *small group program.* A group in which depth relationships can grow through transparent dialogue is like an oasis in the usual desert of superficial relating. There is wisdom in having two parallel sets of groups—the ongoing network of "normal" church groups, and small *ad hoc* groups aimed at personal growth through depth communication and enhancing interpersonal skills. Many types of groups exist, e.g., a depth Bible study group to stimulate the maturing of functional theologies;

[5] In *Joy, Expanding Human Awareness* (New York: Grove Press, 1967), William Schutz declares:

"Our institutions, our organizations, the 'establishment'—even these we are learning to use for our own joy. Our institutions can be improved, can be used to enhance and support individual growth, can be re-examined and redesigned to achieve the fullest measure of human realization." P. 223.

groups to aid preparation for normal crises such as retirement, middle age, marriage, childbirth (Caplan calls these "emotional innoculation groups"). Growth groups for persons with particular problems in living, such as handicapped children, singleness, or chronic health problems, are valuable. Mental health professionals in the church or temple and community can be recruited as leaders or co-leaders (with the clergyman) of groups, and to help train lay leaders for all kinds of groups—e.g., supportive, growth, inspirational, study, and action groups. The ultimate impact on persons of "normal" church groups and of growth-healing groups is determined by the skills, sensitivity, and caring of leaders. Therefore, participation in an ongoing interpersonal skills group under the most competent leader available should be expected of *all* group leaders. The goal of every church and temple should be to have a constellation of small groups varied enough to meet the special needs of every age grouping and major life circumstance.

Another fruitful program area is dynamic *marriage and family life training*. The churches and temples have a direct entree to more pre-parents and parents of children under six (when personality foundations are laid) than any other institution in our society. Thus, they hold the major key to developing a comprehensive program of primary prevention through enriching family relationships and enhancing parental effectiveness in meeting their own and their children's personality needs. The emotional climate of families can be enhanced profoundly by the nurturing relationships within a dynamic, caring church in all the light and the shadows of a family's life cycle.

Education which strengthens parents and families is designed on the emotional growth model utilizing small sharing groups as a major instrument. The most vital groups of my parish ministry was an ongoing child study-nursery group for mothers of preschoolers. Films, lectures, and field experiences were blended with sharing of the fears, hopes, and joys of being parents of young children. Emphasis was on creative ways of satisfying one's own needs in relationships (especially marriage) and on recognizing and satisfying the particular inner hungers of each child. This group would have been even more effective if the fathers could have been involved frequently.

Growth groups for adolescents can be useful in the identity struggle, providing the adult leaders are secure in their adulthood and reasonably comfortable with youth. Parents of adolescents need a growth and nurture group to deepen marriages, resolve conflicts about releasing their teen-agers, and cope with the compound crises of middle age (the pressures of death of parents, menopause, and the grief of the emptying nest). Interpersonal skill groups for young adults (married and unmarried) help them lower barriers to interpersonal intimacy, their life task in that stage. Marital growth groups for couples in each of the major phases of marriage can be highly productive. Rapid changes in male-female roles and the search for depth companionship in marriage make such groups essential in a church program oriented around unmet needs. Groups for pre-married and young married couples also are productive. In addition to groups for individuals and couples, groups for whole families—e.g., family camps and retreats—are invaluable.

Relationship-centered preaching and teaching is another thrust in churches and temples with the growth-healing commitment. Teacher training by the use of interpersonal relationship groups increases the growth potential of church school classes. Preaching maximizes personality values when it is dialogic (with opportunities for talk-back) and when it presents the religious message in ways that are life-affirming. The message is communicated best in a relationship in which acceptance, caring, and confrontation are blended. The quality of the teaching or preaching relationships determines the effectiveness of communication—the "medium is the message."

Religious communities with growth-healing motifs frequently are found to be experimenting with innovations to make corporate worship more alive and meaningful. New structures of involvement and participation are emerging. Several California churches are experimenting with dividing their worshiping congregations into groups of six for guided interpersonal encounter and awareness training during a part of the service.

COMMUNITY MENTAL HEALTH

Pastoral care and counseling are a vital aspect of the growth program of churches. Two developments of particular mental health significance are the *clergy specialist in pastoral care and group development* as a part of a multiple ministry, and the growing use of lay *"pastoral care teams."* Well trained clergymen in specialized ministries of counseling (in local churches, denominational programs, and pastoral counseling centers) are an important new resource for mental health. Their functions include making available new training opportunities in counseling for parish clergymen.

The discovery that certain laymen are *natural therapeutic persons* opens a fresh dimension in congregational pastoral care. When carefully selected, trained, and supervised, such persons can triple a church's ministry to those in crises and to the chronically dependent. Working closely with their clergyman, two laymen from a "grief team" quietly surround a bereaved family with caring as long as they are needed. Trained laymen can be of practical and emotional help to the family of those hospitalized for mental or physical illness. With earlier releases from treatment facilities, a few churches and temples are responding to the need for after-care by sponsoring halfway houses staffed by trained laymen. New methods of pastoral counseling which stress short term, reality, and relationship-oriented approaches and crisis intervention techniques are good news for both the general parish minister and the lay pastoral care team member. All these new developments can help to make churches or temples what they should be—caring communities. When persons become "members one of another," their positive mental health flourishes.

For additional reading

Clinebell, H. J., Jr. *Mental Health Through Christian Community.* Nashville: Abingdon Press, 1965.

McCann, Richard V. *The Churches and Mental Health.* New York: Basic Books, 1962.

6.
PASTORAL CARE AND
THE CRISES OF LIFE

Homer L. Jernigan, B.D., Ph.D.

Albert V. Danielsen Professor of Pastoral Care and Counseling; Director of the Danielsen Center for the Pastoral Care and Counseling, Boston University School of Theology, Boston, Massachusetts

A Crisis Approach to Pastoral Care

The church or synagogue as a caring community should be concerned about people at all ages and stages of life. Religious ministry should be relevant to the needs of individuals, families, and communities. The growth and welfare of persons should be important at all times. Our religious traditions and contemporary studies in mental health recognize however, that there are certain critical times in life which are particularly significant for the emotional and spiritual growth of persons. Religious ministry has long recognized the importance of such experiences as birth, puberty, marriage, sickness, and death. Empirical studies by men like Gerald Caplan and Erik Erikson have brought new understanding of the significance of life crises.

We now have an opportunity to bring together the historic wisdom of our religious traditions and customs with the findings and insights of the behavioral sciences. The religious leader is a key person in this process. Ministry to persons in crisis has long been part of his role, and now he has new understandings and resources to help him. Our opportunity includes the development of more effective approaches to the care of persons in crisis and also the development of programs to prepare people to meet the inevitable crises of life more effectively. Pastoral care, as the total ministry of the religious community to individuals and families in crisis, should include both ministries of healing and comfort and ministries of preparation.

The strategic significance of a crisis-oriented ministry becomes apparent to the hospital chaplain or the student in clinical pastoral education. The minister or rabbi of a local congregation may also experience the readiness of some persons in a crisis situation to reexamine the meanings and values of life and the nature of close interpersonal relationships. Pastoral experience bears evidence that a crisis experience may mean a real effort to change and grow or it may mean a reinforcement of old patterns which limit and distort health and growth.

Gerald Caplan's studies in community psychiatry confirm pastoral observations and add new evidence of the influence of crisis experiences on interpersonal relationships in the family. Caplan describes a crisis as a time

> When a person faces an obstacle to important life goals that is, for a time, insurmountable through the utilization of customary methods of problem-solving, a period of disorganization ensues, during which many different abortive attempts at solution are made. Eventually some kind of adaptation is achieved, which may or may not be in the best interests of the person and his fellows.

Caplan goes on to say, "The important point . . . is that disturbances of interpersonal relationships between mothers and children, and also within the total field of forces in a family, can often be seen clinically to originate during a certain crisis period, or subsequent to a certain crisis period." [1]

Dr. Caplan talks about periods of crisis which are of relatively short duration (four to six months) which are related to significant losses or threats of loss, such as experiences related to birth and bereavement.[2] Erik Erikson, on the other hand, has developed a theory of crisis which is related to personality development through various stages of life. Erikson emphasizes the interaction between the developing individual and his social environment and identifies crucial points and stages of such interaction.[3] Both the crises noted by Caplan and those defined by

[1] Gerald Caplan, *An Approach to Community Mental Health* (New York: Grune and Stratton, 1961), p. 18.

[2] *Ibid.*, p. 41.

[3] Erik Erikson, "Growth and Crises in the Healthy Personality," in *Identity and the Life Cycle: Psychological Issues,* Monograph 1, Vol. I, No. 1 (New York: International Universities Press, 1959), pp. 50-100.

Erikson are important in the development of mental illness, according to studies of family diagnosis conducted by Grunebaum and Bryant.[4]

In a crisis approach to pastoral care it is important to include both the situational and the transitional forms of crisis which occur in families, since both may exert significant influence on the direction of growth of family members and of the family as a whole. Such crises, which happen to most families, include experiences related to birth, adolescence, vocation, marriage, middle age, old age, sickness, and death. Many other crises may occur and may be significant for pastoral care, but it is important to focus the program of the church or synagogue on what might be called the "normal crises" of life. These are the times which influence the life and health of most members of the congregation. Pastoral care which is oriented primarily toward the pathology in the congregation tends to be a quick and inadequate response to emergency situations and has little effect on the welfare of congregation and community. Even a focus on normal crises of families is not sufficient expression, in itself, of a community which really cares about what happens to persons. To care about persons means to care about the social problems which influence their lives, such as poverty, war, discrimination, and political corruption. Pastoral care may need to emphasize personal and family crises because of their significance for the mental and spiritual health of congregation and community, but a total program of caring goes beyond individuals and families to the conditions in the world which interfere with the growth of persons.

Dimensions of a Life Crisis

Each of the normal crises of life which has been mentioned needs careful study in order to identify the nature of the crisis and the resources for preparation and treatment. The analysis of

[4] Henry Grunebaum and Charles Bryant, "The Theory and Practice of the Family Diagnostic, Part II. Theoretical Aspects and Resident Education," in Irvin Cohen, ed., *Family Structure, Dynamics, and Therapy* (Psychiatric Research Reports of the American Psychiatric Association, Washington, D. C., 1966), p. 151.

one such crisis may serve to illustrate the many dimensions which need to be considered and the implications for the life and work of the local congregation.

One of the common tasks of a congregation and its leadership is the provision of an appropriate wedding ceremony for a young couple. This is such a familiar occurrence that little thought may be given to it beyond the necessary details of a "lovely wedding." If, however, a congregation really cares about the young couple and what happens to them in their marriage and what happens to the family which is established by the marriage, then much more thought needs to be given this particular marriage and to the responsibilities of the congregation for marriage and family life in the community. The marriage ceremony, as a symbol of God's concern about marriage and of the congregations' concern about this couple, should symbolize a total program of guidance and support for marriage and family living. A focus on the wedding ceremony is strategically important, because the wedding marks the beginning of a new family. This is one of the crucial places to begin with the development of a comprehensive program of pastoral care.

Some observations about marriage and preparation for marriage can be summarized briefly as a background for discussing a comprehensive pastoral care approach to the crisis of marriage. These observations are based on a variety of reading and experience.

1. Preparation for marriage begins at birth and is influenced by many things. Some of the more significant influences—expectations of marriage and attitudes toward marriage that the couple have developed in their own families, the ability to give and take they have learned at home, their social adjustment outside the family, the opportunities they have had for gradually increasing experience with the opposite sex before this courtship, and their understanding of facts, values, and attitudes related to love and sex.[5]

[5] For a brief introduction to some of the problems involved in preparation for marriage see Evelyn Duvall, David Mace, and Paul Popenoe, *The Church Looks at Family Life* (Nashville: Broadman Press, 1964).

2. Approaching marriage arouses anxieties, and sometimes guilt, about personal adequacy for marriage, closeness with another person, sexual adjustment, ties to parents, new responsibilities, etc. Such anxieties (and guilt) need to be faced as openly as possible *before* marriage.

3. Preparation for marriage is much more than the readiness of two individuals to participate in a ceremony. The couple prepare themselves for marriage by the kind of relationship they develop with each other before marriage. Most important are the patterns of interaction they are developing in sharing positive and negative feelings, facing conflicts, making decisions, and handling their relationships with other people (especially their future in-laws).

4. Our society tends to foster unrealistic attitudes and expectations about courtship and marriage and confusion about husband and wife roles.

5. Many couples, whether or not they have grown up in a religious community, have little idea of the religious meaning and significance of marriage (as well as the psychosocial realities).

6. The wedding ceremony is often seen as a social occasion for which it is "nice" to have a religious service. Meaningful participation in the ceremony as an act of worship of the religious community requires education of the congregation as well as preparation of the couples requesting the marriage service.

7. Adjustments to marriage is an ongoing process, and many important problems cannot be faced realistically until after marriage. Before marriage the couple may be helped to face the problems and resources they have in their courtship, particularly the potentialities and limitations of their own relationship. The couple may also need help after marriage to face problems they could not realistically anticipate before marriage.

8. Marital and premarital problems often involved the interaction of unconscious attitudes and habit patterns which a couple cannot recognize or change without outside help.

9. Marital problems are interwoven with social problems such as education, medical care, housing, employment, race and war.

Such observations could be documented in detail. They do not constitute a total picture of the problem of marriage in our day. Much more needs to be said about that problem; but these brief observations do suggest some of the things a congregation that is concerned about people and about the significance of its wedding ceremony needs to consider. A number of implications for a program of pastoral care emerge.

1. The congregation needs to develop a climate of concern about people and about their marriages. This climate needs to be based on facts about the problem of marriage in our day, the various dimensions of the problem, and the role of the religious community in dealing with this problem.

2. The congregation needs to understand the religious significance of marriage and the meaning of the marriage ceremony.

3. Policies and procedures need to be developed to protect the marriage ceremony from being used by persons who do not accept its meaning or being exploited by those who want to put personal or social values above religious values.

4. The congregation needs to develop a program of family life education which will strengthen families in their efforts to prepare their children for coping with the realities of life (including marriage and family living).

5. Single congregations need to join with other congregations and other concerned groups to develop community programs of education for marriage. Such programs are needed to counteract the unrealistic values and expectations fostered by our society and to provide resources for couples to face the issues of courtship and marriage before they are involved in the actual details of the wedding ceremony.

6. Policies and procedures for pre-marital counseling need to be developed which can use the skills of competent lay members of the congregation as well as those of the professional leaders. Such counseling needs to begin early enough and last long enough to help the couple assess and strengthen their relationship in crucial areas. In some cases the potential in-laws may need to be included in the counseling process. Group pre-marital

counseling is a valuable resource which needs more experimentation.

7. Careful attention should be given to the actual marriage ceremony in order to enhance its worship aspects and to make use of the historic and contemporary resources of the religious community.

8. Programs of marital guidance for young married couples should be developed to help them in their adjustment to problems encountered after marriage.

9. Resources for competent marriage counseling should be made available to those couples who cannot, on their own or with the help of information and guidance, develop adequate patterns of coping with marriage and family crises.

10. Congregations and individual members of congregations should join with other concerned individuals and groups to work for the alleviation of social conditions which are threatening marriage and family life.

11. In view of the complex problems of marriage and preparation for marriage, which have been suggested here, and the need for competent professional resources to assist the local congregation, congregations should join together in sponsoring agencies which can provide such professional resources.

A Comprehensive Program of Pastoral Care

Marriage is but one of the many crises which are important for the emotional and spiritual health of individuals and families. The brief analysis of a pastoral care approach to couples requesting to be married in a religious community is only one illustration of the comprehensive approach which is needed to persons in every crisis of life. It is obvious that such an approach goes beyond pastoral care in the limited sense which is often understood. It does not, however, go beyond the kind of care for persons which should characterize a religious community in our Judeo-Christian tradition.

Both the needs of persons in our day and the new resources for mental health which are available to us challenge us to develop more adequate approaches to pastoral care. We, in our religious traditions, have something valuable to offer to the community mental health movement, particularly in our resources for life crises. We also have much to learn.

For additional reading

For some readings on premarital counseling and marriage education see *Pastoral Psychology,* December 1959, and *Pastoral Psychology,* May 1968. See also Aaron Rutledge, *Pre-marital Counseling* (Cambridge, Mass.: Schenkman Publishing Co., 1966), and J. Kenneth Morris, *Pre-marital Counseling, A Manual for Ministers* (Englewood Cliffs, N.J.: Prentice-Hall, 1960).

7.
SHARING GROUPS IN THE CHURCH: RESOURCE FOR POSITIVE MENTAL HEALTH

Robert C. Leslie, S.T.B., Ph.D.
Foster Professor of Pastoral Psychology and Counseling, Pacific School of Religion and Graduate Theological Union, Berkeley, California

The most natural structure for the church to work with is the small group. Most of the significant work of the churches is done through its committees or its study classes or its action projects. When people come together in the life of the church they expect to meet in small groups and feel comfortable in such a setting. But the level of interpersonal interaction in most church groups leaves a great deal to be desired. The potential of church groups for aiding in personal growth is seldom recognized and even less often utilized. The possibility, however, of making use of small groups in the church as a resource for positive mental health is very great.

In order for small groups to be significant resources for growth, personal sharing needs to be a chief characteristic. Whatever else is carried on in the group, there needs to be a real place for the kind of sharing that leads to a feeling of support and closeness out of which relationships are deepened. For example, in one church a group of young mothers, each having small children, was organized for a study class with an expert from the psychological world. After meeting for several weeks for lecture and discussion, the young mothers were asked if they would be interested in continuing to meet in a small sharing group in which they could support each other in their efforts at being adequate mothers. The leadership would be provided by the associate minister. In response to their eager request for such a group, the first meeting was scheduled.

As the young mothers gathered for the first session of their sharing group, meeting in the library of the church, the leader set the mood for their work together. He asked each member what first name she liked to use, inquired into the ages of the children represented, introduced himself, and then said: "Well, how do you feel about being here in this group?" The sharing group had started. The basic pattern of its interaction had been indicated and the tone for the sessions had been set. By meeting in the church, the concerns of religious commitment were implied. By acknowledging each person in turn as a participating member, the focus on individuality had been stressed. By noting the ages of the children, the common bond of being young mothers had been indicated. By posing the opening question in terms of present feelings the orientation of the group had been established and the focus of the group had been indicated.

The expectant waiting of the leader made it clear that the work of the group would be carried out not by him but by the members. In the opening few minutes, as the leader refused to be cast in the role of answer man, and as interaction among members was encouraged, it became clear that this was a new kind of group experience. The members discovered that they were authorities on their own feelings, that their feelings were quite similar to those shared by others, that they did not need to be ashamed of their feelings. Sensing acceptance from the leader, and recognizing support from the other group members, they quickly learned that they could look deeper into themselves and reveal even more of their feelings. Hearing experiences from other young mothers, they discovered new ways of functioning in the mother role. Sensing the support of the group, they could dare to risk experimenting in new patterns of dealing with their children.

Such a sharing group has as its goal the facilitating of personal growth. It is not a treatment group, although it has some of the features of such a group. It is not a study class, although it has some of the features of study. Its distinctive characteristic is that it combines both of these emphases. It draws on research findings from the field of group therapy, and it makes use of the small group as a facilitator of learning. Indeed, the first distinguishing characteristic of the sharing group is that it combines the therapeutic with the educational.

Since the sharing group as we have described it centers on a sharing of feelings, the emphasis is more therapeutic than it is educational. But because the church group is always concerned with assisting the growth of its members toward Christian goals, it always has an educative function. Of course, any meaningful educational experience takes into account the deeper needs of the learner. There is always resistance to any new ideas which might imply a need for new patterns of thought, and until this resistance is taken into account, little learning takes place. Any educational process has a primary responsibility to master a body of knowledge, but this responsibility can be carried out only in an environment which is constantly alert to therapeutic needs.

A second characteristic of the sharing group is its emphasis on communicating feeling. One of the most significant learning experiences that takes place in a sharing group comes when communication of feelings is given a priority over mere socialization. It is characteristic of most groups that communication is conceived of as being at a fairly high level. Even in a large group we like to feel that we have a basic understanding of what the other person is trying to convey. In smaller classes or in committees or in training groups we are even more ready to assert that we are, in truth, a comfortable sort of group in which the flow of ideas and decisions is carried on in an atmosphere of good fellowship. When group activity is analyzed carefully, however, it becomes apparent that some groups have achieved far greater facility in communicating in a fundamental way than others, and that, indeed, some of the groups seldom reach a point where interaction is on a meaningful level.

A large part of the uniqueness of the sharing group lies in the experience of communicating freely, without defensiveness, in as personal and emotional a manner as one desires. Ideally the sharing group is one in which it is possible to be perfectly honest about emotions present as they are recognized in the self and shared with others. One student in a sharing group writes of what the experience meant to him:

> I have felt freer and more able to be myself in that group than in any other I have been in. It wasn't so much being able to express hostility, but being able to express my inadequacies and feel that they were understood and shared to some extent by the rest of the group.

A third characteristic of the sharing group is found in the kind of involvement which the leader permits for himself. Whether one subscribes to the orthodox psychoanalytic pattern of a passive therapist or not, it is very clear that no leader can really encourage sharing until he is willing to share himself. Granting that the leader needs to maintain objectivity in order to function in the leadership role, it is equally important that he involve himself as a participant.

The point is that the able leader is willing to let the group see him as a real human being struggling with problems. One seminary teacher tells of being at his greatest effectiveness during the days that he shared with his students the blow-by-blow account of his dealings with real estate people as he sold his house to a member of a minority group and tried, at the same time, to act responsibly toward his neighbors. In my own experience with group leadership, I believe I was closest to the group with which I shared my anxiety over a long weekend as I waited for a pathologist's report on a tumor taken from my daughter.

A fourth principle for the sharing group makes the present

situation the focus of attention. The situation of the moment, the here and now in this room and around this table, is never lost sight of. This means that investigation into past behavior is not only not encouraged but is even consciously discouraged. By keeping the focus on the present, many of the unfortunate excesses of a confidential nature about past events are avoided and one of the chief complaints against sharing groups in the church is eliminated. Excursions into the past are entered into only to clarify the present. The real interest centers in the immediate, current scene, and past relationships or past events are of only incidental interest.

To keep the focus on the present calls for considerable activity on the part of the leader. I recall a group situation where one of the group members, a mature woman, dominated the first part of the group with a fascinating account of her recent trip to Europe. After permitting her to go on for a short time, I interrupted to say that although what she was saying was interesting it was inappropriate for our task. Later she wrote me a letter in which she demonstrated that she had learned a good deal:

> I want to thank you for what I learned; how to keep quiet and listen to others; the whole concept of what you termed "unfinished business". . . which meant that there was an interpersonal relationship which had not been worked through; the surprising truth that there is no conflict that does not disappear if both people will go into the encounter and face the negatives and articulate them in terms of actual feelings; . . . your continual emphasis on getting rid of the things that keep people from loving each other.

A fifth characteristic of the sharing group in the church stresses personal sharing as opposed to probing for answers. There is a common tendency in any group that is working with feelings to probe for underlying motivation. The inclination is thus to focus attention on other members with the intent of pushing for an answer as to why a person acts the way he does. I am proposing, however, that a far more productive pattern is to develop the capacity to share in a personal way with increasing freedom.

Thus the attention turns from why someone else functions the way he does to sharing the way a person, himself, feels.

It is obvious that the leader plays a major role in helping groups to share their own feelings rather than to probe for underlying motivation. Thus the leader appropriately asks: How do you feel when Tom keeps pressing you for an answer?" but he does not ask Tom: "Why do you press so hard for an answer?" The principle here is that the exploration of motives is not the task of the sharing group, but the disclosure of feelings present always is appropriate.

There is at least one more principle which characterizes the sharing group in the church. Observations are always welcomed, but attacks are avoided. Whereas the natural inclination is to fix blame for feelings on someone else, the sharing group encourages a recognition of the feeling without ascribing a responsibility for it. Thus instead of saying: "You have a very annoying way of interrupting me" (in which the blame is placed on the other person), the group member is encouraged to share his feeling without attaching blame by saying: "I find myself getting annoyed whenever I am interrupted." Here is an observation about personal feelings which leaves open the question of whose fault it is, and which makes possible an exploration of the meaning behind the feeling in a freer and less defensive manner.

I do not mean in this principle to deny the existence of strong negative feelings or to prohibit their expression. I do mean to suggest that negative feelings are dealt with best in an atmosphere in which a person is not on the defensive. A major advantage of the group situation is that support can be so real that angry and fearful feelings can really be recognized and explored. It is my experience that such recognition and exploration seldom take place in the presence of attack.

To recognize sharing groups in the church as a resource for positive mental health does not imply that everyone in the church should be organized into a group. Sharing groups call for a special interest in a personal kind of sharing. Not everyone is prepared to share his feelings, and so not everyone is interested in participating in a sharing group. A more exact way of putting it is that many do not want to risk involvement in a group that will ask for sharing at a personal level. Hence some kind of screening is needed in order to bring together those who are eager to share without raising resistance from those who are too anxiety-ridden to share. To attempt to organize a whole parish into small sharing groups overlooks this importnat factor and dooms the program to failure before it even gets started.

The kinds of groups in the church in which personal sharing is possible are almost unlimited. High school seniors in one church met for breakfast each week throughout the spring to talk with their minister about their place in life and their feelings about the future. Some churches have sharing groups for parents of teenagers, for retired men, for divorced women, for parents of retarded children. We have already noted the possibility of an educational program out of which smaller, more intimate groups can be formed for sharing on a more personal basis. One church held an all-day conference in September for single parents and then announced a continuing group (or groups) to meet weekly during the fall until Christmas. In a similar pattern one church has an annual Marriage Clinic with outside speakers for four consecutive weeks and then provides opportunity for couples to meet together on a less formal basis in small sharing groups over a period of ten to twelve weeks. In each case the goals are the same: to provide an intimate, supportive group in which personal attitudes and feelings are talked out and in which supportive friendships are developed.

For additional reading

Anderson, Philip A. *Church Meetings That Matter,* Philadelphia: United Church Press, 1965.

Casteel, John L., ed. *The Creative Role of Interpersonal Groups in the Church Today.* New York: Association Press, 1968.

———, ed. *Spiritual Renewal Through Personal Groups.* New York: Association Press, 1957.

Clinebell, Howard J., Jr. "Mental Health and the Group Life of the Church," *Mental Health Through Christian Community.* (Nashville: Abingdon Press, 1965, pp. 149-70.

8.
THE CLERGY'S ROLE IN A GOVERNMENT PROGRAM OF PREVENTION OF ALCOHOLISM

Lawrence A. Purdy, B.D.
*Regional Director, Metropolitan Toronto Region,
Addiction Research Foundation, Toronto, Canada*

What has been the experience of a government addiction program in its use of clergy as members of the professional team? The program of the Ontario Addiction Research Foundation illustrates one approach.

The Foundation is an agency of the Province of Ontario and receives most of its budget through the Department of Health. In turn, it is accountable for its program to the government and people of the province.

A multi-million-dollar research and clinical institute is under construction in Toronto, and plans for joint appointments of senior staff with the University and the Institute are underway; a great portion of the Foundation's current program is dispersed throughout the province. Programs in thirty cities and towns seek to serve the nearly 7,000,000 population with treatment, education, research, and community development resources. These services range from highly sophisticated diagnostic and treatment centers to smaller community clinics and one-man information and development programs.

Among the more than 200 professional staff members, 10 clergy representing the major denominations are at work side by side with psychiatrists, physicians, social workers, psychologists, nurses, and others. There is common consent—perhaps in this field the one area of real consensus—that there will never be enough services and professionals to meet all the needs of the alcoholics and the drug addicts. In recognition of this, a great deal of the emphasis on the role of clergy to be detailed here refers to the development and mobilization of concern, competence, and care-giving capacity on the part of the community as a whole. This is based on direct service experience and demonstrated skill at the secondary and tertiary (treatment and rehabilitation) levels of prevention. Its ultimate objective, however, goes beyond the proliferation of specialized services to the improvement and ultimate change of the community climate which produces the problems. The method is to move to the level of secondary prevention by providing more skilled early intervention by community helpers in the health and social services. Ultimately the aim is to achieve the primary level of prevention by effecting the kinds of social change necessary to reduce the problems of alcoholism or drug dependency.

In all these efforts, hard questions continue to be asked, program achievement is assessed and evaluated, new directions are identified and new emphases explored. This research base is balanced by the need to share our experience with others through programs of training, consultation, undergraduate, graduate, and continuing professional education.

Let us, then, describe briefly what the clergy do and endeavor to fit these activities and experiences into the total rationale for their involvement.

The first full-time appointment for clergy in the Foundation was that of the pastoral counselor. The primary task, five years ago, was to identify and validate the role of the pastor in a multi-professional therapeutic milieu. Given the more than forty-year history of clinical pastoral training in North America, this was hardly a pioneering effort. It was, however, a "first" for the Foundation and included responsibilities not only in the treatment field but in the areas of professional education and consultation as well.

The validation of the role of the clergy in a multi-professional treatment setting is challenging to both the personal and professional relationships involved. However, it is even more difficult to duplicate in the community outside. While a great deal has been said about the interprofessional team, it is inevitably more successful when relationships are sustained, visible, and viable within the closed circuit of an institution. The so-called community team has a long way to go to establish and improve its effectiveness. There is still abundant evidence of tendencies among the health and social service professionals to close ranks against the clergy. Priests and ministers are often the victims of stereotyping by other professionals and seen as irrelevant, untrained, even highly suspect in their motivation. As sources of referral and prospects for ongoing supportive care, they are often overlooked or only reluctantly given gestures of approval by the "professionals."

To overcome this state of affairs, one of the major tasks of the Foundation's clergy is not only to meet the needs of individual patients in treatment, and to contribute to the case conferences in consultations with other staff. The pastoral counselor must also continually work *to bridge the gap between the community*—including the clergy—*and the treatment resources.* To this end then, he aims not only at the needs of the patients, but at the needs of professionals with whom he works, to whom he relates both within and beyond the therapeutic setting.

A major deficiency in *recognizing the spiritual component* in the field of addictions has been the lack of clearly defined criteria, based on hard data, that measure up to social, psychological, and medical standards. The Foundation's pastoral counselor, a member of the staff of Toronto's medical unit, has contributed to the overall design of a measuring instrument providing total medical records by computer. The instrument has a religious and spiritual portion, along with medical, psychiatric, psychological, and social histories. Ultimately, this research will answer 6,000 questions of more than 1,200 patients each year. We see this making an important contribution to a clearer definition of what we mean by the "spiritual component" in the cause, course, and consequences of alcoholism. As experience in this field develops and further research is undertaken, we look for clearer guidelines in measuring the role of religion—as asset and liability—in developing effective treatment and rehabilitation programs.

As suggested earlier, the direct service of our treatment resources to alcoholics and other addicted persons is limited numerically by the staff and facilities available. However, we believe these services can be multiplied effectively if the existing resources in the community are motivated, mobilized, and supported by specialized experience. Background information, training resources, and the ongoing coordination of services is undertaken by agents or field representatives of the Foundation engaged in community development.

In several communities professionals have been appointed to such tasks. In three such communities the person selected is a clergyman. The qualities sought in such an individual represent not only the traditional trust and expectations of the community, but also the very special flexibility and skills that the persons have demonstrated in providing a focus for joint action on the part of the community's professional and volunteer helpers. This "agent" role appears to work best in communities of 25 to 50,000 where the visibility and competence of one individual can be reinforced by frequent and informal contacts with professionals in the community care-giving services.

While Foundation clergy in this role are full-time appointees, there is no reason why partnership programs of more modest scale should not provide for part-time appointments to the same end.

Two of the Foundation's clergy serve important and demanding roles as directors of pilot projects. The Foundation's Bon Accord Farm is a rural rehabilitation project located at a splendid century-old farm northwest of Toronto. Here the hard-core alcoholic is brought for long-term (six- to ten-month) rehabilitation. A choice of activities is available including routine farm maintenance, woodworking and metal working shops, and regular domestic and household chores.

In the city, the Foundation's Halfway House program is also supervised by a clergyman. Responsibilities for this work include not only the administration of the large residential center in Toronto, but a consulting role with church and community-sponsored halfway houses throughout the province. When caring, flexible, and diligent staff persons were needed to get these programs off the ground, the church provided them. Not only the leadership, but the rationale and philosophies of the reinforced family, the supporting community, the corrective living experience, come through with theological as well as sociological bases in these programs.

THE CLERGY'S ROLE IN A GOVERNMENT PROGRAM

To many in the field of addictions, the history and the role of the temperance movement remains a curious and increasingly irrelevant phase in society's attempt to cope with alcoholism. To the Foundation it represents an authentic and legitimate attempt to meet a problem head-on. One of the Foundation's clergy, for some years deeply involved in the temperance movement in Canada, is writing a history to be published under our auspices.

The information being gathered, both anecdotal and statistical, represents a major and significant contribution to the field. It is, moreover, a task being undertaken barely in time to avoid the irretrievable loss of direct contact with some of the few remaining great personalities identified with this phase of social change.

The largest regional program for professional education and training in the province is under the direction of a clergyman. This involves the development of seminars, workshops, professional internships, and community consultations, together with the ongoing flow of information and experience to the agencies and organizations serving the community.

Two of the Foundation's clergy are responsible for the direction of comprehensive regional programs embracing the three thrusts of treatment, education, and research. One of the regions thus directed represents the largest portion of the province's population and the greatest single program investment in terms of manpower and money.

It must be said that only part of the multi-faceted involvement of the clergy in our program is the Foundation's recognition of individual and professional competence. A good portion of the involvement must also be attributed to the ferment and change within the church and the current search for new and relevant ministries. In discussions with the Foundation clergy it has been agreed that the object of this search is not to establish an elite cadre of specialists. Nor is it simply to suggest a rejection of the church and its traditional systems and structures. Rather it is a reconnaissance—perhaps too a renaissance—a rediscovery of the role of the church in society with a particular and urgent emphasis on the cure of souls. The task will not be complete with the discoveries, the identification of roles, the development of

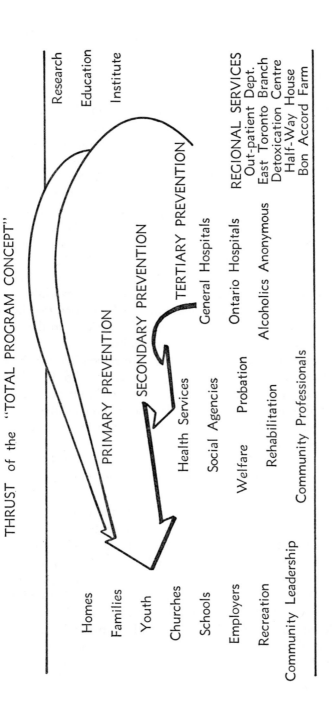

THRUST of the "TOTAL PROGRAM CONCEPT"

PRIMARY PREVENTION

SECONDARY PREVENTION

TERTIARY PREVENTION

Homes
Families
Youth
Churches
Schools
Employers
Recreation
Community Leadership

Health Services
Social Agencies
Welfare   Probation
Rehabilitation
Community Professionals

General Hospitals
Ontario Hospitals
Alcoholics Anonymous

Research
Education
Institute

REGIONAL SERVICES
Out-patient Dept.
East Toronto Branch
Detoxication Centre
Half-Way House
Bon Accord Farm

skills and insights, or even with the clarification of status and relationships with the other professions in partnership programs and community care-giving services. This is only the beginning.

The task approaches a useful point of measurement when the experience gained is interpreted and relayed back to the church to effect modifications in its attitude, structure, and service. The introduction of courses at the undergraduate level in colleges and seminaries, the promotion of graduate serminars, together with more than a decade of specialized training for clergy sponsored by the Foundation, reinforce this experience of ours by adding to the experience of others.

Major shifts in church policy and programming will come, however, only when the religious community, historically opposed to tyrannies of all kinds, recognizes the nature of one of the more subtle and insidious tyrannies of our time—the tyranny of the chemical age. Those of us who are privileged to be on the firing line wih our professional partners have a duty to help the church community articulate a message that meets this need.

What has been described thus far has largely been functional—the way the clergy work in a government addictions program as counselors, administrators, educators, consultants, teachers, and field workers. Perhaps our greatest role is still being shaped by our experience—that of the *prophet*—to be spokesmen out of our experience, insight, and concern, to "tell it the way it is" to the church and, through the church, to the world.

9.
CLERGYMEN IN A PREVENTIVE MENTAL HEALTH PROGRAM

John A. Snyder, B.D., Ed.D.
*Associate Director of Education and Consultation,
Pennsylvania Hospital Community Mental Health
Center, Philadelphia, Pennsylvania*

Too often, pastoral counselors are like a group of men at the bottom of a cliff. People are stumbling off the cliff and getting hurt. Some come miraculously away from the fall without serious injury—perhaps a sprained ankle—and need a little assistance that can easily be given. Others, however, are more seriously injured and require a great deal of attention because of broken limbs. A few are quickly hustled away because of even more serious injuries. The whole scene is such a busy one, and the men so preoccupied with their healing tasks, that no one seems to be able to give any attention to what would seem a logical move: to build a fence at the top of the cliff to keep the people from falling off.

Until very recently, psychiatry has been concerned primarily with "bottom of the cliff" activity—that is, treating the mentally ill and the emotionally crippled. Appropriately, then, much of the effort in psychiatry has been devoted toward elaborate description of the pathology and categorization of the problems to insure treatment in as systematic a fashion as possible. Psychiatrists, as physicians, have been specially trained to recognize, diagnose, and treat mental and emotional illness, and have made a major contribution with their skill.

What has happened in the 1960s is a rapid shift of attention from healing the brokenness at the bottom of the cliff to trying to build preventive fences at the top. The whole mental health movement is an example of this shift. However, all one need do is pay close attention to the precision with which a psychiatrist can define mental illness, and the fuzziness with which he defines mental health, and one becomes aware that our problems are not going to be solved entirely by *that* profession.

The real significance of this confusion is that psychiatrists have started acting like clergymen and clergymen have started acting more like psychiatrists. I am not one to get terribly upset by this. In many cases where the clergyman is specially trained or usually sensitive and perceptive, he may be able to provide healing in many cases of functional mental illness as well as, or better than, many psychiatrists. On the other hand, many psychiatrists with a religious desire to save men and nations can help us interpret what goes into the full, rich, and abundant life.

In our training programs for community clergymen at the

A PREVENTIVE MENTAL HEALTH PROGRAM

Pennsylvania Hospital Community Mental Health Center we have been interested in mutual exchange: (1) We believe that psychiatry and its allied professions can help the clergyman do a better job with his healing ministry (at the bottom of the cliff). (2) We believe clergymen have something unique to contribute to psychiatry in the whole business of prevention (building fences at the top of the cliff).

It is widely accepted that psychiatry can contribute to the clergyman's ministry to troubled people. The real question is, How can a community mental health center and community clergymen work together toward the prevention of emotional disturbances? Resistance comes from both sides—from clergymen who would prefer to talk about schizophrenia than talk about how their Christian education program might be more effective from a mental health standpoint, and from some psychiatrists who have considerable difficulty in visualizing how religion could prevent any of the problems they deal with. In the latter case, the problem is not that these psychiatrists believe that religion is harmful; but rather having themselves grown up in a culture where religion was innocuous, they cannot see the significance of religion for good or ill. We have worked very hard over the last fifteen or twenty years to establish a good working relationship between clergy and psychiatrists in healing troubled people at the bottom of the cliff. If we think, however, that having solved the problem of cooperative effort at the bottom of the cliff we also have solved it at the top—in prevention—we are greatly mistaken.

The first step toward a good program of prevention is to establish a relationship of trust between the community mental health center staff and community clergy. Once some mutual sharing begins to occur, it is amazing what happens.

The clergyman may begin to realize that the mental health professional has a contribution to make to his total pastoral ministry. This may be more important than the mental health professional's help in strengthening his pastoral counseling techniques, especially if the clergyman can realize his unique position of contact with people when problems are just beginning to become serious. We have discovered that the clergyman will often see only those problems for which he knows a solution. By broadening his knowledge of community resources, we broaden his vision. For example, in the beginning of the program one clergyman reported that he simply did not see people with problems. His visitation amounted to administering the sacraments and leaving as soon as possible. However, once he became aware of the help that he could receive from the mental health center for both consultation and referral, he started overwhelming us with calls about the troubled people he was visiting.

Second, the clergyman may find support and encouragement for his own unique style of intervention. In our program we had a black store-front clergyman from the ghetto who was viewed by our mental health staff with some suspicion because of his lack of credentials. He was self-educated and self-ordained. He lacked any formal clinical training, although many troubled people were turning to him for help. It was unexpected that he would become one of our best *teachers*. His lesson of how to prevent suicide in the ghetto is a classic. One of his lay leaders had made a serious suicidal attempt and had been hospitalized. The man was a puzzle to the hospital staff because of his depression; the staff was reluctant to discharge him or to move toward a long-term confinement. The usual approaches of individual and group psychotherapy seemed to be pointless with this man, who neither appreciated nor respected "all this talk-stuff." When allowed, the black clergyman moved in with some very direct intervention. He had discovered that the man's two teen-age daughters were pregnant by him and that there was some community knowledge of this fact. He said his goal with the man was to give him a choice whether he would live or die. Right now, he said, the man will have to die. After having first arranged abortions for the two girls, he brought the layman in front of the congregation and asked the congregation: "Should he die?" The congregation responded in a booming voice: "No." The clergyman repeated the question, and the congregation echoed its response. The clergyman then directed the congregation toward a healing ministry to the man and his family but with a heavy emphasis on the man's "sin." While we might question this clergyman's techniques, it is obvious that he is able to use the resources available to him, and his style seems to be very effective with his people. It is with active intervention like this that some crises are contained rather than allowed to explode with more destructive consequences.

Finally, we have learned that prevention of mental and emotional problems must include concern for the economic, social, and environmental problems which trouble entire communities and form the foundation for specific instances of mental illness and breakdown. In terms of the figure of the cliff, we found that it was not enough to concern ourselves with building fences, even though in the beginning this was the way we defined our task. Far too many of the people who were ending up in the brokenness of life were being driven off the cliff by dogs yelping at their heels. An ideal program of prevention would imply cooperation between the mental health center staff and community clergy in attacking these wider community problems. In the long run this aspect of prevention is probably more important than all the rest. Community clergymen can therefore move into action in the prevention of mental and emotional disturbances in each of these three areas: (1) by using the mental health center resources to make their total pastoral ministry more effective in the early detection of problems; (2) by becoming more comfortable in the use of their own style of helping troubled people so that some crisis situations can be contained; (3) by using the rich resources of social concern in the churches to attack the wider problems out of which so many individual cases of emotional disturbance arise.

For additional reading

Action for Mental Health (by the Joint Commission on Mental Illness and Health) gives the background for the development of mental health programs and suggests the importance of clergymen in the mental health field. For a more specific treatment of preventive programs, see Gerald Caplan, *Principles of Preventive Psychiatry* (New York: Basic Books, 1964). For the application of these principles of prevention to the role of the clergyman, see J. A. Snyder, "Clergymen and Widening Concepts of Mental Health," *Journal of Religion and Health,* July, 1968.

PART II
the church's roles
in treatment

Through the centuries, churches and temples have had a continuing concern for helping the burdened and the crisis-stricken. The one to whom Christians look as founder of their tradition and model of their style of life was called "great physician." Long before he was born, the wise men of Israel functioned in guiding the troubled. The ancient emphasis on healing and helping has received fresh impetus and resources in the contemporary scene. Time-tested wisdom about relationships, in the Hebrew-Christian tradition, has been confirmed and enhanced by insights from the sciences of man and skills from the counseling arts. Consequently, clergymen and laymen have an *unprecedented opportunity to participate effectively in the treatment dimension of the community mental health movement.* By so doing they can be *in mission,* using the "gifts of healing, or ability to help others or power to guide them." (I Cor. 12:28 NEB.)

This section illuminates several salient aspects of the church's many faceted opportunity in counseling and pastoral care. It begins with an overview chapter by a psychiatrist (Knight) of the therapeutic ministry of a church. This is followed by a discussion of crisis counseling with special reference to suicide prevention (Pretzel). In succeeding chapters the nature of the churches' ministry to persons in special need is probed—the poor (Browning), the gifted and retarded (Kemp), the bereaved (Grollman), the alcoholic (Dominick), the mentally ill (Kempson), and the ex-inmate (Klink). One chapter (Bushfield) deals with a vital new mental health treatment resource—the church-related counseling service. The final chapter in this section (Oman) describes a local church program which takes the therapeutic ministry seriously.

Through only scratching the surface of the potentialities of clergymen and churches in the counseling field, these chapters point to some of the major trends and opportunities for reducing human suffering through such a ministry. They reflect some of the new insights and methods which are emerging in this renaissance period in pastoral care and counseling.

10.
THE THERAPEUTIC OPPORTUNITY OF THE CLERGYMAN AND THE CONGREGATION

James A. Knight, B.D., M.D.
Associate Dean and Professor of Psychiatry, Tulane University School of Medicine, New Orleans, Louisiana

There is no institution more community-centered than the church. The church's capacity to involve itself in every aspect of community life has served as a model for the development of certain aspects of the community mental health centers. There has been a growing awareness that the effective church has identified with the total culture of a community and all of its people. Her history has shown involvement and identification with poverty, discrimination, illness, loneliness, imprisonment, persecution, as well as with wholeness.

In the Judeo-Christian tradition, the church has never separated its message of salvation from its concern for concrete service to human beings, including the healing of sickness. At present, community mental health brings a new set of challenges and possibilities to the church. Cooperative efforts of the church and the community mental health center will bring about a better utilization of the new healing powers and methods available for dealing with human ills.

McNeill in *A History of the Cure of Souls* mentions that one of the difficulties in the effective correlation of "religious and scientific psychotherapy" has been the lack of the institutional means of cooperation.[1] The comprehensive community mental

[1] John T. McNeill, *A History of the Cure of Souls* (New York, Harper, 1951), p. 322.

health centers, to a large extent, may furnish the institutional means and thus provide a new pathway to cooperation.

Community mental health programs are being built on the concept of a necessity for an integrated fabric of mental health services in which all the available and appropriate resources of the community are mobilized for prevention, diagnosis, treatment, and rehabilitation of mental and emotional disorders. The focus is on the community where the individual, regardless of age or socioeconomic status, quickly and easily can obtain the services needed without transferring to institutions located in other communities.

In the development of the comprehensive mental health center, the entire community is being involved in identifying and taking action with respect to its own problems. The emphasis is on cooperative and collaborative work among the various groups in the community to the end that they may develop the capacity to work together in dealing with mental health problems. There is increasing attention to the concept that mental health and mental illness can be best understood when there is focus upon the relationship between the individual and the community in which he lives. The centers are not to be just central repositories of professional skills, waiting passively for patients to appear, but will reach out to identify illness in all its psychic and social variants and bring it within the centers' therapeutic orbit through consultative, educational, and preventive efforts.

The clergyman is related to the field of community mental health primarily on three levels: promotional, supportive, and therapeutic. Through recreational, social, and family education programs, he helps promote and maintain mental health.

Through pastoral care and counseling, the clergyman functions in a supportive or sustaining role, and often a therapeutic one. Such a ministry is geared toward early help with minor emotional disturbances, crisis situations, parent-child relationships, and critical life experiences such as birth, death, illness, marriage, school, and work adjustment. Most of our population can be classified in the essentially well group. Often, however, even the healthy person may be in need of practical mental health information and assistance. If the person gets help during crisis periods in his life, a chronic disturbance may be avoided. Caplan has shown that the poor handling of a life crisis often sets the stage for a more inadequate handling of the next crisis by the individual.[2] Thus, the path of breakdown may begin with a poorly handled crisis.

In the configuration of mental health services in the community, efforts are made to identify the clergyman's therapeutic skills. He can provide spiritual support to emotionally disturbed people in times of stress and crisis; counsel on religious matters, applying all the psychological insight at his disposal; listen and identify cases with problems outside the religious framework, and refer them to proper community resources; counsel on personal or interpersonal problems with little emotional content if his training in pastoral counseling is limited; counsel persons with more serious mental and emotional problems if he has had training in clinical practice under expert supervision.

A clergyman's degree of effectiveness in counseling will depend, to a considerable extent, upon his ability to relate to people; his sensitivity and insight in recognizing the nature of the problem; his non-judgmental acceptance of the person in distress; and his knowledge of whether, when, and where to involve other helping resources.

The complex and flexible nature of the community mental health program calls for fully trained persons in *all* disciplines. Comparable competency among the professions helps dissolve artificial hierarchies and helps relate responsibility to talent.[3] The diversity of local demands and problems underscores ability and accomplishment more than professional background. Particular abilities and talents do not necessarily follow professional stereotypes in hierarchical fashion, nor should functions in mental health programs be rigidly defined by profession. Commendably, there has been less strict division of rules and responsibilities among professions in this type of program be-

[2] James A. Knight and Winborn E. Davis, *A Manual for the Comprehensive Mental Health Clinic* (Springfield, Ill.: Charles C. Thomas, 1964).

[3] Gerald Caplan, *An Approach to Community Mental Health* (New York: Grune & Stratton, 1961).

cause generalization is frequently required on the part of the staff.

The congregation is an instrument of therapy. The message in the Gospels discloses that an intimate relationship was taken for granted between physical, mental, moral, and religious health. Incidents are recorded in which a physical affliction was healed and sins were forgiven in one and the same act. Nobody attempted to split human health into a multiplicity of functions, and likewise nobody attempted to promote the welfare of one individual in abstraction from the salvation of the community. Each person saw and felt the spirit of God working through the religious community and knew himself to be a part of the priesthood of all believers.

In the Gospels of the New Testament more attention is devoted to the healing ministry of Jesus than to any other subject except the passion story of the last week of Jesus' earthly life. One may ponder why the art and practice of healing, central to the biblical record, has until recent times been peripheral to theological education and to the central concerns of the organized church.

In studying the biblical healing stories one discovers several basic conditions operative in almost all the cases described. Among these, none is more appropriate for emphasis in a discussion of community mental health than the observation that healing seems to have taken place almost invariably in some corporate context. An example of this is the story of the sick man who had to be let down through the roof into the room Jesus occupied because the door was blocked by large numbers of people (Mark 2:1-5). It is significant that apparently the friends and not the patient himself sought the healing and had the expectant trust. The group atmosphere in the New Testament healing episodes was a most significant factor in the preparation and support of the healing process. In the life of the early church, where healing became more and more associated with the corporate worship and the sacramental life of the believing community, the element of group atmosphere became a factor of major importance.

The implications of this are obvious for the pastor who opens channels of communication between his church and the mental health center. A neglected area of church activity is the use of the congregation as an instrument of therapy. The church as a therapeutic and redemptive community can have profound influence upon the health of the individual and the group. It would not be difficult to show how the congregation could function in a variety of healing capacities. Consider what a great force the congregation would be if it functioned with the devotion and dedication of Alcoholics Anonymous, for the group life in this organization is similar to the group life which the church could furnish to many people with a variety of problems and illnesses.

The mental patient is lonely and isolated, desperately needing to feel a sense of community with others. The congregation has within its very structure the ability to heal his isolation, to rescue the alcoholic, to answer the cry for help of the suicide candidate, to give direction and fellowship to the adolescent. The church also has a great opportunity with the "marginal" person who is living on the edge of life and who is in danger of dropping out of his family and out of society. By recognizing the "marginal" individual and including him in its group life, the church may well "rescue" him who lives on the borderline between sickness and health. Also, the church can function as one of the finest stabilizing forces for senior citizens, providing a sense of purpose and significance to their lives and incorporating them meaningfully and creatively into the religious group life of the church and community. And above all, as the individual in psychotherapy moves from an analysis of his condition to a synthesis regarding his value system, he runs head on into the religious question. He often turns to the church, especially if encouraged to do so, to explore fundamental questions related to the nature and destiny of man and his ever-present existential anxiety and guilt.

In the church one finds many people who have suffered severe adversities. Some have healed scars; others have open wounds. Often there is healing in these people as beautifully illustrated in Thornton Wilder's one act play, *The Angel That Troubled the Waters,* based on the biblical story of John 5:1-4. The play tells of a physician who comes periodically to the pool of Bethesda, hoping to be the first in the water and healed of his remorse when the angel appears and troubles the water. Everybody at the pool also hopes to be the first in the water and thereby healed of his malady. The angel appears but blocks the physician at the moment he is ready to step into the pool and be healed.

Angel: "Draw back, physician, this moment is not for you."

Physician: "Angelic visitor, I pray thee, listen to my prayer."

Angel: "Healing is not for you."

Physician: "Surely, surely, the angels are wise. Surely, O Prince, you are not deceived by my apparent wholeness. Your eyes can see the nets in which my wings are caught; the sin into which all my endeavors sink half-performed cannot be concealed from you."

Angel: "I know."

.   .   .   .

Physician: "Oh, in such an hour was I born, and doubly fearful to me is the flaw in my heart. Must I drag my shame, Prince and Singer, all my days more bowed than my neighbor?"

Angel: "Without your wound where would your power be? It is your very remorse that makes your low voice tremble into the hearts of men. The very angels themselves cannot persuade the wretched and blundering children on earth as can one human being broken on the wheels of living. In Love's service only the wounded soldiers can serve. Draw back." [4]

The person who was healed rejoiced in his good fortune and turned to the physician before leaving and said: "But come with me first, an hour only, to my home. My son is lost in dark thoughts. I—I do not understand him, and only you have ever lifted his mood. Only an hour . . . my daughter, since

[4] Thornton Wilder, *The Angel That Troubled the Waters, and Other Plays* (New York: Coward-McCann, 1928), pp. 147 ff.

her child has died, sits in the shadow. She will not listen to us." [5]

Since mental health planning authorities foresee every geographic area in the country being served by a comprehensive center, the opportunities for collaborative endeavor now exist. The pastor should get involved in the activities of the center and become a part of its leadership. He should spell out in some detail what he would like from the center, what the mental health needs of his people are, what training and educational experience he would like to receive, his ideas of cooperative projects between his church and the center, and the time and talents he has to offer. A clergy consultation service is already evolving as an important function of the mental health center, and such a program should not be overlooked in planning.

Remember that the pastor and the staff members of a center have something very much in common in that they are all submerged in the immediacy of caring for a host of broken or potentially broken people. The community center is not a theoretical ivory tower where hairs are split lovingly, but is primarily a clinical setting where the delivery of specific services takes place.

As for reading material, the Director of the National Institute of Mental Health will send on request a packet of the latest material on comprehensive centers. If particular areas of interest are pinpointed for the Director, an effort will be made to send material dealing specifically with one's interests.

11.
THE CLERGYMAN'S ROLE IN CRISIS COUNSELING

Paul W. Pretzel, B.D., Th.D.
Pastoral Counselor and Psychologist, Suicide Prevention Center, Los Angeles, California

Charlie Johnson is a big man, well over six feet tall, with coarse, rugged-looking features.

[5] *Ibid.*, p. 149.

THE CLERGYMAN'S ROLE IN CRISIS COUNSELING

He had come to the Suicide Prevention Center in Los Angeles because his physician had told him to, but he had little hope of being helped. He even doubted that he wanted help. His life had been unsatisfying for years, and now with this latest stress there was no reason or desire to go on. He was forty-seven years old, married for twenty years to a woman whom, he felt, offered him no warmth. His two children were now grown and gone, and he seldom heard from either of them. He had no close friends and few interests. The one thing he did well, he felt, was his work. For seventeen years he had driven a truck for a Los Angeles firm, and he took some pride and felt his self-esteem increased because his near-perfect work record.

Two weeks ago, after a fight with his wife, he had gone to a local bar and begun drinking. Driving home, he was arrested for drunk driving, and since this was a second offense he was sure he would lose his license. Without a driver's license and therefore without his job, he did not want to live. Charlie's plan was to wait until he received the final court decision, then drive his car to a deserted place and sleep his life away with carbon monoxide. It was a lethal plan. He had the car, the necessary length of hose, and the location already selected. All that was left was for the time to run out, and next Monday, after the court hearing, was the time.

The pastoral counselor to whom Charlie spoke at the Suicide Prevention Center recognized him as a high suicidal risk. Having temporarily lost the ability to deal with the conditions of his life and to cope with the stress that he was facing, he was in a state of emotional crisis. He felt that life no longer held any satisfaction for him and there was only one solution that he could now see—only one way out—suicide.

The experienced crisis counselor, in this case a pastoral counselor, although recognizing Charlie as a serious suicidal risk, also knew that the situation was not as hopeless as it first appeared. Although the person in an emotional crisis is overwhelmed and feels as though his situation will never improve, experience indicates otherwise. Acute feelings of hopelessness, helplessness, and depression are seldom of long duration. They usually abate within a few weeks. In addition, the person in crisis, because he is overwhelmed by his own feelings, may magnify the difficulties that he is facing and, at the same time, underestimate the possibilities and resources that he has. The crisis counselor makes an important contribution by more realistically assessing both the dangers and the possibilities inherent in the crisis situation and adding the elements of perspective and stability.

Crisis theory, as developed by Erich Lindemann and Gerald Caplan, holds that when a person is in a state of crisis, he is especially vulnerable to change. This change may take either a negative or a positive direction, depending, in part, on the influences that affect the individual when he is in crisis. Crisis intervention has to do with exerting the type of influence which will encourage personal growth.

Crisis intervention takes place whenever one person responds to another human being who is overwhelmed by his own feelings and is unable to function in his normal manner. The alert parish clergyman routinely functions as a crisis counselor when his people come to him at times of stress in their lives. Most clergymen have many experiences in dealing with people who are reacting to a crisis by expressing psychological panic, paralysis, or depression, which is distorting their judgment and leading them either into inappropriate action or into an inability to make any response at all. The clergyman who is familiar with the theory and techniques of crisis intervention is well equipped to help his parishioners turn their crises from disaster into creative solutions where personal growth can take place.

Although the long-term result of good crisis intervention is often a significant improvement in the individual's overall adaptation to life, the specific goal of crisis intervention is to help the individual to deal with the specific stress that has brought about the crisis. Whenever the crisis counselor deviates from this goal, he is no longer involved in crisis counseling. In Charlie's case, the goal which the crisis counselor adopted had to do with the immediate suicide feelings springing from his fear of losing his driver's license.

Method of Crisis Intervention

The method of crisis intervention can be organized into four steps: the assessment of the problem, planning the nature of the intervention, the intervention itself, and the resolution and withdrawal.

1. *The assessment of the problem.* When first faced with a crisis situation the counselor needs to make two kinds of assessments.

a. First he must determine whether or not there is an immediate physical emergency. Relevant questions are: Has the person already ingested pills? Has he already cut his wrists? Has he already wounded himself with a gun? If the counselor determines that there is a physical emergency, then he must respond to it by providing what is needed. In some cases, he will help the patient get to an emergency hospital; in other instances he may involve the help of the police.

b. If the counselor decides, however, that there is no imminent physical emergency then he will be free to move into the second kind of assessment and determine, in detail, what kind of crisis is now in effect, what the stresses are, and what they mean to this person at this time. If the person has experienced similar kinds of crises in the past the counselor will want to know how they were resolved.

At the same time that the counselor is assessing the nature of the crisis, he will also be assessing the strengths of the person's resources. The resources will be of two kinds. (1) The internal characteriological resources—the ego strength and the rationality that the patient still possesses. (2) The external resources. The counselor will want to know something about who the person has in his life who can be counted on to help at such a time. Does he have a family? Is he married? Does he have a doctor, a therapist, a clergyman, an employer, a drinking friend? Does he have money? Is he employed?

In the case of Charlie Johnson, it was clear to the pastoral counselor that there was no physical emergency. Charlie had not yet done anything to harm himself, nor was he chaotically out of control. Upon inquiry, he found that Charlie had never been suicidal before, and that this was a new and frightening experience for him. He had no idea of how to cope with such feelings. His resources seemed tenuous. His ego strength was low, and there seemed to be few people in his life who cared for him. It was only after questioning that the counselor discovered that Charlie's mother and father lived locally and might be of some help.

2. *Planning the Intervention.* Once the assessment of the problem has been made, the counselor begins discussing with the person what might be done to alleviate the stress or otherwise adapt to the stressful situation. Thus the patient begins to have the feeling that stress is something that can be dealt with, and there grows in him the hope that the situation is not as overwhelming and as hopeless as he had at first experienced it. The counselor and the counselee explore the possibilities and alternatives, turning them over and over, discussing ins and outs while taking all the limitations of the situation seriously. At this point, there is a commitment being made by the counselor that a solution will be found and that the discussion will continue as long as it takes to find a solution. If this cannot be accomplished in one interview, then appointments are made for subsequent interviews.

The role of the person in the intervention into his own crisis needs to be carefully considered. The person should be encouraged to do everything that he can realistically be expected to do for himself. It is only when he has reached the limits of his own present ability that the counselor will take the initiative to perform some action. When it is clear that the person is temporarily unable to function in some area for himself, the crisis counselor will take responsibility. It is not unusual, for example, for a crisis counselor to take the initiative to speak with some significant other person in order to mobilize help for his counselee.

The important thing is that whatever decision is made about

intervention should be carefully planned. The temptation is to overemphasize the need for speed and to begin intervention without careful planning. This frequently has the effect of confusing an already confused and involved situation. It is important, therefore, that the crisis counselor take whatever time is necessary to gather the information he needs and to carefully evaluate the situation, working out an intervention plan with the person that seems to stress economy of movement and yet promises maximal results.

Although Charlie represented a high suicide risk, the counselor felt, at the end of the first hour, that there was time to work and that Charlie had been able to involve himself enough in the problem-solving process that there was no need for urgent action. A subsequent appointment was set up for three days later.

3. *The Intervention.* Crisis intervention can take such a variety of forms that it is impossible to list them all. Each individual situation carries within itself the seeds of its own resolution. The process of crisis work consists of carefully and doggedly sifting through the possible alternatives until the intrinsic solution is discovered. Sometimes it is enough for the person to be able to redefine his own problems with a different perspective. Failures that he now experiences as being monumental often diminish in importance when compared to other important factors in his life, and he may then find himself able to cope with them. At other times crisis intervention is carried on by helping the person to gain cognative control of his own thought processes—by helping him to structure, to outline, to list in an organized and rational way the different elements of his life. Sometimes crisis intervention can take place simply by the counselor reminding the person that he has experienced similar crises in the past, and that the way he resolved them then may still be applicable now.

At other times, crisis intervention calls for more direct activity, either on the part of the counselee or the counselor or both. If the counselee is immobilized to the point of inaction, the crisis counselor will take the responsibility to contact resource persons in the counselee's life—a spouse, parent, a friend, or doctor—and facilitate their involvement in the crisis situation.

In Charlie's case, although the counselor stood ready to phone his wife or his parents, if necessary, it was decided that Charlie could do this for himself, and he decided that what he should do was to attempt to reestablish his relationship with his parents, which he did with some success.

4. *Resolution and withdrawal.* Crisis theory holds that the counselor begins to plan his withdrawal from the situation as he enters it. Crisis intervention is never a long-term activity, and the counselor must continually be aware that although he will become intimately involved in the person's life for a short time, he must be prepared to withdraw from it at the earliest possible moment. Usually, this will be when the counselee or one of the resource people is able to take responsibility for the situation. Premature withdrawal from a crisis situation, especially a suicidal situation, can have disasterous results. In such cases, the clergyman should have the benefit of competent consultation and good coordination with other helping persons. In some cases, the counselor will want to maintain contact with the particular person over a long-term period, but when he does this, he should be aware that he is no longer fulfilling the function of crisis intervention, but has moved into a different role—one of ongoing emotional support or of helping the person deal with underlying problems.

The resolution of Charlie's crisis came when he reestablished his relationship with his parents and made plans to enter counseling to work through his marital difficulties. He discussed these plans at length with the crisis counselor, who was able to help him by suggesting a qualified therapist. Once Charlie began this new relationship the crisis counselor withdrew from the situation.

Crisis Intervention as a Tool for the Clergyman

Crisis theory has some important characteristics which make it especially applicable for the use of clergymen, both those who function in a local parish and those who function in other kinds of settings.

THE CLERGYMAN'S ROLE IN CRISIS COUNSELING

a. Crisis intervention calls for minimal knowledge about personality theory. Long and detailed psychiatric histories have no place in crisis intervention, and the crisis counselor finds that he can function in an effective way with minimal theoretical or psychiatric knowledge. What is needed in place of this is what most clergymen already have—an intense interest in helping someone who is in trouble, the ability to conceptualize a problem, and the ability not to be overwhelmed by the person's feelings of depression or confusion.

b. Crisis theory affords a way of providing significant help to people, while demanding a minimum of long-term commitment. The clergyman who is interested in being a counselor is continually being frustrated by the great time demands that the counseling normally takes. Crisis intervention is by definition time limited, and offers the advantage of producing maximal results with minimum time involvement.

c. Clergymen have an almost unique access to certain resources that can be mobilized on a person's behalf. Whereas it is very difficult for certain professional therapists to learn to take initiative by contacting people on a patient's behalf, the clergyman usually is very much at home in taking such initiative. In many communities it is expected that when the clergyman hears of somebody in crisis he will take the initiative to seek them out and offer what help he can, and he is used to mustering community support for people in need. Such activity is integral to crisis intervention and is particularly pertinent to the normal functioning of the clergyman.

d. In crises where suicide is an issue, the clergyman is frequently the recipient of the cry for help that suicidal people customarily make prior to their suicide attempt. This places the clergyman in an important position in that if he can recognize the existence of an emotional crisis in one who is communicating to him, he can often take the initiative and begin his work of crisis intervention early in the developing crisis and often forestall serious suicidal behavior.

For additional reading

Caplan, Gerald. *Principles of Preventive Psychiatry*. New York: Basic Books, 1964.

——— *An Approach to Community Mental Health*. New York: Grune & Stratton, 1961.

Farberow, N. L. and Shneidman, E. S. *The Cry for Help*. New York: McGraw-Hill, 1961.

Lindemann, Erich. "Symptomatology and Management of Acute Grief," *American Journal of Psychiatry,* September, 1944.

Parad, Howard J., ed. *Crisis Intervention*. New York: Family Service Association of America, 1965.

Shneidman, E. S. and Farberow, N. L. *Clues to Suicide*. New York: McGraw-Hill, 1957.

12.
THE CLERGYMAN'S ROLE IN GRIEF COUNSELING

Earl A. Grollman, M.H.L., D.D.
Rabbi, Beth-El Temple Center, Belmont, Massachusetts

There is no time when the minister is more sorely needed than during the crisis of grief. He is usually the first one to be called. He officiates at the funeral. He visits the family after the service. In Erich Lindemann's words, the clergyman may be instrumental in emancipating the survivors from their bondage to the deceased, assisting them in their readjustment to the environment in which the loved one is missing, and aiding them in the formation of new relationships.

The pastor is most effective when he acts as a pastor, not as an amateur psychiatrist. He should not forsake his own traditional resources and spiritual functions. His is a fellowship with a past, a present, and a future tied together by rites, theology, and a religious ethic. He has his own unique framework of viewing and handling guilt, forgiveness, conflict, suffering, and hostility. The practice of psychotherapy as the only real ministry to their congregation has led the Suffragan Bishop of Washington, Paul

Moore, Jr., to write: "Too many priests forget their priestliness when they learn some of the basic skills of counseling—or perhaps they have not been trained properly in the use of priestly techniques and therefore are not confident in their exercise. These clergy become 'clinical therapists' who happen to have the prefix 'Reverend' in front of their name."

The clergyman may be of unique assistance to the bereaved. He represents a concerned religious community. His truest function is revealed in terms of years and decades, as he watches children grow, marries them, and teaches their children in turn, and as he stands beside loved ones around the deathbed of a patriarch whom he has come to admire and respect. In addition to crises of faith, people turn to him because of marital questions, parent-child problems, and a variety of inter- or intra-personal needs. He is minister, pastor, counselor to individuals and families in joy and adversity.

When a death occurs the pastor ascertains the emotional state of the bereaved not through cross-questioning but rather through empathy and understanding. The spirit of caring and compassion must communicate itself to the bereaved. Very often the most effective counseling comes after the funeral service. Before the ceremony itself, there may be incredulous disbelief and the needed expenditure of time for the physical arrangements of the burial.

The funeral offers an opportunity to comfort the mourners. It is the rite of separation. The "bad dream" is real. The presence of the corpse actualizes the experience. The process of denial is gradually transformed to the acceptance of reality.

When the funeral is over, the religious leader has the task of reconciling the bereaved to his loss. In the process, he should pay particular attention to possible grief reactions which could lead to personal disintegration and mental illness. When the grief work is not done, the person may suffer morbid grief characterized by delayed and distorted reactions. He may show great fortitude at the funeral but later develop symptoms of somatic disease or agitated depression. This may include the actual denial of the death, with schizophrenic tendencies, or psychosomatic disease such as hypochondriasis, ulcerative colitis, rhematoid arthritis, or asthma. Obsessive-compulsive behavior may manifest itself where the bereaved appeases his guilt through extreme cleanliness, or an unwillingness to terminate the effects of the funeral service—e.g., "Tell me the eulogy again." There may be self-punitive behavior detrimental to his social and economic existence.

It must be noted that the line of demarcation between "normal psychological aspects of bereavement" and "distorted mourning reactions" is thin indeed, just as is the hiatus between "normality" and "neurosis." Each symptom must be viewed not as a single and decisive entity but in the framework of the total composition and of the schematic formulations.

The family way still feel guilty and very much to blame even after a terminal illness. The guilt may take the form of self-recrimination, depression, and hostility. A tendency is to look for a scapegoat—e.g., the minister, physician, or funeral director. Inwardly the indictor may accuse himself, but he turns anger outward in the attempt to cope with his own guilt.

In this area, the clergyman can be extremely effective. The helplessness that assails the grief-stricken often leads them to envisage the role of the religious leader in a symbolic aspect as the representative of God. As such, the clergyman can assuage intense feelings of guilt by offering a meaningful concept of forgiveness as well as help them transform the errors of the past into a loving memorial by more noble living in the future.

The importance of ritual is dramatically portrayed in the French film, *Forbidden Games*. A girl's parents died in an air raid. She received comfort by constantly playing a game of "funeral" and providing every dead creature with an elaborate interment of flowers and ornate casket. "Playing" at burying things helped her to relive, digest, and ultimately master the shock of her parents' death. The child had succeeded in doing something for the dead and bringing relief to herself.

Ceremonials play an important part in helping people of all ages face death and face away from it. Religious rituals are community rituals. They are performed only by those who share a religious sameness and by no one outside it. The traditions create a sense of solidarity, of belongingness, the feeling that one is a member of the group with all the comfort, gratification, pride, and even pain that such a sense brings. For the ceremony is the same for all. It is definite and prescribed. Here he can be made to understand in clear-cut, unmistakable terms what is desired of him. Perhaps by carrying out the religious ceremonials, he will feel that he has regained the love he has lost, that he comes to peace with his own conscience which could personify for him the highest internal ideals. Even rituals which might seem irksome and pointless to others may be heartily welcome. They could be the sought-for punishment, the neutralizer, the deprivation that could balance off the imagined indulgence at the bottom of the guilt.

Certainly, the one-to-one relationship between person and pastor is necessary and beneficial. However, this is not the only approach. Grief work in *groups* is also therapeutic in assisting the bereaved to overcome their separateness and abandon the prison of their aloneness. Just as there is a Golden Age Club for the aged, an Alcoholics Anonymous for the inebriate, why not a place for those who have suffered the grief and dislocation of death? Especially do they need to share with like-minded people their feelings, troubles, and hopes.

A pilot program is being pioneered in Boston as a result of the efforts of Dr. Gerald Caplan, Director of Harvard Community Mental Health Program. He has enlisted an ecumenical bereavement team where clergymen of all faiths meet to discuss their own varied experiences with grief and death.

A widow-to-widow program has been established. Women whose husbands have died within the past year meet periodically to participate in discussions of their personal losses. To assess the accomplishment, one must first remember how they appeared at the first meetings. Their faces were drawn. Most were nervous and shy. Some just sat and stared and were totally uncommunicative. As one of the leaders, I observed an amazing metamorphosis. They became animated. They discovered that one touch of sorrow had made them all kin. They were able to participate with others who were also suffering the emotional trauma of bereavement. They belonged to the largest fraternity in the world—the company of those who had known suffering and death. This great universal sense of sorrow helps to unite all human hearts and dissolve all other feelings into those of common sympathy and understanding. Problems may be singular to each person but there are others present who have faced similar troubles and together they seek to work them out. Each gives of her own understanding, compassion, and supportive concern.

I have met with widows of varying faiths and even participated with women of particular denomination, for example, at Catholic Retreat Houses. I am convinced that each church and synagogue could well form an organization to assist widows and widowers in reconstructing their lives and their homes. Together with interested members of his congregation, the clergyman could be of inestimable value in personal as well as group counseling during their difficult period of loss and aloneness. The bereaved should be claimed for the useful citizens that they are and their talents utilized as part of the larger fellowship of their respective faith and house of worship.

The religious leader's primary objective is to aid in the emergence of a new self which has assimilated the grief experience and grown because of and through it. With the aid and encouragement of a pastor who is kind, sympathetic, and understanding, the bereaved may be helped to accept death through a more profound and meaningful religious approach to life. By the clergyman's evaluation of the experience, by catharsis, confession, remembrance, and release, the members are guided to new purposes. Their introspection may bring new value judgments of life and love and meaning. Even the synagogue or church will no longer be an impersonal entity, since the members have extended their hands in warmth and affection. But most important is the comfort they will gain from a new and abiding concept of God: "Even though we cry in the bereavement of our hearts when our beloved are taken from this earth, may it be as a child cries who knows his father is near and who clings unafraid to a trusted hand. In this spirit, O Thou who art the Master of our destiny, do we commit all that is precious to us into Thy keeping." [1]

Thus, the clergyman has an important part to play in grief counseling. As he helps others, he is himself helped in his dialogical exchange. The I-Thou relationship is, according to Martin Buber, "a religious experience" beyond the most knowledgeable theology and psychology. In the parable of the Chassidic Rabbi, Moshe Leib of Sasov: "How to love man is something I learned from a peasant. I was at an inn where peasants were drinking. For a long time all were silent until one person, moved by the wine, asked a man sitting beside him, 'Tell me, do you love me or don't you?' The other replied, 'I love you very much.' The intoxicated peasant spoke again, 'You say that you love me but you do not know what I need: if you really loved me, you would know.' The other had not a word to say to this and the peasant who put the question fell silent again. But I understand the peasant; for to know the needs of mean and to help them bear the burden of their sorrow, that is the true love of man."

For additional reading

Allport, Gordon W. *The Individual and His Religion.* New York: Macmillan, 1960.

English, O. Spurgeon, and Pearson, Gerald H. *Emotional Problems of Living.* New York: W. W. Norton, 1963.

Feifel, Herman, ed. *The Meaning of Death,* New York: McGraw-Hill, 1959.

Freud, Sigmund. *Mourning and Melancholia.* Collected Papers, Vol. IV. London: Hogarth Press, 1925.

Fulton, Robert ed. *Death and Identity.* New York: John Wiley & Sons, 1965.

Gorer, Geoffrey. *Death, Grief, and Mourning.* Garden City, N.Y.: Doubleday, 1965.

Jackson, Edgar N. *For the Living.* New York: Channel Press, 1964.

Johnson, Paul E. *Psychology of Pastoral Care.* Nashville: Abingdon Press, 1953.

Liebman, Joshua L. *Peace of Mind.* New York: Simon and Schuster, paperback, 1965.

[1] *The Union Prayerbook,* newly revised, Part I, p. 367.

Lindemann, Erich. "Symptomatology and Management of Acute Grief."
American Journal of Psychiatry. No. 101, 1944, pp. 141-48.

Linn, Louis and Schwartz, Leo W. *Psychiatry and Religious Experience.*
New York: Random House, 1958.

Osborne, E. *When You Lose a Loved One.* New York: Public Affairs
Committee, 1958.

Ostow, Mortimer, and Scharfstein, Ben-Ami. *The Need to Believe.* New
York: International Universities Press, paperback 1969.

13.
THE CHURCH'S ROLE
WITH THE GIFTED AND
THE RETARDED

Charles F. Kemp, B.D., Ph.D.
*Professor of Pastoral Care, Brite Divinity School,
Texas Christian University, Fort Worth, Texas*

"Unto one he gave five talents, to another two, and to another one; to every man according to his several ability." (Matthew 25:15) The findings of intelligence tests are now new. Men like Plato, Plutarch, and Galton recognized individual differences and the presence of genius long ago. What is new is the perfection of instruments by which mental ability can be measured with a fair degree of accuracy.

When large segments of the population, like the children in a school system, for example, are tested, it is found that their abilities are distributed fairly consistently along what has been called the normal, or bell-shaped curve. Why this is so we do not know, but it has been established again and again.

We are concerned here with those persons who are at the two extremes of this distribution—those who are unusually bright and are known as gifted, and those who are quite limited and are known as retarded.

Statistically speaking we are talking about approximately one percent who score 130 or above on a standard mental ability test, and those who score 70 or below on the same or a similar test.

THE CHURCH'S ROLE WITH GIFTED AND RETARDED

These are the gifted, and these are the retarded. One percent does not sound like a very large figure until you take into account the population of America; then you realize you are talking about several million in each category.

For all practical purposes these figures have to be enlarged. To consider how it relates to the church, the school, the community and the home, we must include the top 5 or 6 percent, those above 120 or 125 I.Q. These are called "rapid learners" by the schools. Their problems are essentially the same as the few who happened to score five or ten points higher. At the other end of the scale we must add a like number, the borderline retarded, the "slow learners." Now we have increased our figure many times, and have included every community and almost every congregation.

These two groups, so very different in many ways, have some similar problems. Each can be understood better by comparing and contrasting it with the other.

Both groups have been misunderstood. Until recently both have been largely neglected by the church; in fact, the gifted still are. Even though many provisions have been made for the retarded, such as special church school classes, camps and conferences, confirmation classes, and so forth, they only reach a small percentage of the number that could benefit from such help.

Let us compare and contrast them in terms of four areas of a person's life which have a great bearing on community mental health.

Let us consider two boys. One we will call boy *A* and the other boy *B*. Boy *A* has an I.Q. of 133. This puts him in the gifted range. Boy *B* has an I.Q. of 67 and would be considered retarded. *A* grasps ideas quickly. He does abstract reasoning easily. He is well in advance of his years. *B* is just the opposite. He cannot do abstract reasoning; ideas come slowly; he has to struggle to keep up and then usually cannot make it. It becomes very graphic when we speak in terms of mental age rather than I.Q.

Let us assume that both *A* and *B* are the same chronological age. When *A* is five years old he will have a mental age of six years and six months, but when B is five years of age he will have a mental age of three years and four months. When they have reached the age of ten years, the division will be even greater. A will now have an M.A. of 13 years and four months, but B will have attained an M.A. of only six years and eight months. When they reach the high school age of 15, A will now be thinking with those who are 20 years of age, but B will only be able to compete with those of 10 years. How this affects them academically is obvious. They live in two different worlds intellectually. They have a different vocabulary, different interests different levels of attainment and possibility. A's problem in school is boredom and lack of interest. Much of the material he is already familiar with, for gifted children invariably do a great deal of reading. He finds it so easy to compete with his peers that he has no challenge. He may cause trouble, develop poor work habits, and look down on others. B's problem is just the opposite. He is under constant strain just to keep up. Pressured by home and a system which rewards the able, he is in a constant state of frustration. He never attains the satisfaction of achievement, recognition, or approval.

The schools recognize this problem and through special education classes and projects attempt to provide the opportunity for each person to function at the maximum level of his capacities. At least this is the ideal. Not every school attains it, but in principle this is what they try to do. When this is accomplished, the children are provided with learning tasks commensurate with their ability. They gain not only knowledge from academic experience, but satisfaction, challenge, and self-fulfillment as well. It is the latter which have so much to do with mental health. Except in a few noteworthy instances the church and church school have done relatively little.

When A and B have completed their education and move on into the vocational world, we again see the contrast. It begins long before they finish school. It begins as they make plans, select courses, decide on college, graduate and professional school. For A there are so many things he could do and do well that vocational choice is difficult for him. His interests invariably are wide; his abilities are such he could not only succeed but excel in more than one area. In these days of specialization and longer and longer training, he must make a choice.

Say, for example, *A* is active in the church. He is interested in becoming a medical missionary. He also is interested in scholarship—he would like to teach in a seminary. Both fields appeal to him. His professors and his vocational and mental ability tests indicate he could do either. Both are long and expensive training programs. One requires an M.D.; the other, a Ph.D. His life will be very different if he finds himself in a missionary hospital in Africa, or in a seminary classroom in America. This is but one example. We see gifted young persons who are interested in the arts and in science, who are drawn to a career in social work or a career in the church. Some have great skills in the laboratory and equally significant talents for public service. A choice must be made—it is not easy.

B, however, has a different problem. His choices are very limited. There are so few things he can do and do well that he should be helped to make his choice early and receive training. The problem is more complicated if he is in the borderline group. His friends may be going on to college, but with today's standards he cannot be admitted. He may even think he wants to enter one of the professions. Many such persons express a desire for a vocation which requires training they could not possibly master.

Even so, *B*'s situation is much brighter than it was just a few years ago. Many who were once left in almost complete inactivity are now living useful lives, doing useful things. The retarded, contrary to what was once thought, can be productive vocationally. Some of them, it is true, are limited to sheltered workshops, but it has been found that many can be trained to do routine tasks in industry and do them well. This not only gives them income but also a sense of belonging, of usefulness and importance. To be able to earn one's living in our culture is a mark of maturity and worth.

All of this has a direct bearing on community mental health. Nothing is more important for mental health than for the people in the community to find satisfaction, meaning, and purpose in their work. One's vocation has implications far beyond the income that is involved, as important as that is. When one sees his job as something that he enjoys, something to look forward to each day and in anticipation in the years ahead, if he sees the thing he is doing as meaningful and important and worthwhile, then his whole life has meaning.

Unfortunately not many people are so fortunate, and some have an experience that is quite the opposite. The thing they do each day and look forward to tomorrow is dull, uninteresting, and offers no real challenge or purpose. In this sense it is a mental health problem for people of all levels of intellectual ability, but the very brilliant and the very limited do have special problems finding meaning and satisfaction in their vocations.

While *A* and *B* have been going to school, preparing for vocation, going to church, playing on the playground, they have been associating with other children and with various adults. This, too, has a bearing on mental health. Psychological literature in recent years has been saturated with such words as "acceptance," "identity," "rejection," "estrangement," "self-actualization." All of which is to say that the person who feels accepted by his peers, loved by his family and other persons who are significant to him is most fortunate. Those who are not must find some means to compensate for this lack. It is absolutely essential for mental health.

Both *A* and *B* may have a similar problem at this point. Both may be misunderstood by adults and rejected by their peer group and for the same reason—both are different from the norm. For the child or the teen-ager there can be no greater evil. This accounts for such problems as a very gifted person who feels very inadequate. It accounts for some of the delinquent and antisocial-behavior of the retarded. At least in this way they can gain some recognition and acceptance from those in their age group.

We hasten to add that this does not mean that all gifted children feel inadequate, rejected, or hostile; on the contrary; many are well adjusted and well liked. It certainly does not mean that all retarded children are delinquent. Most of them are not. It does emphasize the fact that while both *A* and *B* do have differences from the norm in terms of ability, both also have the same need of acceptance, attention, affection, and love.

Both *A* and *B* conceivably might belong to the same church. It certainly is not unusual to have a youngster with an I.Q. of 130-plus and a youngster with an I.Q. of 70 in the same congregation. I have known cases where they were in the same church school class. Both also have spiritual needs. If the Christian faith, the fellowship of the church, the significance of prayer and worship, the challenge of Christian service are important for that large segment of the population that fall in the range between 80 and 120, then it is important for these two youngsters who happen to be above and below that group.

Here again we see the contrasts. If we go back to the difference in mental age, it will shed some light on the problem of their religious development and training. *A* will be asking questions much sooner than *B*, even than those in the middle range. His mind is inquiring, and it inquires about spiritual matters quite as much as any other. The problem is that he is so seldom helped. Parents, church school teachers, and pastors find he can ask questions nobody can answer. They may discourage him, brush him off, evade the issue, tell him to wait until he is older. The result is that he gets the impression it is wrong to ask questions, or adults do not have the answers.

B's problem is quite the opposite. The things that are discussed in church, or even in a graded church school class, are in advance of him. He does not understand. It does not mean he cannot understand some religious concepts. It does not mean he cannot have religious feelings. He can, but he needs to be helped by people who have infinite patience, who can simplify, who will explain, repeat, and explain again.

All of religion is not knowledge. It is also feeling, worship, challenge, fellowship, trust. Both boys need these for mental and spiritual health, but each must be helped in his own way.

The challenge of working with *A* is his great potential. If he can be helped to work through his frustrations, to attain a humble but realistic conception of his own capacities, to dedicate and commit himself to a life of service and faith, the whole future may be affected. The challenge of *B* is that his needs are so great; the problems he faces are so many that to be able to help him surmount just a few of them is most worthwhile.

I began with a verse of Scripture. I conclude with two more. "Every one to whom much is given, of him will much be required" (Luke 12:48 RSV). "Truly, I say to you, as you did it to one of the least of these my brethren, you did it to me" (Matt. 25:40 RSV).

For additional reading

Ayrault, Evelyn W. *You Can Raise Your Handicapped Child.* New York: Putnam's, 1964.

Copa, Cornell, *Retarded Children Can Be Helped.* New York: Channel Press, 1955.

Kemp, Charles F. *The Church; The Gifted and the Retarded Child.* St. Louis: Bethany, 1957.

Palmer, Charles E. *Religion and Rehabilitation.* Springfield, Ill.: Charles C. Thomas, 1968.

Petersen, Sigurd D. *Retarded Children: God's Children.* Philadelphia: Westminster, 1960.

14.
PASTORAL CARE
AND THE POOR

Don S. Browning, B.D., Ph.D.
Professor of Religion and Personality, The Divinity School, The University of Chicago, Chicago, Illinois

To raise the question of the pastoral care of the poor at this point in history is something of an embarrassment for the pastoral psychology movement. To raise this question now necessitates the confession that the pastoral psychology movement has not heretofore adequately given it the attention that it deserves.

This book and the essays within it are a product of the so-called pastoral psychology movement. The pastoral psychology movement is a consequence of the relatively self-conscious and systematic attempt to strengthen the ministry of the church by making use of the insights and expertise of the social and psychological sciences. It has concerned itself with many issues and problem areas—the church's ministry to marital discord, alcoholism, youth, the elderly, the emotionally disturbed, and the delinquent. But little attention has been given to the poor.

There are specific reasons why the pastoral psychology movement failed to direct its attention to the problems of those afflicted by poverty. The reasons are more sociological than ideological. From the beginning the pastoral psychology movement attached itself to principles which, if consistently applied, would have brought it to an early and fruitful confrontation with the special situation of the economically deprived. But, because of certain reasons related to the sociological origins of the movement, it was often not faithful to its own best motivations and insights.

The pastoral psychology movement was developed by sincere and far-sighted churchmen who were, for the most part, members of the mainline, middle-class denominations in the United States. The first classes in pastoral psychology were taught in those more progressive and liberal seminaries where both the professors and the students espoused middle-class attitudes and values. Its companion disciplines were primarily clinical psychology, psychiatry, and social work, and pastoral psychology itself soon took on the trappings of quasi-professionalism with its emphasis upon the white collar, appointments, structured interviews, and so forth. Much of this was for the good, but it unwittingly led the pastoral psychology movement to isolate itself from the lower classes. Whether we are speaking of pastoral psychology as a more or less loosely organized body of principles which informed the daily work of increasingly larger numbers of ministers educated in the better seminaries, or whether we are talking about pastoral psychology in its more professional manifestations in the form of institutional chaplaincies or church-related counseling centers, the sociological origins of the movement tended to render it ineffective in relating to the specific problems and life-styles of the poor. Just as the ground-breaking book of Hollingshead and Redlich entitled *Social Class and Mental Illness* demonstrated that the helping professions of psychiatry and clinical psychology were likely to be less attentive to and less effective with people from the lower socioeconomic strata of our society, a similar book and a similar indictment could be written about the pastoral psychology movement.[1] Today, pastoral psychology, just like clinical psychology, psychiatry, and even social work, must admit that it faces a "crisis" in self-definition—a crisis which must be resolved before it can break through the barriers which have been limiting it from becoming a positive force for the betterment of the poor of our nation.

From the beginning, the pastoral psychology movement concentrated on the principles of working with individuals and small groups. It borrowed freely from the knowledge about individual counseling, group dynamics, and group therapy which the secular disciplines of psychology and psychiatry had discovered. It transposed, not always uncritically, into its own setting a variety of therapies which had yielded some success in secular psychiatric and psychological clinical settings. Most of these therapies emphasized "talk," "insight," and the so called structured interview. From the beginning it was recognized by the more discerning leaders in all the helping professions that some people did not seem to be able to make much use of these "talking therapies." But this was often thought to be their problem and not necessarily an indictment exposing the implicit shortcomings of these therapies. The poor, the uneducated, the activistic, were often judged to be poor prospects for therapy or counseling. Such people seemed to have high resistances against gaining self-understanding or insight. They seemed unable to keep regular appointments. They often tended to externalize their problems—something which all good counselors guarded against. They often said such things as "What good does it do to talk about it?" As a consequence, such people were often written off as poor investments for the counselor's time and energy. Only

[1] A. B. Hollingshead and F. C. Redlich, *Social Class and Mental Illness* (New York: John Wiley, 1958).

gradually was it recognized that the talking therapies were really more consistent with the introspective and verbal styles of the middle-class and upper middle-class people they were originally developed to help. It slowly was recognized that lower-class people were less verbal, less introspective, less abstractive and more concrete than most middle-class persons. *But this did not mean that the poor could not be helped; it simply meant that help had to come in a different form than most psychological, psychiatric, and pastoral counselors were accustomed to providing.*

The question must be asked: who are the poor? This question is a large one and cannot be handled adequately in this essay. Our purpose here is to make a few generalizations which will help us orient ourselves toward a concrete understanding of what pastoral practices with the poor might involve.

First of all, the poor are people without money, or at least, without enough money to live adequately within the context of Western society. But there is more. The poor are also those without power. By this I mean that they have less control over their lives, less latitude in decision-making, and less influence over political, educational, and economic institutions which impinge upon their lives, than is the case with people in the middle classes. It is becoming increasingly clear that to help the poor is not only to solve their shortage of money, it is also to help them develop more responsible control over the direction of their own lives. This last point has great significance for the strategy of pastoral work with the poor.

There are other things to be said about the poor. Certain distinctions should be made. There are different types of poor people. There are certain important differences between rural and urban poor, be they black or white. There are crucial differences between Puerto Rican poor and Appalachian whites. Herbert Gans has developed a typology of the poor and draws distinctions between (1) so-called maladjusted, (2) the routine seekers, (3) those who are striving to get into the working class or into the middle class, and (4) those who are action seekers striving to maximize excitement and gratification within their present status.[2] And of course, there are both important similarities and differences between the lower-class poor and the lower-income working class.

In spite of these differences, there are some important general characterizations of the poor which can be made. We will look at these features of the poor both from the standpoint of how they may constitute liabilities for the poor and, at the same time, implicit strengths which can be used in their behalf by the sensitive minister trying to be of help.

Social scientists have learned a great deal about the language patterns of the poor. Certain facts are clear. Their language is more directly attached to concrete action and to practical and immediate problems of everyday living than is the case with the middle-class.[3] This is why middle-class talk therapies are inadequate and why the poor may not do well in middle-class–oriented school systems which emphasize verbal skills, abstract reasoning, and knowledge for knowledge's sake.

Although the language of the poor is more concrete, more action-oriented, and more bound to pragmatic and utilitarian concerns, it is not necessarily more limited. Frank Reissman points out that the language of the poor may be rich and flexible, quite capable of expressing the experiences and attitudes that are real to the poor.[4] It is a language somewhat different from that of the middle-class; and middle-class teachers, therapists, and ministers may not be able to understand it. Yet Riessman believes that this language, if taken seriously, can be used to the advantage of the educational and therapeutic process if the proper methods and sensitivities are used.[5]

Many poor people have a different attitude toward time than

[2] Herbert Gans, "A Survey of Working- and Lower-class Studies" in *Mental Health of the Poor*, ed. by Frank Riessman, *et al.* (New York: The Free Press, 1966), pp. 119-27. *Mental Health of the Poor* will hereafter be referred to as *MHP*.

[3] Daniel Miller and G. Swanson, *Inner Conflict and Defense* (New York: Henry Holt, 1960), p. 24; Basil Bernstein, "Social Glass, Speech Systems, and Psychotherapy," in *MHP*, pp. 194-209. Frank Riessman, *The Culturally Deprived Child* (New York: Harper, 1962).

[4] Riessman, *The Culturally Deprived Child*, pp. 1-25.

[5] *Ibid.*, p. 14.

do middle-class people. The poor tend to live more in the present and the past, are less able to tolerate delay, and are less inclined to plan for the future.[6] On the other hand, middle-class people tend to live almost completely for the future and have considerable capacity to make sacrifices today in the hope for a better tomorrow. This emphasis upon the present and the past among the poor may be born of a lack of hope; but in some cases it may be a product of an honest cultural difference indicating a more self-accepting and less acquisitive style of life, a style which should be respected and not automatically deemed inferior to the more ambitious future-oriented activities of the middle classes.

Many of the poor are more likely to use and be responsive to punitive and physical expressions of authority than is true with the more permissive middle class.[7] They are likely to be more sensitive to the demands of the extended family and are more likely to stay within its jurisdiction. One the other hand, there may be, among the lower classes, more mutual helpfulness between members of the same extended family or even between friends and neighbors.[8] Although this may be true, the effects of this stronger family solidarity are often nullified by the general disorganization of the neighborhoods in which the deprived live and their general reluctance to give political expression to their grievances.

Let us conclude by listing some principles and describing some strategies which should be kept in mind when ministering to the poor.

1. Pastoral work with the poor should take place in the context of a well-integrated total program designed to both (a) integrate the poor into the larger society and (b) transform society to better respond to and encourage the unique contributions which the poor can make to the rest of society. The poor need individual attention and assistance. But individual pastoral care is most meaningful when it takes place in the context of a larger at-

---

[6] John P. Spiegel, "Some Cultural Aspects of Transference and Counter-Transference," in *MHP*, p. 308.

[7] Melvin Kohn, "Social Class and Parent-Child Relationships: On Interpretation," in *MHP*, p. 166.

[8] Riessman, *The Culturally Deprived Child*, p. 48.

tempt to analyze and correct the social forces which perpetuate poverty. More than this, individual and direct attention to the personal problems of the poor should proceed simultaneously with an effort to stimulate *them* to become active in analyzing and correcting the conditions which have created and sustained their poverty.

2. To stimulate the poor toward active participation in finding a solution to their own problems means starting where the poor perceive themselves to be. This means taking their everyday problems very seriously. Their problems may vary. For some, their problems may be expressed around difficulties in providing child care for mothers attempting to pursue part-time work. For others, it may involve problems in dealing with the complexities of a welfare system upon which they are dependent but which they cannot comprehend. Other problem areas may center around skill deficiency, substandard housing, household management, and may necessitate job training programs, tenant unions, or homemaking assistance. These are strategies presently being tried in various places with differing degrees of involvement by representatives of the church. The pastoral care movement should be able to add a new dimension to these efforts. Not only is there great promise in such programs for stimulating the poor to increase their own potential for dealing with their problems,[9] they also provide both an opportunity and a meaningful supportive context for more direct and personal pastoral care if the minister is there to help handle the frustrations, disappointments, and anger which will undoubtedly surface. This is what is often missing from some social action strategies—the sensitive handling of the personal substratum of meaning and conflict which often is brought to and precipitated by such action. Of course, social action on the part of the poor can be ego-building and therapeutic in itself. But just as ego therapy must generally be accompanied by some attempt to handle deeper anxieties and conflicts, so must

[9] For stimulating discussions of how social action can help develop the human potential of those who participate, see the following articles: Peggy Way, "Community Organization and Pastoral Care: Drum Beat for Dialogue," *Pastoral Psychology*, March, 1968 pp. 25-36; Rudolph M. Wittenberg, "Personality Adjustment Through Social Action," in *MHP*, pp. 378-92.

social action and the kind of therapy that it provides be accompanied by auxiliary resources to handle the deeper human problems which an unsophisticated program of social action can unwittingly repress and deny.

3. Therapies which emphasize role-playing, dramatic action, and concrete problem-solving are generally more consistent with the cognitive styles of the lower classes. Although the pastoral care of the poor should take place in the context of larger strategies of social action such as community organization efforts, tenant unions, job-training programs, and the general politization of the poor, there is clearly a place for more direct and person-oriented work with small groups and individuals. As Frank Riessman writes, "low-income people tend to *work out mental problems best when they can do things physically.*" [10] In his important article entitled "Role-Playing and the Lower Socio-Economic Group" Riessman gives several examples of the successful employment of role-playing in working with the poor. For instance, role-playing can be used to rehearse how an unemployed person might learn to relate to a new employer. It has been used successfully with juvenile delinquents to help them work through problems of handling authority. It has proved exceptionally beneficial in the training of indigenous non-professionals who are being used with increasing frequency to help bridge the gap between educational or social service projects and the communities they are attempting to serve. Role-playing involves the total person in a learning process and appeals to cognitive, kinesthetic, emotional, and experiential levels of human existence. For this reason, it is nicely adapted to the more action-oriented, motoric, and concrete styles of the poor. In addition, it can often be used in "marginal situations" in the very midst of other more or less non-therapeutic activities as a learning interlude which should help increase the capacity of a person or group to deal with current problems. It can be used in the context of discussion groups or talk-oriented therapies as the subject matter of group reflection.

[10] Frank Riessman "Role-Playing and the Lower Socio-Economic Group," *Pastoral Psychology,* March, 1968, p. 51.

Games can also be used with therapeutic efficacy. Rachel Levine tells of her use of family games as a device to stimulate family interaction.[11] Pathological or self-defeating patterns of interaction can be readily elicited and identified by such an approach and then can become topics for fruitful discussion and clarification.

In general, the so-called behavior therapies and ego-building therapies, which emphasize decision-making, integrity, and the active synthesis of conflicting impulses, seem most congenial to the styles and needs of the poor.[12] Any program of individual and small-group counseling with the poor should attempt to minimize red tape, needless professionalization, and other types of structural frustrations often accompanying more standard services—frustrations such as complex and frightening diagnostic interviews, excessive use of referrals, and delays in the availability of the sought-for service.

4. Whenever possible, structural professional counseling with the poor should be sanctioned and guided by the poor themselves. The poor should have seats on the boards of the counseling centers, be they religious or secular, which attempt to serve their communities. For example, the Woodlawn Mental Health Center on the southside of Chicago has sitting on its board of directors representatives of all the major groups within this predominantly lower-class Negro neighborhood. Although the Center is staffed by highly competent professionals, the basic goals, philosophy, and procedures of the Center are worked out by representatives of the Woodlawn community. In this way, the Center becomes an integral part of the community itself and not just another agency coming in from the outside, competing for power and clientele and in this way further fragmenting an already badly disorganized community.

[11] Rachel Levine, "Treatment in the Home: An Experiment with Low Income, Multi-Problem Families," *MHP,* pp. 329-35.

[12] Howard Clinebell, *Basic Types of Pastoral Counseling,* pp. 189-205, 222-43; William Glasser, *Reality Therapy* (New York: Harper, 1965) Perry London, *The Modes and Morale of Psychotherapy* (New York: Holt, Rinehart, and Winston, 1964).

15.
THE CLERGYMAN'S ROLE
IN THE TREATMENT OF
THE ALCOHOLIC

George P. Dominick, B.D.
Chief Clinical Chaplain, The Georgian Clinic Division, Georgia Mental Health Institute, Atlanta, Georgia

About a year ago, on the night before Christmas, I answered the phone at my home in Atlanta. The caller was a local clergyman asking for help with a woman who was drunk and sick in an Atlanta hotel room. The story, as it unfolded, had a distinctly ecumenical flavor. Ill and alone in a hotel, this woman had called a friend in London. The English friend immediately called the only American he knew—a Catholic priest in Baltimore. The Baltimore priest then called an Atlanta priest who, in turn, called me. Nor was this the end of the broad web of involvement. Within the next eighteen hours, operating around the key role of the local priest, we involved a physician, a hotel clerk, a member of Alcoholics Anonymous, and the facilities of a hospital emergency room.

Obviously, not all clergy contacts with alcoholics are so dramatic or so ecumenical. More often contact comes in the form of the familiar plea of the alcoholic's wife: "Please see if you can talk to him. He knows he needs help but he just won't do anything about it." Or, again, it may be the late-night call from the alcoholic himself. Lonely and remorseful in the midst of his drinking, he may just want to talk to somebody. Sick and scared, he may demand immediate relief from what he feels is a life-or-death crisis.

These common experiences pose questions with regard to the clergyman's attitude and role. Is the clergyman willing to be involved with the alcoholic? How does the clergyman begin to become an effective helping person? How can he sink his roots into that sense of professional competence so necessary for dealing with the crisis pleas of the alcoholic? How can he learn to recognize the alcoholic's tremendous capacity to stir up anxiety, frustration, and anger without at the same time throwing up his hands in despair? How can he offer compassion without becoming overly protective or manipulative? And, finally, shall the clergyman offer himself to the alcoholic as one who is only incidentally a representative of religion or as one who recognizes the significance and value of his specifically religious heritage and role?

These questions are the same as those to which we have addressed ourselves in a five-year National Institute of Mental Health Research and Training Project for the training of clergymen in the field of alcoholism conducted at the Georgian Clinic (1964-69).[1]

The Georgian Clinic, having developed an interdisciplinary staff over a period of fifteen years, recognized the clergyman's potential. This has come into focus through the extent to which the Clinic has used clinically trained clergymen in its treatment program. These clergymen were equipped for, and took seriously the responsibility of relating to these isolated people (alcoholics) in such a way that the alcoholic became aware of his own capacity to relate. These clergymen were equipped to accept this responsibility as a *long-range* project (perhaps a lifetime). They helped to conceptualize the illness as expressing a feeling of "caughtness" about life which called for a pastoral or shepherding response. They saw the treatment process as the opportunity to provide patients with a "community of concern," a microcosm of healing forces which would offer the patient regular opportunities for facing those issues of human existence which lie below his alcoholic symptoms. The key issues were and are:

1. The alcoholic's struggle between living and dying—whether or not to make a commitment to life.

2. The patient's struggle to trust or to have faith in himself, in others, and in God—as opposed to the temptation of hopelessness.

3. The patient's struggle to find some worthwhile and at-

[1] "Pilot Project for Clinical Training of Clergymen in The Field of Alcoholism" NIMH Grant #8589, staffed by: George P. Dominick, Co-Director; John M. Crow, Coordinator of Training; Melvin B. Drucker, Clinical Psychologist for Evaluation.

tainable meaning or purpose for life—versus flight into an anesthetized purposelessness.

4. The patient's struggle to step out into the mainstream of life—as opposed to his shrinking back in face of the anxiety, guilt, and tension of the human situation.

The clergyman with training, therefore, brings to the field of alcoholism an awareness of the person behind the bottle, an awareness of the central existential question behind the long list of situational questions and pleas. He brings this orientation to the crisis demand of the immediate situation and to the slow process of growth which is the lifelong business of the alcoholic and his family.

The most graphic, although obviously limited, characterization of this pastoral role is the familar shepherd image. Implied in the shepherding role and function are a perspective, a life-style, and a healing orientation.

The shepherding perspective is based on the search for the troubled person beneath a plethora of symptoms and diagnostic labels. This perspective takes seriously that fundamental sense of lostness which echoes through so much of the alcoholic's conversation, and it accepts as fundamental reality the alcoholic's struggle between life and death. Shepherding involves an attitude which takes seriously man's responsibility for his own choices, yet maintaines faith in man's capacity to grow and change. It is an active calling which sees its work as a lifelong relationl process. It is a professional stance which puts less emphasis on "gaining insights" and "making adjustments" while putting more emphasis on a supportive "standing with."

The shepherding function also implies a life-style. The shepherd does not stand apart from his sheep, offering suggestions from another plane of life. Nor does the effective pastor. The effective pastor is one who has learned as a result of his own involvement in the human predicament and can admit to his own experience of "caughtness." He is a person who needs neither to flee nor to explain away the basic anxiety involved in human existence. A good pastor may, for instance, be considerably more at home with the alcoholic's ever-present death wish than is the physician. The physician tends to react to death exclusively as the alien intruder, whereas the pastor looks upon it as a part of the bundle of human existence—an inevitable dimension of the life process which is to be faced with realism and faith. One of the pastor's basic contributions, in fact, lies in his ability to accept the life/death ambivalence in the alcoholic—particularly during the initial struggle for sobriety.

Finally, the shepherding function involves a rather distinct healing orientation. This healing orientation concerns itself with *caring* rather than *curing*. Caring accepts a person where he is and as he is. It is an offer which refuses to be contingent on mutual agreements to change or to improve. The offer contains possibilities for growth but remains a valid offer even if every possibility is refused.

The shepherd's healing orientation finds its focus in *understanding* rather than in *adjusting* another person. Understanding is seen as a broader offer, aimed at promoting a sharing and an interaction at depth. Understanding may lead to change, but its thrust is relational—increasing the capacity of two human beings to stand together.

The essence of this healing orientation is the pastor's offer to support the alcoholic's inner strengths—even those strengths which the alcoholic may not yet have recognized in himself. Such support may begin on as rudimentary a level as literal hand-holding whereby the pastor accepts the alcoholic's present weakness and supports the only strength that is available—his potential strength. Further along in the process, this same support may be offered by a total refusal to intervene or to reassure, thus affirming to the disbelieving alcoholic his own capacity to endure tension and to shoulder his own burdens. The operational principle is identical in both cases—the pastor's acceptance of present weaknesses and his support of potential and emerging strengths.

As an important postscript to the pastor's healing orientation—his acceptance of the alcoholic's inalienable right to procrastinate or even to fail totally—needs to be mentioned. This is one of the tough tenets of theology which in actual clinical practice becomes a liberating therapeutic principle not only for the pastor but for the alcoholic as well.

My thesis has been that, given adequate clinical training, the clergyman can become the key member in a team approach to alcoholism. The obvious discrepancy between clergy potential and practice has been traced to the minister's attitudes toward the illness and to his own inhibiting insecurity about his professional competence. His definitive contribution, nonetheless, lies in his capacity, however dormant at present, to respond to the alcoholic's demonstrably pastoral needs. Building on this thesis, let me suggest some rather particular contributions which may be made by parish clergy.

Early Intervention. The clergyman who is alert to his pastoral responsibilities has the opportunity, as well as the responsibility, to know in considerable detail the pulse of his community. He still enjoys the respect of the citizenry. He is seen as one who is concerned about the preservation and implementation of the ethical and human values in community life. He is, in addition, a person who has an entree into the homes and family life of his parishioners, as well as many other persons in the community. He is looked up to as a person who can give guidance, counsel, and genuine concern from a perspective that transcends the relative values of present-day culture.

This means that the pastor—to the extent that he has eyes to see and ears to hear—can pick up the early signs of problem drinking. Along with the family physician, he finds himself in a unique position to work at early intervention. Sometimes this intervention will take the form of direct efforts to motivate the alcoholic toward early treatment and care. Frequently, it will mean helping the family of the alcoholic relate to him (or her) in such a way that he will be confronted with the reality of his alcoholism at an early stage.

Too often, however, the pastor becomes a person whom we might describe as the "happy fixer" or, on the other extreme, the "finger pointer." The happy fixer is the pastor who sees the solution for the alcoholic in terms of solving his immediate problems. His thinking is that he is thereby really aiding in a recovery from alcoholism. The happy fixer stays busy getting the alcoholic out of jail or out of jams. He works at getting him a job to replace the one he lost last week and labors at patching up quarrels between husband and wife. What the happy fixer fails to understand, of course, is that the alcoholic lives by a series of crises and dependency demands. Thus, the happy fixer unwittingly perpetuates the alcoholic's sick patterns of living.

The finger pointer is the pastor with all the answers. His answer may be a hell-fire-and-brimstone condemnation or it may be a very enlightened explanation of the latest theories on alcoholism. At either extreme, the idea is that handing the addictive drinker the *right answer* will do the job. The difficulty, of course, is that the alcoholic's problem is precisely his inability to translate other people's answers into his actual scheme of living.

Early intervention actually begins with the pastor's ability to accept the alcoholic where he is without making unrealistic demands, while setting firm limits. The alcoholic needs to know that our concern is genuine, but he has to learn that we will consistently refuse to make his decisions for him. He needs to experience our respect for his potential strength. Such respect comes through in our willingness to let him face the consequences of his own behavior. The task is to offer compassion without getting bogged down in sympathy, to offer consistent limits without falling into moralizing judgments. It is the task, also, to recognize both the child and the adult within the alcoholic.

One aspect of early intervention is what might be called the availability of the minister—meaning more the attitude than the situation. There is no other profession that advertises its offer to be used in the sense that the clergy does. Frequently, however, we associate this being used with our experience of being made an easy touch. The rather natural human reaction is to become angry, resentful, and suspicious of persons who dare to accept our invitation—who dare to attempt to use us.

I am convinced, therefore, that we need to take a long, hard look at what it means to be "used" so we can begin to set it in its positive perspective. It is obvious that nothing significant is going to happen between us and the alcoholic if we attempt to change his way of life without at the same time permitting ourselves to become genuinely involved. This brings us to the question: How does the alcoholic seek involvement with us? The alcoholic's first move is frequently to try to manipulate us, to make us a patsy who will meet his sick dependency needs. We need, therefore, to be aware that these attempts at controlling us are the alcoholic's characteristic way of asking for involvement. Any real relationship with the alcoholic, therefore, inevitably opens us to a whole series of manipulative demands. But this behavior, including even his acts of drinking, is basically his sick, desperate attempt to relate to other people.

Our role then becomes, first, to learn to recognize the ways in which the alcoholic tries to involve us, and, second, to make some constructive use of that involvement. The criterion is whether we are being used appropriately or inappropriately. It becomes the responsibility of the minister to utilize the involvement for growth away from sick dependency and toward the mobilization of potential strength and responsibility.

Treatment. In order to understand the treatment role of the clergyman, we must determine our basic pastoral goals in relation to the alcoholic. It is my belief that both long-term and short-term goals are best viewed as the development of a relationship rather than as a process of problem-solving. The development of a relationship marked by (1) mutual respect, (2) an acceptance of the alcoholic as he is, and (3) a response to the person beneath the mask is basic to effective counseling with the alcoholic. Such a relationship is also basic to help him accept the fact that he has an illness; it is essential to an eventual referral process and to an ongoing or follow-up pastoral care.

The alcoholic, however, regularly complicates the situation by asking us to solve his problem. He frequently seeks us out during a crisis, bringing a great hunger for dependency: "Take care of me," he says. Unless we understand that he is really asking for a relationship, we will miss the key factor. To solve his problem—to fulfill his dependency needs on his terms—will inevitably lead him to find some excuse for becoming very angry with us. Dependency simply works that way.

The answer, of course, is a realistic relationship of respect in which we accept our responsibility for determining the appropriate and inappropriate use of our involvement. Once such a relationship has been established, the next step is that of referral. To refer an alcoholic to other helping agencies should never be seen as ducking our pastoral responsibilities. On the contrary, it is a recognition of our professional responsibility in the team approach to alcoholism.

Meaningful referrals must be based on a genuine knowledge of community and regional resources. We need to know more than just the name and telephone number of a clinic or a member of A. A. As the minimum essentials for adquate referrals the pastor should have a firsthand, working knowledge of available detoxification facilities, local A. A. groups, nearby rehabilitation centers, and those social agencies which can render service to the alcoholic and his family.

Successful referrals are never simply the handing out of information or the making of telephone calls. Timing is extremely important. A premature referral to A. A. or to a hospital or rehabilitation center will be interpreted by the alcoholic as rejection.

Once a satisfactory referral has been made, the pastoral function becomes one of following through as a member of the helping team. Here again we see the pastor's need for some real knowledge of the rehabilitation program to which the alcoholic has been referred. It is the pastor's responsibility to keep in touch, to keep the lines of communication open, and to offer his support even though some other person or agency has assumed the primary role in treatment.

Another important aspect of the pastor's referral work is the support and interpretation he can offer the alcoholic's family during the rehabilitation process. Resident patient care for a breadwinner may place additional pressure on the family's financial squeeze. A slip during the rehabilitation process may seem to the family to wipe out all their earlier hopes. Even when rehabilitation is most successful there are the strains of accepting the alcoholic as he experiments with new patterns of relating to his wife and children. In all these cases the clergyman can be a key member of the treatment team as he responds to alcoholism as an illness involving the whole family.

The clergyman also needs to bring to his referral efforts the attitude which says: "If one approach doesn't work, we'll try something else." The pastor cannot afford the luxury of putting all his eggs in one basket. There simply is no such guaranteed basket available. No one facility, resource, or approach has all the answers to this particulr disability. If at first you don't succeed, join the club and try again.

In addition to those services which the pastor can render personally, there are the resources of his church. Sermons, church-school groups, and youth groups offer regular opportunities for the pastor to state his interest in and support of the alcoholic and his family in their struggle for sobriety and meaningful living. Larger churches or clusters of smaller churches might even form special groups for alcoholics, their spouses, or their families. Alanon and Alateen have shown very clearly that the spouses and children of alcoholics have a special need for support during the strains and stresses of the long rehabilitation process.

Finally, there are specifically religious resources which the clergyman has to offer the alcoholic. But a word of caution is needed here. Most alcoholics in the early stages of treatment and care have difficulty in the appropriation of the traditional resources of Scripture, prayer, sermons, and worship. Out of their deep feelings of guilt and their fear of rejection, they back away from these resources—feeling more threat than comfort. It is not uncommon, however, for these same alcoholics to begin, at a later point in their rehabilitation process, to seek the answers and resources of their faith. The best rule of thumb at this point is to wait patiently—listen more and talk less.

Education. Few people in the community occupy so favorable a position as the minister in terms of opportunities to aid in eduction about alcoholism. Each week he enters into a series of dialogues with individuals and groups, each dialogue offering an opportunity for speaking to the facts and attitudes involved in this aspect of the human condition. Unfortunately, ministers have tended to sit back and wait for other professionals to take the lead. My suggestion is that ministers should take the lead in educational efforts. Where other professionals of a community are indifferent or disorganized, the minister can work toward arousing an interest in the team approach to alcoholism. In those communities where the professionals are already engaged in a team approach, the minister can be of real service in interpreting these professional resources to the community at large. In many of our smaller communities the place for the clergyman to begin is to develop a line of communication about people with problems of alcoholism with at least one local doctor. Out of this working relationship other doctors and ministers can gradually become involved. Bear in mind that doctors, like pastors, get lonely and discouraged, and begin to wonder what they really have to offer the alcoholic. The two should sit down together and talk. As a team, these two members of the helping professions can find endless opportunities to transmit the message of the alcoholic's need—and his hope.

Prevention. The prevention of alcoholism is a function in which clergymen are already involved. Every effort made by a pastor or a church group to strengthen the roots of personal or family living is an effort toward the prevention of alcoholism. To put it another way, our traditional calling to make men whole and our traditional ministry of reconciliation constitutes a fundamental effort in the area of prevention of alcoholism.

The alcoholic, even before he takes his first drink, is a fragmented person, plagued by guilt and ever fearful of rejection. Thus, even in the nursery department of the church school the teacher who genuinely accepts and cares for a little toddler makes a significant contribution to the future life of a man or woman. Honest and straight-shooting youth leaders can help young men and women to break through their incipient shells of isolation and to know the value of sharing their feelings with others. Warm, accepting groups of members in any local church can provide a constructive alternative to the alcoholic's flight into the bliss of the bottle.

Thus, each time we communicate *good* news to persons oppressed by the fears of bad news, we have joined the fight against alcoholism. We can help our congregations to move beyond the structures of a burdensome, legalistic morality. We can lower the barriers of prejudice and judgment against the weaker brother. By so doing we contribute to the prevention of alcoholism.

For all the dangers of simplification the principle is clear: a person either learns constructive ways of handling the stresses of life, or he is tempted to learn destructive escape techniques. Alcoholism is one such escape technique. And persons learn these constructive alternatives from other people—family, teachers, minister, friends. The clergyman is in a key position to teach men and women, boys and girls, that real living comes to us when we give up hiding and begin to turn toward other people, toward life, and toward God.

All I have said points directly and unmistakably to the fact that parish clergy desperately need expanded training opportunities in the field of alcoholism. The potential is great. Unfortunately, however, most of this potential presently lies dormant. It is my conviction, moreover, that this will continue to be the case until increasing numbers of clergymen can receive additional training within a clinical setting.

In a five-year period the training project at the Georgian Clinic has exposed approximately 1,300 pastors and seminarians to the problem of alcoholism. A small number of these, approximately 30, entered into six or more months of full-time training. We used the clinical training model in which trainees primarily work directly with alcoholic patients under close pastoral supervision.

We have visualized the dynamic nature of the training process—where the heart of learning and teaching of pastoral care lies—by seeing the trainee surrounded by: (1) the community of patients, (2) the staff (representing all other helping professions), (3) a peer group of trainees, and (4) the chaplain supervisors. Our aim was to equip the clergyman to become involved in a more meaningful way with alcoholics and their families. Evaluation studies have indicated that we have effected such change.[2]

For additional reading

Alcoholism, A Source Book for Priests. Indianapolis: National Clergy Conference on Alcoholism, 1960.

Clinebell, H. J., Jr. *Understanding and Counseling the Alcoholic.* Nashville: Abingdon Press, rev. ed., 1968.

Keller, John E. *Ministering to Alcoholics.* Minneapolis: Augsburg, 1966.

Shipp, Thomas J. *Helping the Alcoholic and His Family.* Philadelphia: Fortress Press, paperback, 1966.

16.
FUNCTIONS OF COMMUNITY CLERGY WITH THE EMOTIONALLY DISTURBED

J. Obert Kempson, B.D., M.A.
Pastoral Consultant, Department of Mental Health, State of South Carolina, Columbia, South Carolina

As our cybernetic culture emerges, crisis pastoral care will consume greater portions of the parish minister's energy and time. His parishioners' expectations will demand deeper sensitivity about human concerns, and increased understanding and skill about pastoral care.

Emotional disturbance is a crisis situation which commands the attention of the community clergy. As the minister functions pastorally, several obvious factors may be borne in mind. First, the disturbed person is a child of God and a fellow human being. Second, he is experiencing an intense stress situation which may isolate him from himself, others, and God. Third, he may need to recognize his worth and preserve his dignity as a person. Fourth,

---

[2] A more complete description of these areas of involvement is contained in a three-year report "Pilot Project for Clinical Training of Clergymen in the Field of Alcoholism," which may be obtained by writing Georgian Clinic Division, 1260 Briarcliff Road, NE, Atlanta, Georgia 30306.

he may be preoccupied with a way of meeting his needs and what he perceives as life's demands. Fifth, he may need to become more aware of his God-given potential and realize the actualization of it.

Among mental health professionals it is generally agreed that the clergyman is a significant helping person. In the study, *Americans View Their Mental Health*,[1] it is reported 42 percent of persons who sought help turned to clergymen, 29 percent went to physicians, 18 percent to psychiatrists or psychologists, and 10 percent to social agencies or marriage clinics. This same report also reveals that of those who sought help 42 percent reported their problems centered around their marriage, 18 percent dealt with personal adjustment difficulties, and 12 percent related problems about their children. It is noted that 65 percent of those who sought assistance from clergymen claimed they received some help. These statistics indicate the significance of the pastoral function in emotional crisis and places upon the clergyman a heavy pastoral responsibility.

Chaplaincy Service in South Carolina State Hospital sponsored a study, "Chaplaincy-Community Clergy Developmental Project," [2] for the purpose of exploring the contacts between mental patients and their churches and clergy in South Carolina, and of offering guidelines to assist community clergy in providing more meaningful pastoral care to mental patients upon their return home. The survey, by interview and questionnaire, explored interactions between pastors and patients before, during, and after hospitalization. Information about the pastoral care skills used by the clergyman and his background was also secured. The social framework of the church as it related to the patient's experience and the pastor's outreach in helping the person were also data items.

Among the results secured from the study were several of par-

[1] Gerald Gurin, *et al.*, *Americans View Their Mental Health* (New York: Basic Books, 1960), pp. 305-7, 319.

[2] "Chaplaincy-Community Clergy Developmental Project," S.C. State Hospital Columbia. Mental Heath Project Grant OM-499, National Institute of Mental Health. Emily A. Spickler Program Consultant. J. Obert Kempson, Program Director.

ticular interest. The number of patients in contact with both pastor and church before, during, and after hospitalization remained about the same. Overall, only a small portion of the patients had a long-term relationship with their pastors. Over half the patients of the 438 who supplied information had very little or no contact with their ministers. It was also noted that more than a third of former patients expressed discomfort about being present for or participating in the programs of the church, nor were they able to participate in community activities. About a third of the patients consciously sought help from their ministers. Lack of contact with their pastors or feelings about themselves or their pastors appeared to interfere with their attempts to seek help. Data revealed that 63 percent had never asked for pastoral help, that 27 percent had made no attempt at contact, that 12 percent were ashamed to seek help or felt the pastor would disapprove, and that 12 percent said he was unable to help.

About half the pastors of the 523 supplying data were providing pastoral care for disturbed persons who were not hospitalized, and about 40 percent said they were involved pastorally with hospitalized persons. These ministers were relating with disturbed persons in churches which were stable in membership, with regular worship and a moderate to full program each week.

The pastors' initial contacts with the emotionally disturbed were ordinarily made by referral from others or because of the pastoral functions of the ministers. Half of clergy felt, as pastors, they must deal with persons' religious and psychological needs together. The pastors recognized some lack of understanding existed between themselves and the community resources to which they might refer distressed persons. This matter of emotional distance was one of the areas which they felt was open for further exploration.

Some summary comments by Emily A. Spickler, who was Research Consultant of the project, are:

> Protestant pastors of stable churches, less than 800 in membership, without special training in dealing with mental and

emotional problems are in contact through their role as pastor with people inside and outside their churches who have mental and emotional problems. The goal of their pastoral activities is to help people develop a quality of relationship to God, man and self.

The ministers expressed the need for more available pastoral care resources. One-fourth of them desired help in the form of training for themselves, aid in methods of work or in preventive measures. The data revealed that pastors do not necessarily take on a new or unprecedented role in being concerned with emotionally distressed persons hospitalized or not hospitalized. Their pastoral care must take on a particular emphasis or extension in order to be effective with people who have special difficulties. Effectiveness in the pastoral role can be aided by understanding how the ill person's reactions are affecting his contact with pastor and church, and in what areas pastoral methods and procedure can take this into account.

Another part of this particular survey reveals data which point up the clergyman's functions as he ministers pastorally to emotionally distressed persons. This information was secured from interviews with forty-five pastors, fourteen patients, and two patient groups, one of which was followed over two months. The data describes several categories for pastoral care functioning.

The pastor can foster group-belonging which relates the distressed person to the church. This can be accomplished by the pastor's maintaining his personal availability and also the availability of the church to people in distress. As several patients said, "We may not need to call on the pastor, but we know he is there. He is available twenty-four hours a day." Building a long-term relationship encourages confidence. This, in itself, would certainly discourage changes and interruptions in pastoral relationship. Fostering continuing contacts with disturbed persons who are unable to make these contacts themselves is a most important aspect of pastoral outreach. Church members also will need to be guided and instructed in making contacts. This kind of education for crisis pastoral care ministry would involve understanding about emotional distress, interpreting what the crisis situation is, preparing the members of the church in giving support, and maintaining relationship with the person in some way while in crisis and later.

The rehabilitation of the distressed person's participation in the church comes through encouraging and supporting his responses. Acceptance provides an atmosphere for give and take between church groups and the person who may use the church as a family substitute. Furthermore, it is important sometimes that foster roles be provided these persons so as to avoid some of the intense conflicts which they have had in closer relationships with members of their families.

Another function focuses on pastoral care for the disturbed individual. In this supportive ministry the minister watches over the distressed person on a long-term basis but not in an overly solicitous manner, and cooperates with professionals in the treatment effort. The clergyman is available consistently regardless of how the patient responds or behaves. He listens to those who need to talk, and in particular to those who have no one else with whom to talk. Also he guides and interprets the uses of religious processes. Counseling can be provided persons who have expressed their concerns to the minister on levels where he is comfortable and possesses skill. Consultation from professionals can enhance his counseling. He refers, with pastoral skill, those whose siuations are beyond his time and training. Sometimes distressed persons are unable to relate to other professionals. Here the minister has an opportunity to provide pastoral care to these persons. The clergyman can serve an important function by enabling the person to make more adequate community adjustments.

In providing for the pastoral care of the distressed person's family the minister has an opportunity to help them understand their relationship to the person and something of the illness background. He can provide counsel in resolving guilt and in meeting their frustrations. The family needs to maintain hope instead of feeling that little can be done to help the person find a stable place in society again.

The minister guides and educates the membership of the

church in understanding and dealing with mental and emotional illness. A long-term process of education needs to be undertaken in the average church to enable people to realize that in crisis they can turn to the pastor to secure help. The minister, representing God and the moral structure of the church, functions to help the family, the disturbed person, and the church understand the stress situation.

Preventive intervention in mental health may also be a facet of the minister's educational and pastoral function. In his pastoral calling and other activities he can become aware of the need for providing the necessary counsel and guidance in order to prevent more serious trouble from developing. His sensitivity and concern can prompt him to enable the congregation to meet its pastoral care responsibilities as a redemptive community.

The pastor can provide first aid in crisis for both individuals and their families when, for varying reasons, they have been unable to contact or use community resources. Some persons recognize the minister's availability on a twenty-four-hour basis for emergencies when other resources are unavailable. The minister may be perceived as the advocate of the poor, the dispossessed, and others who, not aware of community resources, need his counsel.

The effectiveness of the clergyman is influenced by his expectations, the expectations of others, the various demands on his time, and his own understanding and skill. His own church's understanding of emotional illness will have a direct effect upon his efforts and how he functions pastorally. Most people see greater value in matters which the pastor and the church endorse. The minister is expected to be dependable, trustworthy, and to render no hurt. It is generally assumed that the pastor will not turn away from human need or seek to escape it. This places on him a great responsibility, a responsibility that needs to be shared with the total congregation as a caring community.

From the data supplied it becomes evident that a minister, to function more effectively with the emotionally disturbed, needs to formulate his concept of the pastoral function. Some guidelines are therefore suggested. The pastor, as a symbol of God and a symbol of the church, develops with a person a unique relationship characterized by understanding and acceptance of him as a child of God with potential which can be actualized. The pastor can assist in providing an atmosphere for the person to deal more adequately with his basic attitudes toward himself, man, the universe, and God through pastoral care (counseling, visiting, and group work) and worship experiences thereby enabling him to develop a more satisfactory style of life.

The several aspects of pastoral care for the emotionally disturbed described above set forth some principles and structure for the functioning of community clergy as they become involved with crises in the parish and in the community mental health setting. While the minister's helping role in crisis is generally recognized by both professional and lay persons, he realizes his need for counsel and educational opportunities to develop his potential more fully. His desires, the expectations of his parishioners, and professional recognition stimulate cooperative endeavor on many levels by both religion and mental health leaders for crisis pastoral care intervention.

17.
THE RELIGIOUS COMMUNITY AND THE RETURNING INMATE*

Thomas W. Klink,** B.D.
Chaplain and Director, Division of Religion and Psychiatry, The Menninger Foundation, Topeka, Kansas, 1959-1970

"Inmate" is not the usual term to identify a patient in a mental hospital. It is not the familiar term to describe youngsters in correctional institutions or, usually, the term for adult prisoners. But it does have the virtue of being generally applicable to persons who spend some significant segment of life

* Adapted and abridged from material originally presented to an Institute on Social Welfare Services for the Clergy, La Crosses, Wisconsin, 1966.
** Deceased

within an institution. This paper concerns the functions of religious communities—churches and congregations—in the effective reintegration of inmates into the open community. Thus, this paper deals with the "tertiary preventive" segment of a comprehensive system of care—that is, those efforts which tend to reduce the likelihood of a recurrence of disorder.[1]

Inmates discover that returning home can be a complicated and frustrating process. Two collect prayers, products of ministry to inmate congregations, reveal the complexity of the process.

"Almighty God, loving Father of us all, we acknowledge before Thee our shortcomings and our impatience. We know so much in solitude. We fall so short of making others understand. Forgive us our isolation behind the walls of fear and doubt, for with Thee and and Thy people there is that love which is perfect understanding. Perfect love casteth out fear. Give us the grace to communicate ourselves and the patience to wait for healing understanding."

The second prayer reveals the inner experience of being an inmate.

"Oh, God, the strength of those who suffer and the repose of them that triumph, we rejoice in the communion of saints. We remember all who have faithfully lived, all who have passed on into Heaven. We remember especially those who have been important to us. We have not always lived true to their ways. We have found that their ways are not our ways. We have tried to be more obedient to them than to Thy living spirit. We have borne the burden of bondage to the past. Forgive us our missteps. Grant us the freedom to stand strong in our heritage, and the wisdom to discern the newness of Thy creation in us."

Although there are important differences among inmates, there are two similarities: all have been inmates, and nearly all return

---

[1] Gerald Caplan, *Principles of Preventive Psychiatry* (New York: Basic Books, 1964), pp. 113-27.

home. These similarities frame the opportunity for the religious community in its service to the returning inmate.

The basic study of the inmate's experience is Goffman's *Asylums: Essays on the Social Situation of Mental Patients and Other Inmates.*[2] He discusses the situation of those who spend some time in "total institutions." There are five categories of total institutions: (1) for the care of the harmless but incapable (sick, blind, aging, etc.); (2) for those threatening to the community (tuberculous, leprous, and some mentally ill); (3) for those against whom the community seeks protection (criminals, political or social deviants, *and* some mentally ill); (4) isolated work organizations (including military posts, boarding schools, work camps), and (5) organized retreats from the world (monasteries, cloisters, and other asylums).

Goffman's analysis makes evident the similarity of all inmates: they have been isolated from their pre-inmate world, they have been inducted into another world. Meanwhile, in some degree, something has happened to the world "outside." The dogs barking at the returned Ulysses or the children ridiculing Rip Van Winkle are symbols of the invariable changes during a person's period as an inmate (or wanderer).

The dissociation of streams of events is revealed in an excerpt from a pastoral contact with the wife of a mental hospital patient who seeks marriage counseling:

"We tried so hard not to have John go to the hospital, and then it just couldn't go on and he went and you have no idea how we've had to scrimp to make it possible, but we managed by everybody taking an extra load. But after a while John's letters were disinterested. He seemed to have found a place for himself in the ward. He's coming back home weekends now but he seems in a hurry to get back. He doesn't seem to appreciate how we've taken over his load. Last Saturday, Reverend, he called to say he would be discharged in two weeks, but he wouldn't be home this Sunday because his ward government group was in charge of an open house for an

[2] (Garden City, N.Y.: Doubleday, 1961.)

138

infirmary ward at the hospital. (And here she breaks down into tears.) What do you think has happened?"

A comparable insight into the effect of separation is found in the following statement to a parish clergyman by a paroled prisoner returned to his family after eighteen months in an adult correctional institution:

> "Reverend, I thought I was better off than some guys. My wife stayed steady; no divorce, no running around. She kept the station open. She hired some help. She cared for the kids. She even managed to get the lawn mower started once or twice. I am so grateful I can't see straight. That's what gets me about how mad I get about little things. I've never felt so angry before as about a little thing that's going on now. I wonder if I am going off my nut. While I was gone she and the boys rearranged the seats at the dinner table—it sort of makes sense—closer for her to the kitchen and to the phone but *my old place is gone.*

Such quotations illustrate rather than exhaust the significance of the inmate phase of a treatment or correction process. It may be hard to believe—given our preconceptions about hospitals and prisons—but, however well-staffed or ill-programmed, such institutions are organized societies. For inmates who have been alienated from the larger society the institutional society may often be more satisfying or secure. The religious community or clergyman who would be of help to the returning inmate or his family needs to be aware—as in the illustration above—that a weekend pass at home may be less attractive than responsible participation in a ward project.

If we can understand the positive involvements in an inmate society we may also be able to understand its negative results, the recidivists or chronic inmates. They are a small but important minority who cannot tolerate having their human needs for food, shelter, work, and companionship satisfied unless they can at the same time be mutinously hostile at the personal or institutional provider. The dynamics of such nursing and biting by immature persons makes it clear that pastoral or religious services to inmates must support a redirection of hostility as well as meeting their needs.

Motivation for the clergyman or religious community is important in insuring effective service to returning inmates. Easy and presumptuous compassion, undisciplined pity or guilt, even "love" are poor motivations for significant work. The process of re-adaptation for nearly all inmates involves stressful work which he alone must be encouraged to do. Those who would be of service to him must be willing to administer a tolerable dose of such strong medicine fully as much as they are moved to be "his friend." [3]

The religious community dare not presume that to be released is an unambiguous occasion of joy or achievement. Ex-inmates need frank, open responses. They need to be free to reveal, for example, "just how crazy-mixed-up I was and what happened to me in the hospital," or "how tempted I am by the non-responsiveness of the new outside world."

A church men's group went to a weekly prisoner-citizen fellowship meeting in an adult prison. They were made uncomfortable by, "how unfair the law is which demands a prisoner have a job or a sponsor before he can be discharged even though he has been approved for parole." In their guilt and anxiety this group volunteered to be a sponsor. When the discharged prisoner was fired from his first job for abusing fellow employees, the group increased financial assistance! When he met their visitor at his living quarters drunk, they bought him a coat! When he wanted to break parole conditions by taking a job as a cab driver, the vocational circumstances which led to this original troubles, they intervened with his parole officer. It was only when they discovered, with help from the prison chaplain, how guilty and angry their motivations were for dealing with this man and how immobilized they were in responding rather than giving that they were able to discover limit setting, goal setting, responsive listening. Then they found more charitable pastoral acts than just destructive guilty giving.

[3] See T. W. Klink, *Depth Perspectives in Pastoral Work* (Englewood Cliffs, N.J.: Prentice-Hall, 1965), p. 58.

THE RETURNING INMATE

An inmate prayer from a psychiatric hospital reveals this desperate need for responsiveness:

> Our Father, God, whose watchful care extends to the least of Thy creatures, to the utter-most parts of the earth, we confess our temptation to feel neglected. We have been in need, and our needs have seemed not to have been met. We have done wrong and our wrong-doing has gone unpunished. We have set forth plans and our dreams have aroused no enthusiasm. We acknowledge our temptation to feel that there is little response to us. Forgive us for blinding our eyes to the fullness of Thy response. Understand our efforts to carry on a dreary monologue. Restore us to confidence in Thy patient attentiveness, to all that we do, or need, or dream. Amen.

Inmates are the butts of very traditional, often derisive humor. Such humor is revealing, not obscene. They have been "drunk," "crazy," "in jail," or "in the clink." Ex-inmates know the quality of humor. Until the religious leader or community can be free to accept such humor we will be as stiff and unhelpful as starched and fearful Gray Ladies passing Kool-Aid across a table at a ward bingo party.

This is a creative pharmaceutical age. Thousands of modern inmates are able to leave hospitals because of regular and often continuing dosages of anticonvulsants, tranquilizers, energizers, hormones, or alcohol-sensitive compounds. I have met a few ex-inmates back in hospitals because they have heard such wonderful potions derided at church or from the pulpit as evidence of modern corruption, comparable to subway rapes or God-is-dead theology. A minor but not insignificant element in the function of the religious community with the returning inmate is its understanding of the functions of drugs.

The inmate's situation is fraught with ambiguity. For example, Mr. A. has a serious drinking problem. Once, this was dealt with punitively (a police charge for driving-while-intoxicated). His family was puritanically religious; he knew that they regarded his drinking as a sin. This led him to seek pastoral help to "put down the devil." His enlightened religious leader properly rejected this idea and encouraged him to seek help for a medical-psychological problem. In the alcoholic treatment institution he was exposed to a group-oriented program in which his problem was identified as properly shameful before the official group standards.

Most inmates have experiences comparable to Mr. A's. They meet an ambiguous or conflicting set of evaluations of their trouble. Hopefully, by the time of their discharge, some dominant judgment has emerged. But as they return to the community they meet the varied or ambiguous judgments again. They need support in maintaining that judgment which has proved most useful for *their* recovery.

Treatment institutions are intended to change inmates. It is not easy to change, we all know that; inmates are no exception. Inmates resist the power of the treatment institution to effect change. A subtle and universal device for resisting genuine change is to accede to change because somebody or something bigger or stronger is making you change. At least that defers the issue of stable change until the power of the institution is withdrawn at the time of discharge. At that point, when the institutional supports and sanctions, group encouragement, and/or behavior reinforcements terminate, the inmate emerges into the arena of personal choice. Rarely can a clergyman or religious community pick up the change-supporting function of the treatment institution. What can be done is to support and aid the ex-inmate to make the changes his own rather than those which have been forced on him by the power of law, drugs, confinement, shock therapy, or control of privileges. To be free is never easy, but no group or individuals should be more prepared for aiding others to use freedom than clergymen and religious institutions who teach or preach of the *yetzer tov* and the "grace of God."

18.
A CHURCH-SPONSORED CRISIS COUNSELING SERVICE

Donald C. Bushfield, B.D.
Chaplain of the Help Line Telephone Clinic, Los Angeles, California

On April 1, 1965, the incoming lines were activated at the Help Line Telephone Clinic in Los Angeles, California. It was the first denominationally sponsored crisis counseling service in the United States to offer help to all areas of human need, caring for the whole man. It is a project of the Los Angeles Baptist City Mission Society, a division of the American Baptist Convention.

Help Line was guided into being through the creative leadership of the Rev. H. Leslie Christie. He was inspired by the pioneering effort of the Life Line Centre in Sydney, Australia, in 1963 at the Central Methodist Mission, led by its superintendent, Dr. Alan Walker. Mr. Christie caught a vision of how the telephone could become the vital link between the masses of troubled people in Los Angeles, and the loving concern of the Christian church with its good news of God's love and willingness to help. Impressive evidence in this direction was obtained in the summer of 1963 when he led in the training of a battery of telephone counselors. The counselors were being prepared to help those responding to an invitation to discuss their personal needs which was made at the conclusion of a pre-taped telecast of a Billy Graham Southern California Crusade meeting. The response was overwhelming; calls continued coming in until late into the night. This experience convinced Mr. Christie of the potential of such a service. The success of these past three and a half years has vindicated his decision to proceed.

Hopeful of securing a broad ecumenical base of support, the Los Angeles Council of Churches was approached, but the needed funding was unavailable, so it was decided to underwrite the support within the American Baptist structure.

We found that a preparatory period prior to the opening of the service is very strategic. To communicate to your constituency the need, relevancy, and efficacy of such an operation is vital. In most denominations the pastor is the key figure, the one at the local church level who can best determine whether the plan will get a fair reception.

The recruitment of telephone counselors, lay and clergy, also is very important. An open invitation should be made to all who are interested to attend a series of preparatory training sessions. Our policy has been to accept as volunteers only those who have been endorsed by their pastor after they have applied through him. The pastors should be informed of the personal qualities needed to be an effective telephone counselor, such as sensitivity, healthy motivation, concern, stability, cooperativeness, dependability, willingness to learn, and a non-judgmental attitude. They should be accepted into the program on a provisional or probationary basis. This serves at least two purposes. It is a reminder that they remain a member of the team only as long as they continue in the ongoing training program. It also leaves a door open in case a volunteer just does not measure up as an effective counselor after there has been an opportunity to observe and evaluate. We have used the term "enlisted staff," rather than volunteers, a term which might imply that all who apply will be accepted. The final decision as to who was accepted was made by the Director. Another safeguard as to a volunteer's acceptability could be to require the taking of the Minnesota Multi-Phasic Personality Inventory or some other similar test. Yet another could be the requiring of an autobiographical sketch with questions asked to determine how they have responded personally to stressful situations in the past.

To prepare these potential workers, a series of training sessions was scheduled. Meetings were held once a week for eight weeks prior to the beginning of the service. Resource persons from the specialities of social work, law enforcement, communication (the telephone company), pastoral counseling, alcoholism treatment, and care for the aging were invited to share their insights, answer questions, and make suggestions. In addition, a field trip was taken to the office of the Los Angeles Police Department where special attention was given to their telephone center through which all incoming calls of a crisis nature are routed. These training sessions were helpful in illuminating vital areas in the wide scope of human problems. It was also decided to have, as a minimum, quarterly training conferences and an annual conference which would include staying overnight at a church conference ground in the mountains.

In the meantime, rapport was being established with the various helping organizations in the community. Information was being gathered as to the names, addresses, telephone numbers, services offered, and eligibility requirements of the various agencies. It was then recorded on Rol-o-dex files, to be kept within easy reach of the person handling incoming calls.

Our professional staff consists of a *director* (supervisor) who oversees the operation, arranges for publicity, schedules the interpretation of our work to individual churches and other groups, and recruits volunteers. He also supervises the professional staff members and participates in case review sessions periodically to keep a sensitive ear tuned to types of cases we have been handling and then notes their disposition and progress.

The supervisor coordinates various phases of the operation. It is he who ferrets out information regarding the new helping agencies that are forming almost every week in our area. He maintains a liaison with them and sees that our information and file system is kept current while doing the major part of the work of referring our clients to the specialized helping agencies. On a weekly basis he confers with the consultant and the chaplain at the case review sessions, both to review recent cases and to preview those coming up.

The *staff consultant* counsels almost exclusively over the telephone with those clients who have been referred to him by the intake worker. He also plays a vital part in the ongoing training program for the volunteers. He helps them to be more skillful in handling different types of problems, utilizing some of the "idle" time when they are serving but when the phones are not busy. His responsibility also includes the vital "call backs" to people who have previously contacted us, been helped, and referred to a special helping agency. His friendly call of concern for their current progress and needs is received with appreciation.

The *chaplain* is assigned those cases that have been referred to the staff consultant because of the depth of the problem, and it has been determined by the consultant that a face-to-face visit from the chaplain is needed. The supervisor obtains consent for a visit by the chaplain, and the appointment is set up. The chaplain's schedule is usually filled up two or three days in advance. However, occasionally the urgency of a particular problem—e.g., case manifesting signs of a high suicide potential—may necessitate the juggling of his schedule. We feel that having a chaplain available for face-to-face home visits is vital for our organization, since it was founded in the spirit of One who incarnated Himself to minister to human needs. The chaplain seeks to be the client's friend helping him to clarify the causes of his problem, to focus on some constructive alternatives of action, and to be aware of the helping resources available. A brief report is made on each visit and is kept with the original intake sheet.

Two secretaries give a portion of their time for filing, typing, and other miscellaneous tasks.

The public is informed of our services in a variety of ways. We run ads in both metropolitan newspapers on alternate days. Also, we buy space in suburban papers. Free public service time is granted to us by eleven AM and FM radio stations. Occasionally we have been interviewed on radio and television, and special newspaper articles have featured our ministry. In addition, brochures and small business-size cards have been used and distributed by churches and other groups.

As has been noted, Life Line was the first church-sponsored comprehensive crisis counseling center in the world; Help Line was the first in the United States as far as we have been able to determine. At present, The United Methodist Church is establishing some centers like this. Some individual churches and religious groups presently offer services to people who have special problems such as alcoholism, suicide, unwanted pregnancies, narcotic addiction, juvenile delinquency, blindness, old age, illness, and so on.

A good way for a church to proceed in starting such a service is to examine the needs of the community. A survey could be helpful. A committee of concerned and responsible persons could serve to stimulate interest in the membership. A study would help determine the manpower and funds needed. It would be well to project realistic needs for a five-year period to avoid a cutback later because of insufficient funds. The securing of a skilled, competent professional staff is a vital part in the forming operation also. The church willing to give to such a venture the time, effort, and expense required will be repaid manyfold by the knowledge that many people have been helped to better, happier and more purposeful lives.

Like any new venture, we encountered problems and have profited from wrestling with them. Among these has been a difficulty in maintaining an adequate number of competent volunteers. Also, we had a struggle finding an effective training program that would meet the particular needs of all the volunteers with their varying degrees of skill. Again, the churches' interest seems to lag at times in spite of our sending out periodic progress reports and occasional case summary illustrations. Also, we have had some difficulty in setting down designated areas of responsibility in our "clinical process" within the professional staff, while also trying to have some degree of flexibility in special instances. Some of our volunteers have difficulty operating as members of a team and have caused problems by encouraging some clients to become dependent on them.

Vital to an effective service is a skillful professional staff who work well together. They need to be able to function not only within their own sphere of responsibility, but also to "double" in training the volunteer staff. A maximum of "live" coverage of the telephone should be provided during the week with the electronic recording "secretary" used only when staff members are not available. Another necessity is adequate advertising placed strategically to reach the largest number of people. An added benefit would be to get permission to have the service listed in the front of the local telephone directory with the other recognized emergency agencies, such as police, fire, and ambulance services. Also mandatory is a good working relationship with the other community helping agencies; the referral list must be constantly revised and updated. An effective training program is a requisite, and included should be appropriate recognition and awards given periodically to remind volunteers of their importance and your appreciation. Our training program has inspired several of our volunteers to enroll in college classes in human behavior, suicide preventive seminars, and pastoral counseling courses. Case review sessions scheduled at least weekly are necessary for the professional staff. Records need to be kept and the inactive cases periodically shifted to prevent the files from becoming too cumbersome.

It is imperative to stress the need for the wholehearted backing of your constituency before you begin. We have found it very difficult to make up later what we did not get at the outset in interest and support. It is important to set goals high enough to challenge, yet realistic enough to be accomplished. There should be an understanding with the volunteers that they will have to meet certain standards of involvement in the training program to maintain their active status. Included as a part of these standards should be the serving of a minimum number of hours on the line during a set period, attending a certain minimum number of training conferences a year, and complying with requests to come in for special individual conferences relative to problem areas. We have found that volunteers tend to lose their interest in the program more quickly by idleness than by being overly busy answering calls. To help them avoid boredom, we try to arrange for them to have something useful to do when not on the phone, such as stuffing envelopes or typing records.

It is best to determine and explain to all involved the "clinical approach" to be used. Our method is to have all incoming calls handled by the volunteers; the more serious ones are referred to the staff consultant, and those whom he feels could profit from a home visit are turned over to the supervisor, who arranges an appointment for a visit from the chaplain. This approach avoids confusion, but flexibility even here is necessary, since overlapping in certain cases will be unavoidable. Another lesson that will be learned as one proceeds is what is the appropriate time and method of referral and when it is best to continue in a supportive role until the client is able to accept a referral and not misinterpret it as rejection.

It is hoped that some readers will be encouraged to initiate the formation of a crisis counseling service in their communities. They will find the challenge exciting, the experience rewarding, and the accomplishments fulfilling. God speed you on your way!

For additional reading

National Institute of Mental Health. *Manpower: Utilization of Non-Professional Crisis Workers,* by Samuel M. Heilig. Planning Emergency Treatment Services for Comprehensive Community Mental Health Centers, 1967.

Pretzel, Paul W. "The Volunteer Clinical Worker at the Suicide Prevention Center." Los Angeles: Suicide Prevention Center, 1968 (mimeographed).

Rioch, Margaret; Elkes, Charmian; and Flint, Arden. Pilot Project in Training of Mental Health Counselors. U.S. Department of Health, Education and Welfare, *Public Health Service Publication* #1254.

Verah, Chad. *The Samaritans.* London: Constable, 1965.

Walker, Alan. *As Close as the Telephone.* Nashville: Abingdon Press, 1967.

CLERGYMEN IN MENTAL HEALTH CENTERS
19.
ONE PARISH'S EDUCATIONAL COUNSELING PLAN

John B. Oman, S.T.M., D.D.
Pastor and Director of the Counseling Center, Wesley United Methodist Church, Minneapolis, Minnesota

A round-faced toddler with wheat-colored hair bounded onto the stage and smiled happily at an audience of about seventy- five people. Behind him, although taller and two years older, his sister walked slowly and edged backward to a chair, sat down, and stared at the toes of her black patent leather shoes. The assembly could not see her face at all, only the perfectly even part in her hair and the twin ponytails tied with blue bows. Now and then she smoothed out her skirt or twisted the bracelet on her arm, but she did not look up.

"What's your name?" the director asked the small boy, and was rewarded with a grin and the clear announcement that his name was "Tommy" and that he was "free years old." When the question was asked of his sister, she did not indicate any awareness but continued to study her shoes. So Tommy provided the director with her name—Becky—and age—five.

The conversation between director and boy revealed that "yes, he and his sister fought sometimes," and they sometimes hit each other. Momentary contrition clouded the little boy's face, but he brightened up, telling about the pet dog he had been promised.

As the two left the stage, Tommy was leading as before. The director turned to the audience and commented, "This is an obvious power struggle," then asked, "What's the story here?"

A grandmotherly type raised her hand and said, "Tommy has found the 'charm route' to getting his own way. He's obviously the boss in that home."

A father with two pre-teen children sitting beside him made the next observation, "He's clearly the mother's favorite. The little girl has given up. She's the one who needs help first."

Some people in the audience remembered the first visit of Tommy and Becky and their divorced mother to the Wesley Methodist Church's Parent Education Center. They recalled that the mother, trying to handle the overwhelming responsibilities of earning a living; finding competent, warmhearted babysitters; and being a double parent, had sought guidance from the Center. Several suggestions had been made to her at that time, including the director's guideline: "Don't interfere with the children's fights. They are trying to involve you. Let them settle things by themselves, without you being judge."

ONE PARISH'S EDUCATIONAL COUNSELING PLAN

The mother's current problem was the difficulty of coping with the little girl, who repeatedly wanted to hug the mother, to follow her around, to literally cling to her apron strings. The consensus of the audience was that the child was conscious of her brother's charm, his painless method of getting his own way by eliciting attention and smiles and the impulse to love him. She was plainly discouraged, and felt the need for constant reassurance. She should have this reassurance, the audience agreed. Becky must be made to feel secure in her mother's love, must hear the words and see the approval in her mother's eyes, but *not* pity, which would only reinforce her feelings of inadequacy.

After this case, two more parents and their offspring appeared on the stage and set forth their problems—the parents first and then the children; the parents retiring to a room out of sight and hearing so that the children would not be influenced by their presence or their reaction to what the children said. The problems are varied: bedwetting, impudence, underachievement, exaggerated sibling rivalry, to name a few. How they are solved illustrates in classic simplicity and effectiveness the whole theory of education-plus-counseling at Wesley Church.

It *is* possible to learn from the mistakes of others as well as from one's own—this is the premise on which the Wesley program is founded. For activation of the program, Wesley depends upon an informed and dedicated laity. Over 10 percent of the membership is involved in one or more of the counseling-oriented courses of action fostered by the century-old downtown Minneapolis church.

The Parent Education Center, one of the newest of Wesley's activities (not yet two years old), has quickly developed into a community resource that draws observer-participants every Sunday morning and has helped families from all over the Twin Cities area through various problems and conflicts.

Based on the Adlerian theory that problems are best brought out into the open and that those who know will be far less judgmental than the troubled one fears, the counseling and education program has successfully proved that people do care and people will help.

The family with problems is required to attend two sessions of the Parent Education Center (held every Sunday morning, from 9:15 to 12:00, this block of time being divided into two periods to allow for church attendance) before registering and offering its problem for discussion. Sometimes mere attendance and observation will give enough insight so that the family can begin working on its problem.

There is no fee connected with Wesley's Parent Education Center. The children are placed in the playroom where supervisors make notes on their behavioral patterns and attitudes. This is particularly valuable since the observations are made during a time when the children are not influenced by reacting toward parents.

The parents (or parent) take a comfortable place on the stage, which is raised about fourteen inches above the main floor. The audience is a vital part of this entire procedure. Composed partly of parents with problems, it also has a heavy preponderance of the laity in training which figures so strikingly in all of Wesley's endeavors. As the parent outlines the problem, the director will ask questions and so will people in the audience. The director of Wesley's Center is a pediatrician, but if a physician is not available, any member willing to immerse himself in study of today's child-care and psychology literature, and who is of a mature state of mind, flexible, outgoing, and truly interested in people, can do the job. The director guides the discussion along the lines of sound personality and character development—with no less an underlying thesis than the Golden Rule.

Parents are urged to develop an atmosphere of mutual respect; to communicate on levels of fun and recreation as well as on discipline and advice; to allow a child to learn "through natural consequences"—that is, by experiencing what happens when he dawdles in the morning and is permitted to experience the unpleasantness and embarrassment of being late to school; to encourage the child and spend time with him playing and learning (positively) rather than spending time lecturing and disciplining (negatively), since the child who is misbehaving is often merely craving attention and if he gets it in pleasant, constructive ways, he will not demand it in antisocial ways; to avoid trying to put the child in a mold of what the parent thinks he should do and be, or what other people think he should do and be, rather than what his natural gifts and tendencies indicate; to take time to train the child in basic skills—to bake a cake, pound a nail, sketch or write or play a melody—including those things the parents know and do well and are interested in. Even if the child is not talented along the same lines, he will appreciate having the parent share the art, skill, or knowledge with him in a non-demanding way.

If the children are teen-agers, they often appear on stage with the parents and join in the discussion of the problem. But if the children are pre-teen and younger, it is deemed best to present them apart from the parents.

After hearing both sides or *all* sides (grandparents and the public school teacher occasionally appear, too), the director and audience offer a number of suggestions to try during the forthcoming week. The Recorder for the Center keeps a written account of these recommendations, along with a progress report. The parent, on subsequent visits, tells what worked and what did not work, and why. From time to time, reference is made to earlier notations, so that the analysis is a comprehensive one.

Misbehavior is generally separated into four goals: the child is striving for attention, power, or revenge, or he feels inadequate and wants to be left alone. Examining the periphery of the problem generally reveals which goal the child is either consciously or unconsciously seeking and the all-important question of *why* he is seeking it.

The same stage comes into use later in the day as Wesley's public psychodrama is presented. Again, the laity is in charge here, with directors of psychodrama—for the most part lay members of the pastoral care program—conducting these dramatic interpretations of daily problems.

The audience comprises not only Wesley members, but a

wide-ranging cross section of the Twin Cities community—students, housewives, professional men, teachers, and preachers. Again the underlying scope of the program is both counseling and educating. Almost everyone present learns something and takes home some insight to use in interpreting his own life. Later, if problems arise requiring more help and more objectivity than he can muster, he will have a background for the type of counseling done at Wesley and will be more ready and able to benefit from it.

Public psychodrama grew out of Wesley's group counseling program. The principle of a church-sponsored group-counseling program is quite widespread now, but Wesley's group counseling dates back more than a decade. It is an outgrowth of the continuing philosophy that church work is done not just by the minister and the official board, but by a committed congregation following a plan of "tithing of time" which can be as meaningful and productive as the tithing of money . . perhaps more so, considered in terms of involvement and in repair of people's *modus operandi.*

Helpful as group counseling proved to be, with each troubled person in the group (about ten persons) finding himself strengthened, aided, and cared for by the other members of the group, sometimes there were exasperating dead ends—psychological impasses where it seemed that the counselee had developed a blind spot and simply could not visualize his problem objectively, or from any other viewpoint than his own. Nor could he state it adequately, sometimes—whether because he was living inside it and could not, therefore, accurately state its dimensions, or whether he simply lacked the word power to make his fellow group members see what was taking place in his life or what had already taken place.

Public psychodrama was found to be the answer to these and other problem situations. For one thing, it was often found that participating in a psychodrama would give enough insight for a person to begin a practical and progressive onslaught against his own problems.

Psychodrama is a simple device, yet in its very simplicity it often serves many complex human difficulties, doubts, and problems. "God is love" is a simple credo, yet in action its outreach is enough to change the world and every life within it. Putting God's word to work in as many situations as possible is what the counseling program attempts. Its ways and methods are simple, basic. *Help* is the key word.

Psychodrama is simply the *acting out* of a situation, rather than the recounting of it in words. Its principal value lies in its focus. The person with a problem begins to explain the situation as he sees it: "So then my mother-in-law asked my wife, 'What's he going to do about the promotion?' and I'm sitting there like a piece of furniture, wondering why she doesn't ask *me* what I'm going to do. Why does she need an interpreter? I speak the language!" The psychodramatist intervenes at this point, "Don't tell us what happened; act it out. No, don't you be yourself in this case—take your wife's role."

A cast from the audience is quickly assembled so that everyone involved in the original situation is represented on stage—the man and wife, the mother-in-law, a teen-age daughter. The man in this case may play several different roles, changing them in mid-conversation, so that the question he asks as a daughter is answered by himself playing his own mother-in-law. Sometimes the person with a problem chooses (or is advised) not to play his role at all, but to watch and listen. Through dramatization, he is unequivocally removed from within his problem. He has no choice but to see it from other viewpoints. What he sees may vary all the way from his wife's childlike dependence upon her mother's opinion, the mother-in-law's hesitancy to ask him a question directly for fear of his explosive reaction, to the mother-in-law's attempt to downgrade him in his daughter's eyes because of her wish to have a more vital part in her granddaughter's life. Or it may be a combination of factors. Seeing the problem through other eyes, however, gives a fresh outlook, and the man begins to take the measure of his problem.

Next question: What can he do about it? Again, psychodrama will help him choose a more constructive course of action so that his interpersonal relationships will be more pleasant, more enhancing of individual worth.

During the psychodrama there may be not only role-reversal which means that each person may assume different parts in the life-drama, but there may be, quite often, an alter ego. This person will sit or stand beside the protagonist and will express feelings he may have but hesitates to express openly.

While parent-education, group-counseling, and public psychodrama are performing their life-shaping functions, another phase of the Wesley program is beginning where life ends. The Healing Fellowship of Christian Friends was organized three years ago when it seemed that there was a gap in the ministry of the church after the initial period of mourning had passed. Bereaved persons, assisted through the first few days and weeks of grief, were still in need of sustaining help when relatives had departed for distant homes and friends were not in day-to-day attendance. A one-to-one new friendship was devised to close this breach in Christian fellowship. A group of fifty volunteers was assembled, trained, and consecrated into this service during a special ceremony at a Sunday morning church service.

When death occurs, a volunteer (or sometimes two) is assigned to the bereaved. His job is to sustain and comfort. He begins by asking the two most therapeutic questions: When did it happen? and, How did it happen? Then, Tell me about it. He encourages talk about the deceased, about the death, about that part of life shared by deceased and bereaved. Only by going back to the beginning of that shared life can the bereaved begin to reclaim the investment in that life and prepare for emotional reinvestment.

The Christian Friend supports the bereaved in the decisions that were made at the time of the funeral services. Did I do the right thing? is a recurring question, and the Friend does his best to assure the bereaved that his decisions were honestly based. Someone to talk to, confide in, and rely on makes grief therapy a personal thing, developed to fit each individual's needs. A Friend may find himself arranging a birthday outing, helping to fill out insurance claim forms, taking the bereaved to visit the grave site, responding sympathetically to a phone call, helping to find new living quarters for the bereaved.

Throughout all this, the Friends of the Healing Fellowship not only aid sorrowing persons to survive a bereavement without becoming psychologically crippled, but find that they, themselves, in the process of helping others, are finding deeper and more profound interpretations of the Christian life than they could in any other way.

The Healing Fellowship of Christian Friends preceded the establishment of the Academy of the Lay Ministry by about two years and, along with group counselors, formed the nucleus of all the laity interested in forwarding Wesley's programs. The Academy of the Lay Ministry offers opportunity for service in several categories: volunteer group counselors, grief therapists, coffeehouse workers, teachers of parent-study groups, psychodramatists, pastor's assistants.

In the letter which volunteers received, it was emphasized that the Lay Ministry involved real dedication and work: "This is not 'just another committee.' I hope you will be very honest in the decision I am asking you to make, for I want only those who will be wholeheartedly committed to the tasks of Lay Pastors. Otherwise a polite 'yes' on your part will hamper more than help."

Sometimes the Academy has all-member sessions of training; sometimes the sessions are confined to a single area of service (although all members are invited and welcome to sit in). The group counselors will be briefed and have refresher courses by various experts, including members of the staffs of the University of Minnesota. The grief therapists will hear visiting lecturers from one of the local seminaries or perhaps hold discussion sessions on current literature in the field. Coffeehouse workers are trained to encourage reticent, timid people to express their feelings in conversational groups. Teachers of parent-study groups prepare to conduct the small groups which have developed as offshoots of the Parent Education Center's Sunday morning program. Psychodramatists study new techniques in their work. Pastor's assistants are coached to do their work more effectively—that is, devoting one hour a week to visiting in the homes of members and prospective members (a total of 1,080 calls during 1967).

Wesley's coffeehouse, "The Cup," has been operating for two and one-half years in the basement of the church, with its own private entrance around the corner from the Sanctuary entrance. A dedicated husband and wife manage The Cup, which is open each Sunday from 5:00 P.M. until 11:00 P.M. About twenty-five volunteers serve under their direction as conversationalists with lonely people who come to the coffeehouse for fellowship, or as workers to man the food counter, which serves coffee, tea, hot chocolate, and pastries at a nominal cost.

Almost any time one comes into The Cup, he will find informal discussions going on around the red-and-white checked cloth-covered tables in this dimly lit room. At 7:00 P.M. there is always a program, carefully selected by an imaginative program chairman, who gives many hours each month to contacting speakers and discussion leaders in order to insure a varied program that will appeal to all age groups and interests. An advertisement was placed in the local paper inviting critics of the church to come and voice their criticisms and discuss them at the coffeehouse. A Karate exhibition, folk-singing, representatives of various religious and political affiliations, advisors in budgeting finances are but a few of the programs presented. Everyone's opinion is important, and people soon learn that it is safe to speak up freely in this permissive atmosphere.

All of Wesley's outreach has produced a synergistic effect—many times greater, because of the combination, than the sum total of all the individual programs. People have learned and helped others to learn, and with such learning has come an improved pattern of living, a life-style with Christian reference.

PART III

the clergyman's role in community mental health services

The growing network of community mental health services is bringing hope and help to tens of thousands of persons in many parts of our country. The existence of these excellent new resources raises important questions for churches and temples: How should the community pastor, priest, or rabbi relate to the mental health services and programs in his area? What qualifications should be possessed by clergy staff members of community mental health centers? What clinical and academic training should they have? What should be their functions? (This was discussed in a preliminary way in Chapter One.) How should they relate to other staff members and to the religious organizations of the community? How can the churches' laymen cooperate with and support community mental health services? In what ways can these services enhance the effectiveness of the churches with the people they serve?

The chapters in this section throw helpful light on these questions. Each statement is written by a person who has had firsthand experience related to community mental health programs. Two of the authors (Moyer and Beebe) report on their experiences as clergy staff members in mental health programs. The chapter on qualifications of staff members is written from the perspective of a clergyman (Kempson) employed by a state mental health department which makes extensive use of clergymen in its regional programs. This section includes a revealing report (Hathorne) of a study of the patterns of clergy involvement in community mental health services. The final chapter in this section (by Clements) stresses the importance of local control of community mental health centers.

Two important convictions underlie the discussion in this section. First, *no comprehensive community mental health service can be really comprehensive unless it succeeds in involving the religious organizations and leaders of its community.* And second, *to accomplish the effective utilization of the mental health potentialities of churches, a mental health service must have a well-trained clergyman on its staff.* Only such a bilingual person —that is, a person who can communicate across disciplines because he can speak both the language of the ministry and religion, on the one hand, and the language of mental health on the other—can build the necessary communication bridges between the churches and the mental health services. Such bridges allow cooperation to occur. To help acquaint mental health leaders and legislators with these two facts is one of the functions of religious leaders who are informed about community mental health.

20.
THE INVOLVEMENT OF CLERGYMEN IN COMMUNITY MENTAL HEALTH CENTERS

Berkley C. Hathorne, B.D., Th.D.
Suicide Prevention Program, National Institute of Mental Health, Chevy Chase, Maryland

Approximately one-fourth of the comprehensive community mental health centers that were operational in 1968 had clergymen on the staff; another 25 percent had a staff person designated to work with the churches and clergy within the catchment area being served; and the remaining half of the existing centers generally acknowledged that one of their goals was to relate in some helpful way to the churches and clergy, but had not yet formulated any plans for accomplishing this. In a limited study, conducted under the auspices of the Department of Ministry of the National Council of Churches, 18 community mental health centers were specifically evaluated for involvement of clergymen.[1]

Among other aspects of the program of the centers that were evaluated was the nature of relationship and involvement of clergymen with the community mental health centers. There are five ways the clergy were observed being related to centers: (1) in the planning, organization, and administration of centers; (2) as ancillary mental health workers; (3) as consultants; (4) as part-time staff persons; and (5) as full-time staff members.

1. It is apparent that in nearly every instance the clergy has been included in the planning of the community mental health program at the national, state, and local level. Many of the clergy selected for this responsibility were already giving leadership in mental health work through state mental health associations; a smaller number were selected because of their special training and experience in mental health ministries. However, the majority of those involved were ministers, priests, or rabbis who were well known as community leaders, usually in charge of a large influential congregation. Seldom were minority groups represented, and usually the clergy selected were not totally informed concerning current developments in the areas of pastoral care, counseling, or religion and mental health. As the centers themselves have come into being, fewer clergymen have been involved. The majority of the centers are related to existing institutions which already have a board of directors, some of which, of course, have clergymen on the board. Newly constituted centers, organizing a new board, usually include a local clergyman on the board of directors. Again, however, he is usually selected on the basis of community leadership, rather than expertise in matters of mental health, or how representative he is of the community being served.

A small percentage of the functioning comprehensive com-

[1] Berkley C. Hathorne, unpublished manuscript, "The Role of Churches and Clergy in Relation to Comprehensive Community Mental Health Centers," 1968. The centers selected for study either had existing programs relating to local churches and clergy or had clergymen functioning on the staff. Personal visits and interviews were undertaken at twelve centers while written reports and oral presentations at professional conferences gave sufficient information to include six additional programs.

munity mental health centers are sponsored by church-related institutions. In these cases, clergymen are often involved in the administration of the center. For example, the Mennonite Church has established several community mental health centers, and several are adjunctive services of institutions of the Roman Catholic Church. In both cases, professional church workers are largely responsible for the administration. Of course, in all such cases, the centers serve *all* people within the catchment area without regard to creed, and the professional and supporting staff of the center is representative of all faith groups.

2. The staff members of most community mental health centers view the local parish clergyman as an ancillary mental health worker. It is well established that many people go to their minister, priest, or rabbi with their personal and emotional concerns; therefore, the mental health professionals seek to relate to the clergyman as a "mental health gatekeeper" in order to reach people in need of mental health services. To accomplish this, about one-fourth of the centers have assigned a nonordained staff person to foster relationships with the clergy and the churches. In some cases the person is a psychiatrist (as is the case at the Temple University Mental Health Center in Philadelphia) or a psychologist, but most frequently he is a social worker. One of the major purposes of such a staff member is to relate to the local clergy in order to develop a referral net which makes it possible to reach the people the center is organized to serve.

Dr. Robert H. Felix has termed the parish clergyman "the first line of defense in mental health," and stated that he represents an untapped resource for the early detection, referral, and treatment of persons and families in community mental health. As the effort is made to push mental health back into the neighborhood and the family, the role of the clergyman takes on new importance. He is one of the few professional persons who relates to the individual in the context of his family and community. The staff members of the centers generally recognize the potential of the local clergy and the churches as community resources but express bewilderment as to how to relate to the various clergy and local congregations in a manner that will be mutually helpful.

This frustration is illustrated, for example, by the inability to understand the small number of referrals by clergymen to the mental health centers (approximately 3 percent), whereas the expectation is that local clergy should be a primary source of referrals. The major reasons for this discrepancy is the fact that the local clergyman feels that (a) there is no one on the staff of the mental health center to whom he can personally relate, and (b) when he refers a parishioner he feels that his concerns are not adequately represented by anyone on the staff of the center, and (c) he feels that his role and relationship with the parishioner or the family is not recognized or utilized as an important part of the experience of therapy either during the treatment time or in the after-care period.

The idea of the clergyman as a "gatekeeper" is, in some ways, not a very flattering concept. Though not intended, it is quite demeaning, for a gatekeeper is, first, one who is outside, and, second, one who screens who goes in and who comes out, and nothing more. Most clergymen want to be seen not simply as gatekeepers, but rather as partners in mental health development and treatment. They want to be more than part of a referral process for the center. Such clergy would suggest that they might be used not simply as gatekeeprs, but in programs of primary prevention, in some types of treatment, and in supportive after-care. For example, such things as life adjustment counseling; community social action; marriage and family life education and counseling; social, religious, and therapeutic group experiences; and the after-care of patients by means of a supporting, redemptive fellowship contribute to positive mental health. The clergyman performs a historic and meaningful caring and curative role. His primary orientation is working with people through all the experiences of life. He often sees a spiritual dimension bound up in numerous cases of emotional problems, although it is recognized that "only about ten percent of the problems brought to ministers . . . pertain to religious questions. Marriage and family problems are the most frequent of the problems encountered; psychological stress problems are second in frequency; youth-behavior problems, third; alcoholism, fourth; and problems of aging, fifth." [2]

The local clergyman should be involved in mental health in a positive way. He represents a potential for being the first line of *offense* in mental health. The resources of religion and the religious community have not been utilized in an attempt to foster good mental health. The positive aspects of religion have been generally overlooked, the usual approach of mental health workers being that when some people get emotionally sick they often use religion as one of their many defenses. A shift in focus and due regard for the positive utilization of religious sentiment in mental hygiene can be beneficial and will further the goals of the community mental health program. A partnership between the community mental health center and the local clergy should include consultative services with the clergy to assist them with their own pastoral care and counseling ministry with their parishioners; education and training opportunities in mental health, including evaluative and referral procedures in relation to the local mental health center; and the development and supervision of an after-care ministry with patients originally referred to the center by the local minister, priest, or rabbi. Dr. Gordon Allport states for the clergy what many of them feel. "Instead of two major disciplines demanding teamwork in the interest of mental health, there are clearly three: Religion, psychiatry, and the social sciences. Their interrelations are only now being understood." [3] Partnership, not an ancillary relationship, is what is suggested.

3. In some situations clergymen have been engaged as part-time or occasional consultants in relation to community mental health centers. This has not been a typical or common pattern, but it has much to recommend it. Before attempting to relate to the churches and clergy, or to develop a clergy staff position,

[2] Research project by Eugene F. Nameche, under the Harvard University Project on Religion and Mental Health, reported in *The Ministry and Mental Health,* Hans Hofmann, ed. (New York: Association Press, 1960), p. 225.

[3] Gordon W. Allport, *The Person in Psychology* (Boston: Beacon Press, 1968), p. 148.

a few hours of consultation with an objective but highly competent clergy-consultant should be considered. Such a consultation may simply confirm the program that has already been planned, but in other cases, it could lead to a critical examination, revision, and improvement of the proposal.

At least two states have appointed full-time clergy-consultants on the staff of the state department of community mental health. The pioneer, South Carolina, has provided the consultant to work with local communities and religious organizations in the planning, implementation, and evaluation of programs and projects involving the local center and the clergy and churches. A few individual centers have engaged the services of nationally known experts in religion and mental health, such as a theological professor of related subjects, or officers from national organizations such as the Academy of Religion and Mental Health, the American Association of Pastoral Counelors and the Association for Clinical Pastoral Education. The Department of Ministry of the National Council of Churches is now able to recommend to centers the names of such consultants. In most cases, there will be such an expert within a few hundred miles of the center. In addition, the National Council of Churches can provide direct consultation with national, state, and local church and mental health organizations concerning the involvement of churches and clergy in community mental health centers.

There are no known examples of non-staff clergy-consultants being engaged by a center on a permanent basis. Centers desiring some type of ongoing relationship with a clergyman normally provide for a part-time or a full-time staff position. But it is conceivable that a clergy-consultant might be retained, for example, to attend a weekly clinical staff conference, or to conduct occasional seminars or worshops for the clergy. In a rural setting, where clinically trained clergy are not generally available, such an arrangement has much to commend it.

4. Of the approximately 25 percent of centers that have clergy on the staff, about two-thirds of these are part-time. However, if we add to the one-third full-time the number of centers that have the equivalent of a full-time staff clergyman (having

divided the position into two or more part-time positions), we reverse these ratios. In other words, two-thirds of the centers with clergy staff members have either full-time or the equivalent of full-time staff clergymen. *Nationally, this means that one center in every six has provided for a full-time clergy staff position.*

Most centers with part-time, rather than full-time clergy staff, have purposely selected this arrangement. In many cases, they have employed two half-time clergymen, usually one Protestant and one Roman Catholic.

This arrangement appears to be working well in such widely separated centers as Lowell, Massachusetts, and Grand Forks, North Dakota. In the first instance the two clergymen have local church responsibilities half-time, and in the latter situation, both are half-time chaplains at local hospitals. Centers that have been organized as a new thrust of existing institutions often share part of the time of the full-time chaplain of the parent hospital. Although these part-time programs were functioning well in most cases, it appeared that there was not as much happening or as many new and imaginative developments taking place as in centers with full-time clergy staff members. Generally speaking, two half-time clergy do not equal a full-time staff clergyman, assuming that they are comparable as far as training and ability is concerned. A director may feel he is getting more for his money this way, and he may in terms of hours of actual work. Also, the fact that he can have two major faith groups represented may appeal to him, although in this age of ecumenism this generally is not necessary. However, if only one clergyman is employed he must be able to relate to *all* the local clergy on an ecumenical interfaith basis. In actual practice, however, the two tend to duplicate each other's work. They apparently see their task as serving the patients and relating to the clergy of their own faith group, and they lack the total involvement in the work of the center that is needed to be creative. Further, the part-time clergy tend to see their role in traditional, institutional chaplaincy terms and usually do not have the time to get very deeply involved outside the center.

In other words, they are largely center and staff-oriented, rather than church, clergy, and community-oriented.

In a few centers financial considerations dictated a part-time rather than a full-time clergyman on the staff. Where this is the case, would it not be advantageous to explore possibilities of the churches helping with the support of the program? At least one center has a clergy staff person who is supported, in part, by the local Council of Churches. A few of the part-time clergy staff members were engaged to do a particular job—for example, to do marriage and family counseling. Such a specialized role greatly limits the possibility of developing a comprehensive pastoral services and consultation program at that center.

5. The clergymen serving full-time on the staff on community mental health centers are generally well trained for their work, with a few exceptions, having had a minimum of a full year of special clinical and advanced academic preparation beyond graduate theological school. There is no uniformity of title or functional responsibilities. For example, typical titles are: pastoral services consultant, director of pastoral services, community chaplain, coordinator of pastoral consultation, and mental health specialist in religion.

The role of the clergyman on the staff of the center has not been clearly defined. This is seen in the confusion concerning the function of the pastoral specialist, both on the part of the administration and staff of the center, and on the part of the staff clergyman himself. None of the centers studied was utilizing what might be termed a comprehensive, functional approach.[4] The role is still to be defined and developed, but at this stage it is desirable to keep things flexible rather than prematurely structuring a role model. What can be observed is that the following functions are being performed (this is a composite of what now exists, although no one center is providing all functions): (a) *Pastoral services*—in the traditional sense of pastoral care and counseling, religious services, and

[4] Berkley C. Hathorne, "Critical Issues in Developing a Pastoral Services Program in the Community Mental Health Center," *Pastoral Psychology,* May, 1969.

religious education. (b) *Consultation*—to both the center staff and to the clergy and churches in the community. (c) *Administration and community organization*—to develop both the pastoral consultation department and the program of the center. (d) *Education and Training*—in such areas as continuing education for local clergy, in-service staff training, clinical pastoral education by qualified supervisors, and educating of clergy and laymen in programs of positive mental health. (e) *Therapy*—to provide a religiously oriented therapist on the staff of the center when he is qualified by professional preparation. (f) *Research*—to evaluate and improve knowledge of the relation of religion and mental health.

The above functions demonstrate the diversity of roles being undertaken by clergymen on the staff of community mental health centers. For example, at one center, the staff clergyman organized the local clergy and churches in support of a county tax measure that gives permanent support to the mental health program; at another center, the clergy staff member is involved in regular, weekly consultation with local clergymen concerning their own pastoral care and counseling ministry with their parishioners; at another center an extensive training program for clergy has been developed; and at another, a program of therapeutic social action involving local clergy is planned.

Although there is no consensus of what the functions of a clergy staff person should be, what seems to be common is this: The clergyman on the staff of a community mental health center has a dual identity. He is both a clergyman and a mental health specialist, and he should have no confusion about maintaining this dual role. *He should attempt to relate to the staff of the center as a mental health specialist in religion and to relate to the local clergy and community churches as a religious specialist in mental health.* As long as he maintains this dual identity without negating either dimension he will be able to relate the two facets of his professional role. If the center is seeking to facilitate an interdisciplinary team approach to community mental health in which each professional functions within his own specialty and cooperatively relates to the other team members, then the contribution of the dual-trained, clergy-mental health specialist, should be welcomed.

The above is a report of the use of clergymen in eighteen comprehensive community mental health centers and some of the efforts of the centers and the clergy to relate to each other. An effective, relational bridge can best be provided by a clinically trained clergyman on the staff of the center charged with the responsibility of fostering this relationship. Such a program will be of mutual benefit to the local churches and the mental health center in a local community, for it will mobilize the clergy and the resources of the religious community in a creative partnership of community service and improved health.

For additional reading

Pastoral Psychology. Special issue on "Community Mental Health and the Pastor," May, 1969.

Pattison, E. Mansell, "Functions of the Clergy in Community Mental Health Centers," *Pastoral Psychology,* May, 1965, pp. 21-26.

21.
THE COMMUNITY PASTOR AND THE COMPREHENSIVE MENTAL HEALTH CENTER*

Frank S. Moyer, B.D., M.A.
Chaplain-Supervisor, Rockford Memorial Hospital Rockford, Illinois

The development of meaningful relationships between community clergy and mental health professionals is one of several important challenges confronting comprehensive community mental health centers. While the external forms and structures of these relationships vary with each center, all are being made possible by the "new" concepts which centers are

---

* The material in this chapter is based on the author's experience as a clergy staff member of the Community Services division, Nebraska Psychiatric Institute.

bringing to bear upon "old" problems.[1] Among these new concepts are at least three which have opened new potentialities for the community clergyman.

First, the center views the prevention of illness and the fostering of health as of equal importance to treatment. While treatment facilities are important aspects of the organization, centers are more than super-clinics offering multiple services to the mentally ill and retarded. Staff time and professional resources are legitimately involved in assisting other community agents and agencies engaged in various public service programs.

Second, the concept of comprehensiveness has meant an interdisciplinary approach at *all* levels and in *all* facets of the center's program. There has been a recognition of the resources and assets of many other helping professions and occupations, and a utilization of them in the operation of the center.

Third, the centers have recognized the importance of "community" to the success or failure of their development. They have reaffirmed that mental health and/or illness do not exist in a vacuum nor can they be treated in one. Center personnel are actively working in reciprocal relations with other community helpers so that the full potential of both may be realized. Since community clergy and religious groups are also interested in mental health there are many areas for fruitful collaboration. These areas are more easily discerned when seen in relation to the five "essential services" each center must offer.

Consultation and Education. The service of consultation and education is of key importance in the growth of comprehensive community mental health centers. It represents the means whereby the mental health resources of the center becomes linked to the mental health resources of the community in a complementary manner. Prior to the development of this service many community clergy performed their mental health functions in isolation from other concerned professionals. Referrals were usually *from* clergyman *to* mental health facility, and the information accompanying such referrals tended to flow one way,

[1] Lucy D. Ozarin, M.D., "The Community Mental Health Center: Concept and Commitment," *Mental Hygiene,* January, 1968, pp. 76-80.

as if the clergymen had little to offer of practical value to the mental health professional. As centers develop this service they are realizing it must be a two-way process. Because of their involvement in so many community functions, community clergymen possess a wealth of knowledge about the attitudes, feelings, and organizational structures present in the community. Some centers now include clergymen on their ongoing planning committee, which has as its task the responsibility to keep the center relevant.

Consultation also increases the potential value of the clergyman as a care-giver because it affords him professional support. In one center the consultative service was offered each time a clergyman referred a parishioner for treatment. The result was that 80 percent of these parishioners never became clients of the center but were maintained by their pastors.[2]

Community clergy are also being contacted when their parishioners are accepted as clients. Usually these men are able to provide additional information about the client's *lieben sitz* so that the treatment plan may be better geared to meet his needs.

Educational programs for clergy in areas of mental health and illness have involved thousands over the years. Some community pastors have spent whole summers in clinical pastoral education programs as well as graduate degree programs in counseling, sociology, and similar fields. Centers have learned that greater effectiveness is achieved when they involve these local clergy in planning local programs. Also, they are learning that many of these clergy may be of value to the center's own in-service education programs. Few mental health professionals have had courses in theology, comparative religions, or ethics; nor have they had the opportunities to learn the intricacies of their communities as have clergymen.

If consultation and education are done on a reciprocal basis, then a mutuality of concern and involvement is established. In this way the uniqueness of both is respected, and neither runs the risk of being patronized or misused.

[2] Frank S. Moyer, "Shepherd Without a Fold," *The Clergy and Psychiatry,* Community Services Division, Nebraska Psychiatric Institute, 1967.

Emergency Service. The emergency service facility or unit should enjoy a close working relationship with community clergy. The pastors have long had to deal with emergency situations alone and usually welcome any who offer to relieve their burden.

Emotional crises among members of the community tend to be both fragmented and complicated. They seldom follow classic symtomatology or respond to traditional treatment. Yet many mental health personnel and clergymen are still being trained to deal with these crises by classical methods. Let me illustrate: One area pastor recently reported the situation of a female parishioner who became progressively more disturbed. She had been hospitalized previously for an emotional illness and the family had been told to get early treatment should it recur. Being new in the area, the husband called the community pastor for suggestions and referral resources.

This pastor visited the woman, recognized an acute fulminating psychosis, and called the local center. A "team" was convened to meet with the patient, her family, and her pastor to evaluate what treatment was indicated. This team, which did not have present either a psychiatrist or psychologist, decided she should remain at home under medication and with supportive help from the pastor. The decision was made in the erroneous belief that home would be similar to the institution, which had nurses to supply medication and other staff members to help set limits. This woman became worse, refused to take her medicine, and had the whole neighborhood upset because she went from door to door. Whom did they call? The community pastor, wondering what he was going to do about it! When he called the center they still wanted to continue the first plan. Fortunately, this trained community pastor demanded that more competent help be obtained or he would camp on the doorstep with the patient.

The reasons for describing this are to emphasize the many roles the community pastor plays and why collaborative efforts must be made. Collaboration in planning treatment programs helps to avoid many emergency situations and minimize the trauma in others.

We now recognize that immediate assistance for persons facing emotional emergencies increases the prospects for a healthy resolution. Communities have a long tradition of calling clergymen in such crises. Many centers have recognized this and have joined with clergymen in the development of creative programs for emergency needs. These include twenty-four hour telephone service, suicide prevention programs, after-care programs for released patients, and home visit programs.

Partial Hospitalization. The opportunities for more direct service for the community pastor in the partial hospitalization program are manifold. If this service is to be either a bridge between inpatient service and his home or to provide treatment without leaving the community, the pastor should be invited to participate *if* the patient indicates a church preference.

In addition to visitation, many community pastors could conduct groups at the day care center or other partial hospitalization programs. These should be not group therapy sessions, but discussions. As a pastoral function he could introduce studies of the religions, or of current situation ethics. If it is conducted *as* pastoral act, it will be therapeutic.

Some church groups may also wish to operate a partial hospitalization unit as part of the center. This might be a day care facility such as The Threshold in Champaign, Illinois.

Outpatient. The outpatient service is one area where cooperative efforts often have failed. Once the patient is referred for treatment, many pastors are not sure what role to assume. Yet, in between visits the patient-parishioner sees the pastor at worship services and in other areas of activity. Often the pastor is called for little emergencies which need band-aids. Some pastors are told to maintain only a superficially supportive role during this period. This, allegedly, protects the patient from having two therapists who may work at cross-purposes. Others, the majority, are given the green light to continue in whatever manner desired. Here the implication is that the minister's therapy will be of no consequence either for good or for bad.

Neither approach is valid. The hands-off system fails to grasp the pastor's role as a pastor. It does not understand that to offer *only* superficial support means he is not able to involve the patient in the strengths of faith—for faith, to be strong, cannot be superficial. The opposite, or "it's-of-no-account," approach represents a conceit inappropriate to any community mental health professional.

Any community pastor who makes a referral to the out-patient service should be given the opportunity to join the therapeutic effort in whatever role is effective. Some few may be therapists using the center staff as consultants. Most will be able to contribute to the social history. *All* will continue to serve the patient as pastor, and that role may be used therapeutically.

Inpatient. The opportunities for the pastor to be involved should continue once the patient enters the residential treatment program. This is assumed because of the short-term nature of treatment and the community involvement concept. Pastors should do the major share of pastoral visitation, conducting worship, and similar functions. Chaplains, if employed, should be used only where their expertise is required. This helps to insure continuity with the community for the patient.

The future of comprehensive centers depends on our ability to grasp the significance of the community and its resources. Centers must learn how to accept the various care-givers in their natural roles. They must let them treat those they traditionally have been treating—rather than becoming screening agents for them. If they attempt the latter, the manpower needs will never be satisfied.

The community pastor works most effectively when there is open communication, encouragement, mutual trust, respect, and cooperation. If centers will approach the community pastor in *that* atmosphere, a relationship may develop in which both grow toward more effective service in their community.

Local ministerial associations should initiate communications with their centers offering to serve as professional resource personnel. They should assume responsibility for planning and implementing their own educational programs and use the center's resources where applicable. The most urgent need, how-ever, is to develop creative means of working together with centers in the areas of prevention. This working together in preventive education not only lightens the burdens for both groups, it establishes that close sense of community that is a powerful resource for health and against illness.

For additional reading

Consultation and Education, Public Health Service Publication No. 1478, N.I.M.H., Washington, D.C.

Moyer, Frank S., "Consultation as a Pastoral Function," *Occasional Paper,* #681, Lutheran Social Welfare Services of Illinois, January 1968.

Schofield, William, "In Sickness and in Health," *Community Mental Health Journal,* Fall 1966.

22.
THE STAFF CLERGYMAN'S ROLE IN A COMPREHENSIVE MENTAL HEALTH SERVICE

Lloyd E. Beebe, B.D., S.T.M.
Director, Department of Pastoral Services, Henne-pin County General Hospital and Mental Health Center, Minneapolis, Minnesota; Adjunct Professor of Pastoral Care, United Theological Seminary, Minneapolis

People using the services of a comprehensive community mental health center may and often do express their concerns in religious terms. There is a religious dimension to coping with the conflicts of emotional disturbances. For many it is important that they try to find some meaning or purpose in their struggles or to evaluate, perhaps for the first time, the implications of their faith in their crisis situation. It is at this point that the role of the clergyman can be most clearly seen. The clergyman on the staff of a mental health center must not only define his role in relationship to the person having difficulty, but he must also define his role in relationship to the center's staff members, who are also interested in helping this person overcome his difficulties.

The clergyman represents a point of view about the nature and destiny of man. He represents a professional group which is very close to the problems of people, and he also represents a community of people who are interested in the implications of their religious point of view for their daily lives. From this perspective it is imperative that ways be found to share insights on the understanding of man and of helping him to deal with his life, by a cooperative effort between clergymen and mental health professionals. This chapter will present some ways in which the role of the staff clergyman is being worked out at the Hennepin County Comprehensive Community Mental Health Center with the hope that it will offer some suggestions for developing clergy roles in other centers.

While the *clergy staff person* represents the religious dimension of living, he is not a pastor in the usual sense of the word. He does not function or have the same responsibilities as the pastor of a church or temple. He does not have a group of people who have called him to be their religious leader, nor does he have an identifiable flock for whom he is the shepherd. He must necessarily be concerned about the care of all the people regardless of their particular religious affiliation or non-affiliation. He is not interested in converting a person to one particular religious viewpoint. The staff clergyman may perform some traditional pastoral functions (e.g., administering the sacraments), but his main function is to help the patient to identify and use his own religious resources. This role may be difficult for both the staff and the patients to adjust to, because both tend to view the staff clergyman in terms of their experience with his traditional role in the community.

Some community clergy may have their difficulties, also, in understanding his role. It is very important that they understand and support the role of the staff clergyman and not view him with suspicion when his religious views are different from their own or when his goals in working with people seem to be different from their goals. The staff clergyman's job is to help them be more effective in their work with people.

In reality, then, the most helpful stance from which the work of the staff clergyman can be viewed is that of the "religious expert"—to use a helpful phrase introduced by E. Mansell Pattison. This describes his field of interest, his scope of activities, and his relationship to the other staff people and to the patients. By training and experience, the staff clergyman's expertise is in the area of religious knowledge and understanding. While he certainly possesses communicating skills and a basic understanding of social and psychological functioning, he is not a social worker, psychologist, or psychiatrist. His primary job is to bring what resources he can to the total understanding of the person who is experiencing emotional difficulty. This may mean helping a patient deal with the implications of his faith for his problems, raising the issue with the staff regarding the effect of the religious dimension of a patient's life on his present behavior, or in helping the staff to deal with their own religious feelings or understanding.

From this basic role of the staff clergyman as the religious expert, a number of different functions can develop, because his area of competence is recognized and he is not seen as competing with other staff members. Working along with the other staff members, he is free to help develop and implement the philosophy and program of the mental health center. His functions may include:

A. Counseling. How much and what kind of counseling the clergyman does will probably depend to some extent upon his own interest and training. It will also, however, depend upon how he wants the staff to understand his functioning, and this is the crux of the matter. Relationships to individuals are still important even though ideas are changing as to how much time is spent in therapy with individuals, with groups, and with the total social milieu. While I have tried to describe rather carefully the pastoral role of a clergyman working in a mental health center as contrasted to that of a parish pastor, I think it is important that some aspects of his pastoral role be maintained diligently—his openness to all levels of pastoral conversation, his availability at all times, his understanding of and empathy with the deep yearnings of people for a sense of purpose and meaning in life, forgiveness, moral clarity, the sense of the holy, and the importance of confidentiality and continuity in relationships. The staff clergyman is uniquely equipped to function in these areas with people, and he must learn how to use this uniqueness as creatively as he can. Gordon Allport believes that the reaching out for life may be as important as the reaching back into life. He makes the remarkable statement "that what a man believes to a large extent determines his mental and physical health. . . . Religious belief simply because it deals with fundamentals often turns out to be the most important of all."

All this is to say that if the staff clergyman has confidence in the uniqueness of his role and the other staff members begin to understand this role, his counseling will take on a kind of helpfulness that can be very supportive to the staff. When a patient's problems are related to religious or moral conflict, the staff clergyman would be the most likely person for the patient to see because of his authority in this area and because he may be perceived by the patient to be the most appropriate person to deal with these problems.

B. Consultation. Consultation may become a primary function of the entire mental health center staff as more is learned about how to use the resources of community caretakers more effectively. Of the five services considered essential by the Department of Health, Education and Welfare to the functioning of a comprehensive community mental health center, the statement on consultation alone discusses the role of a clergyman. This may be an indication of the importance placed upon consultation, but it may also indicate uncertainty about other possible roles for the clergyman, an uncertainty which needs to be worked out.

Within the center itself, the clergyman may be the consultant for the staff in regard to religious conflicts being expressed by their patients. Questions of a particular religious culture or theological position may be important to understand. Religion can often be a powerful motivating force in people's lives or instrumental in forming attitudes toward illness, conflict, or suffering. The staff clergyman can be helpful in dealing with these areas and in helping the patient to mobilize his religious resources constructively. During staff conferences the influence of religious values is sometimes overlooked. The clergyman can remind the staff of this factor and help to interpret it. The Chief of our Clinical Psychology Department, Dr. Thomas Kiresuk, has noted that once he lets his patients know that he is interested in their religious concerns, his patients frequently will be more expressive in using religious language than when using the language they think he wants to hear. The clergyman can help the staff feel more comfortable in discussing religious material and understanding this religious language.

Community clergy have important information about and relationships to patients being seen by the mental health center. The staff clergyman can keep the center alert to this resource and encourage the involvement of the pastor in the treatment program. Sometimes this clergyman is the key person in the follow-up work with the patient upon discharge from the center. The staff clergyman can help to interpret the work of the center to the patient's pastor so that he will understand more clearly the problems of his parishioner and be able to help more effectively.

Many community clergyman feel inadequate when it comes to helping with the emotional problems of some of their parishioners. A vast resource is available here through developing more effective consultative techniques for use with these clergymen. It is the job of the staff elergyman to help to develop these techniques.

C. Education. There is a good deal of information available in a mental health center that is important for the clergyman to know. It is the responsibility of the staff clergyman to help to make this information available to the community clergymen. He may do this through conducting continuing educational programs, clinical pastoral education, or by leading seminars on special topics such as suicide, grief, or alcoholism. At Hennepin County, for example, seminary students in our clinical pastoral education program have learned a good deal about suicidal people and crisis intervention by participating in our Suicide Prevention Service under the supervision of that staff clergyman. They have learned about the community resources which are available for help and how to use these resources.

It is important that the staff clergyman assume the responsibility for the education of his own professional group. The staff clergyman understands the work of the clergy and can relate his information directly to their concerns. This does not mean, of course, that other staff peple are not involved, but it does mean that the staff clergyman can help to integrate and focus the information so that the community clergyman is functioning as an effective clergyman and not as a clergyman with some mental health information.

D. Special Activities. The staff clergyman may be involved in any number of therapeutic activities. At Hennepin County he has worked closely with the problem drinker and Alcoholics Anonymous. Patients are often referred to him for evaluation and recommendations to the proper resource for help. He has also helped to mobilize the community toward a cooperative approach to the treatment of the problem drinker.

At the Day Treatment Center one group was formed specifically to deal with religious problems. Many patients were expressing religious conflicts, and it was felt that a group should be formed to deal with these conflicts. The group is called the "Philosophy of Living Group," and all patients currently at the Day Center are required to come, as they are to all other group meetings.

The intent of the group is to deal with the cognitive level of helping the patient to integrate what he is learning about himself with his religious values. Some of the group meetings will center around one of the Ten Commandments. We have often explored the meaning of "honor your father and your mother" with patients who are having difficulty with their parents. What does the teaching "to turn the other cheek" mean to the patient who is always being manipulated by others? Sometimes the question is raised about the expressing of anger, because some patients have been taught that this is a sin. Sometimes religion can be used by the patients as an effective defense against facing their problems realistically, but at other times it can be a powerful motivating and integrating force. It is important to understand the difference and help the patient to use his religious resources meaningfully.

I have been trying to describe the role of a clergyman in a comprehensive community mental health service. There is much more to be learned. I have felt the struggle and the uncertainty as I have attempted to organize my thoughts. Mental illness and the facing of emotional crises are much too prevalent for any one group to work with alone. By working together some progress can be made. I believe that the climate is right for a cooperative effort toward our common goals of a more meaningful and productive life for as many people as possible in our society. The staff clergyman can help to make the resources of the religious community available to the mental health center, and he can help the community clergyman use the mental health center more effectively.

Specifically, both the clergy and the mental health professional can work together at the local, state, and federal levels of government in emphasizing the importance of including a well trained clergyman on the staff of each community mental health center.

For additional reading

Allport, Gordon W. *The Individual and his Religion.* New York: Macmillan, 1950.

Caplan, Gerald. *Principles of Preventive Psychiatry.* New York: Basic Books, 1964.

Clebsch, W. A., and Jaekle, C. R. *Pastoral Care in Historical Perspective.* New York: Harper Torchbook, 1967.

Consultation and Education. Public Health Service, N.I.M.H., Bethesda, Maryland.

McCann, Richard V. *The Churches and Mental Health.* New York: Basic Books, 1962.

Pastoral Services Through the Comprehensive Community Mental Health

Center Program. South Carolina Department of Mental Health, Columbia, S.C., 1968.

Pattison, E. Mansell. "Functions of the Clergy in Community Mental Health Centers," *Pastoral Psychology,* May, 1965, pp. 21-26.

Pruyser, Paul W. "Religion and Psychiatry: A Polygon of Relationships," *Journal of the American Medical Society,* Jan., 1966, pp. 135-40.

23.
QUALIFICATIONS OF CLERGY STAFF MEMBERS IN COMMUNITY MENTAL HEALTH PROGRAMS

J. Obert Kempson, B.D., M.A.
Pastoral Consultant, Department of Mental Health, State of South Carolina, Columbia, South Carolina

While the qualifications of a clergyman functioning in a mental health setting may be determined by his peers, professionals from various disciplines, or other persons, his ability to rise to these standards will be influenced to a considerable degree by his motivation. His own involvement in bringing the qualifications into living reality will determine the quality of pastoral care he can offer.

Motivation is a form of anxiety or discontent, as Thomas W. Klink pointed out.[1] It is a disquiet about things, which, when constructively organized, can prompt a person to enter and pursue the process of learning, and also to actualize his insights. It is recognized that heightened anxiety can be destructive, while mobilized discontent can be creative.

Some motivational questions need to be raised as one looks at an individual's qualifications, as these relate to effective pastoral care in a mental health setting:

How does a pastor feel about himself, what he knows, what he wants to learn, and what he does?

Is he motivated to accept emerging pastoral care responsibilities?

[1] Thomas W. Klink, "Relating Objectives and Educational Procedures toward Motivation," an address. Seminar on Adult Learning, Syracuse University, 1967.

Do his pastoral care opportunities generate new insight, new ideas, new attitudes, and new skills?

Are his concepts and work patterns flexible and adaptable?

Does his pastoral care concept recognize individual potential and enhance it?

What is the pastor's tolerance for change?

Can he grow in the awareness of his limitations and accept them?

Will his pastoral care perception transcend the immediate situation?

Can the growing edges of the pastor be sustained and nourished?

Does he have flexibility which enables him to change goals?

Why does he want to be a pastor in a mental health setting?

These questions might suggest that if a clergyman renders service in a community mental health setting it can be an awesome responsibility. However, if the pastor clarifies his motivation it can lead to a more effective expression of his person and therefore to more meaningful pastoral care.

Motivation then is a factor for change. It prompts one to be involved in the learning process. At least three levels of change goals are recognized by Edgar W. Mills for effective learning:

1. *Change in personal characteristics of the minister:* e.g., changed attitudes, greater self-acceptance, growth in insight or knowledge, etc.

2. *Change in ministerial role performance:* better preaching, counseling, other skills; improved relations with laymen, more effective use of community resources, etc.

3. *Change in the social systems of which the minister is a part:* e.g., better leader development in the church, closer bonds among clergy in the presbytery, better mental health in the community.[2]

[2] Edgar W. Mills, "Relating Objectives and Evaluation," address, Seminar on Adult Learning, Syracuse University, 1967.

Such change goals fused into the pastor's motivation can renew and strengthen his ministry. New vistas will be opened. He will become involved not merely in meeting the qualifications of his position but in enhancing his own growth and pastoral care effectiveness.

Certain minimal qualifications may need to be set as a base pointing the way for the minister's growth and pastoral care. For the past quarter of a century efforts have been made to establish and clarify such qualifications. The matter has remained in a fluid state, though there has been general agreement in certain areas. This apparently indicates a healthy policy that qualifications are never permanent but are continually in the process of becoming.

The Association of Mental Health Chaplains[3] has approved standards and a certification process for clergy functioning in mental health facilities. The Association for Clinical Pastoral Education[4] is a certifying and accrediting organization concerned with the proficiency of its training supervisors and with the quality of clinical pastoral education conducted in mental health and other settings. Program objectives and procedures have been established to determine effectiveness. Also, standards for accrediting training centers have been provided. The American Association of Pastoral Counselors[5] is similarly concerned with the training and certification of clergy as pastoral counselors, and accredits counseling centers.

These three organizations in a cooperative effort prepared and endorsed "Recommended Guidelines for Clergy Serving in Comprehensive Community Mental Health Centers." These qualifications were formulated in consultation with the College of Chaplains, Division of the American Protestant Hospital Association; the Department of Ministry, the National Council of Churches of Christ in the U.S.A.; the Jewish Chaplains' Asso-

[3] "Newsletter," Association of Mental Health Chaplains, 400 Forest Ave., Buffalo, N.Y., Vol. 21, No. 1, p. 8.
[4] "Standards," Association for Clinical Pastoral Education, Suite 450, 475 Riverside Dr., New York, N.Y. 10027. pp. 2, 5.
[5] "Manual and Directory," The American Association of Pastoral Counselors, Inc., 201 East 19th Street, New York, N.Y. 10003. pp. 8-10, 22-27.

ciation; and the Division of Chaplaincy Services, United States Catholic Conference.

Recommended Guidelines for Clergy Serving in Comprehensive Community Mental Health Centers

The Mental Health Act of 1963 launched a bold new approach toward meeting the community mental health needs of our citizens.

This approach envisioned a comprehensive and inter-disciplinary involvement of the total community, including the religious sector, to enable people to meet the complexities and stresses of modern life.

In order that the resources of the religious communities be fully utilized, many comprehensive community mental health centers have already employed clergymen on their staffs. In addition, numerous requests have been received for guidelines for the employment of qualified clergymen.

The following guidelines are offered to be of assistance to comprehensive community mental health centers, and to clergymen seeking such positions.

I. *Suggested Titles:* Coordinator, Pastoral Services; Pastoral Consultant; Director, Pastoral Services; or Mental Health Specialist in Religion.

II. *Functions:*

  A. Pastoral Services: to facilitate traditional pastoral functions in the context of the relationship of religion to illness and health; these may include but not be limited to religious services, pastoral counseling and religious education.

  B. Consultation: to provide a religious specialist on the staff of the mental health center to serve as a consultant to the center staff, local clergy and the religious communities.

  C. Education: to foster education in the following areas:

185

1. The larger community—community groups, workshops, seminars and sensitivity groups in order to help persons understand principles of coping with life and thus enable them to better maintain health and prevent illness.
2. The clergy—to utilize sound pastoral care and mental health principles in developing and enhancing their pastoral care and counseling skills.
3. The clergy—to provide clinical pastoral education for them.
4. The center staff—to share in the "in-service training" for members of the center staff.

D. Administration: to participate in the administrative concerns of the center as they relate to the religious community and to implement and coordinate the pastoral services and the consultation and education programs.

III. *Skills:*

A. Ability to maintain his pastoral identity in a setting where there is a great deal of overlapping of roles and functions.
B. Ability to work with troubled individuals and families as an integral part of the staff in terms of diagnosis, conferences, referral and support.
C. Ability to listen, understand and formulate the real needs of persons and structures from all areas of the community.
D. Ability to work creatively with persons of diverse religious backgrounds and religious structures.
E. Ability to work with persons and organizations of different social backgrounds.
F. Ability to participate in and help mobilize community structures for essential social change through a working knowledge of the nature of communities and community structures.
G. Ability to establish and maintain intrastaff relationships and to relate to the various mental health disciplines, i.e.

to understand their professional languages and to speak effectively to their concerns. Central to this task will be the interpretation to the professional staff of the various religious resources, concerns and phenomena.

H. Ability to establish and maintain training programs for clergy and laymen in religion and mental health including, where appropriate, accredited clinical pastoral education programs through the possession of educational and supervisory skills.

I. Ability to plan, project, actualize and evaluate relevant programs.

J. Ability to discover and utilize the best religious resources of the community in the overall care of persons and families who come to the center.

IV. *Qualifications:*

A. College

B. Seminary

C. Ordination or denominational equivalent

D. Continuing ecclesiastical endorsement

E. Three years of full-time pastoral experience

F. One year (4 units) of clinical pastoral education in community mental health, or its equivalent as defined by national certifying clergy organizations professionally concerned with community mental health and community action.

G. Where possible, special teaching credentials, supervisory certification or advanced degrees.

V. *Implementation:*

It is recommended that representatives of the inter-faith community be consulted in the planning of the service and in the selection of the clergyman.

The primary criterion for a staff person would be his credibility in the community in which he works. This means, not only his identification and common background with the people in the community, but the skill to render technical assistance and his basic commitment to "mobilize community structures for essential social change."

In addition to the mental health specialist clergy described in the guidelines, centers should also consider community clergy without specialist training who do have background and skills to work with the community. There is a critical need for community persons without professional accreditation to be members of the staff of community mental health centers because minority groups have been inadequately represented in the mental health professions.

These job specifications for the pastor in a community health ministry emphasize three primary categories for role development. The staff clergyman would provide consultation for the community minister about pastoral care of persons in crisis, about his counseling process, and his pastoral care of families. The community minister would be recognized as a consultant on occasion to the staff clergyman and to the center's other professionals.

A second function would be educational. The staff clergyman would offer such opportunities in pastoral care, counseling, and related areas. In some centers he would plan and supervise approved clinical pastoral education. Other similar efforts would involve him in educational efforts with churches, schools, and agencies on the community level.

A third major function focuses on pastoral services for which he would be responsible and/or in which he would participate. Such pastoral services would include worship services, pastoral visiting, intensive counseling, occasional contacts with relatives, and appropriate group work. He would encourage the community minister to provide pastoral services following the parishioner through his crisis experience whether in the home, mental health center, or institution.

In three-fourths of the plans for mental health reported from all the states in a national mental health planning effort a few years ago, the clergyman was listed as a significant helping person. It was noted that little was offered about using of his resources, little was mentioned about the educational opportunities necessary to release his potential, and few qualifications were suggested for a staff clergyman in mental health facilities. The trained, qualified clergyman can contribute out of his uniqueness in the healing community where, with other trained professionals, he assumes a vital role in crisis care to the troubled person.

24.
COMMUNITY CONTROL OF COMMUNITY MENTAL HEALTH

George Clements, M.A., S.T.L.
Pastor, Holy Angels Catholic Church, Chicago, Illinois

The second Vatican Council has, to put it mildly, generated a revolution within the structure of the Catholic Church. However, no phase of that revolution has been more dramatic than the emphasis that has been placed on the role of the parish council in parochial control. It is interesting to note that the loudest hue and cry for effective parish councils have been sounded by the parishioners of inner-city churches, and more specifically by those in black communities. There are many parishes whose parish councils are floundering because the pastor is giving only lip service to the need for relinquishing much of the administrative control of the parish to the parish council. Today, across the nation we are witnessing the formation of groups that are identifying themselves increasingly with community control. In every major city of our country there has been created, or there is in the process of formation, Afro-American patrolmen's leagues, black lawyers' guilds, black teachers' associations, Afro-American firemen's leagues, black doctors' societies, black ministers' caucuses. I'm not sure—there may even be a black psychiatrists' group.

All these organizations are addressing themselves to the pressing need for community control, particularly among powerless people—Mexican Americans, Blacks, Puerto Ricans, Appalachian whites. The current hassle I am involved in with my own church authorities in the Archdiocese of Chicago is largely a result of the phenomenon of community control. Sparked by St. Dorothy's Parish Council, the black community demanded from church authorities the same recognition for our black community that is accorded, with no question, to the Polish, the Lithuanian, the Irish, and the German communities.

And now we are face to face with the potential of community control of community mental health. It would devoutly be hoped that professionals in the fields of mental health and religion could learn from the mistakes that have been and are being made by other groups supposedly working for the betterment of our communities. Certainly the most obvious pitfall is that of reluctance to, and even hostility toward, listening to the vital components of the community, the residents themselves. Social agencies, welfare groups, religious organizations, commercial concerns, all have marched into our communities—especially our inner-city communities—with preconceived notions of superimposing their structures upon a community, of afflicting a community with a structure that was developed in some think tank without consulting any significant forces within the community itself. We would do well to ask ourselves how sincere are we in our concern for community mental health if we are unconcerned about consulting the community.

Another area of legitimate concern is that of actual involvement of the community in the *administration* of community mental health. It is so easy and so ridiculous for us to slap on a white collar or a white smock and assume that we have the trust of a community. Certainly in the black community nothing could be further from the truth. I am a black man, and yet I am automatically suspect in the black community. Recently a meeting was held in the basement of St. Dorothy's Church in Chicago. Participating in the meeting were members of a young radical, activist, militaristic black group. After several hours of wrangling back and forth—rapping is the term we use—

one of the young black men jumped up and yelled at me, "Father, what you are saying makes a lot of sense—what does not make sense is that white man's collar you have around your neck!" That incident has really made me stop and re-evaluate my position in the community. If that happens to me, a black man striving to be relevant, a fortiori it will happen to Caucasians—excuse the expression—in spades. It is the height of arrogance as well as folly for professionals in the field of mental health to ignore actual involvement of the community in the administration of community mental health.

Also we must be cognizant of the necessity that the community have reasonable *control over allocation of funds* for community mental health. For example, I really wonder how often community residents have been consulted prior to construction of community health facilities in a given neighborhood. Here are people who have lived in the community a great deal of their lives, and yet they are not considered qualified to state their opinions as to how much money should be spent in construction of a community mental health facility and where it should go. We who are professionals are very squeamish in furnishing information to the community about our financial affairs. Very few members of the community know how much money the pastor *really* receives or what the salary is of the professionals staffing our community mental health centers. We tend to shy away from letting the community get too close a look at us for fear that they might begin getting truly serious about this business of community control. Certainly if members of the community held the pursestrings and signed the salary checks of those working in the field of mental health in the community, we then would have a much more enlightened and much less patronizing behavior pattern displayed toward the community.

Furthermore, our efforts should be directed toward community *participation in and sharing in the responsibility* for mental health, not because of any ulterior motives but because this is just and right. There are skills that we professionals possess that are of immense value to our communities, especially our inner-city communities, but we are grossly derelict in responding professionally to our communities if we do not take the lead in giving them an effective measure of control in their own destiny. It is my hope and prayer that we will take heed and listen to our communities before we plunge headlong into them— or we might find that we have plunged into a nest of hornets and will not have any communities left to diagnose. Finally, we ask ourselves possibly the most poignant question of all— Should not the community have a say-so in *the definition of terms of mental health?* Just exactly what is mental health in the context of the community? Is one, for example, mentally healthy if he leaves his family because that family will fare better on ADC than they ever could on the meager unemployment compensation checks he receives?

If there is to be little or no effective community control of community mental health centers, then let us abandon the farce of the appellative designation, "community." Let us call them what they really substantially are—federal, state, or county mental health centers. After all, these are the names given them by the people who actually *live* in the community.

PART IV
training and orga‑ nizing for mental health action

The effectiveness of churches and temples as participants in the mental health revolution will rise or fall depending on the *quality of training* which their clergymen receive in this field, and on their success in training their laymen, in turn. For this reason, nothing is of greater significance in the church-mental health partnership than increasing the number and quality of training programs for clergymen. Clergy training in mental health insights and skills should be widely available on three levels—*seminary, graduate training* (for specialists) and *continuing education* (for parish clergymen). To increase such training opportunities is a responsibility shared by seminaries, denominational leaders, clinical training and pastoral counseling centers, and by mental health leaders.

The first paper in this section (Stewart) deals with the crucial matters of the role and training of laymen in community mental health and pastoral care. Three of the chapters (Howe, Johnson, and Westberg) in this section discuss various aspects of continuing education. Two chapters deal with seminary (Oates) and graduate (Wise) training, respectively. Another chapter (Anderson) discusses several issues in training clergymen in mental health skills, particularly the need for including an emphasis on the physical aspects of mental disturbances.

This section also focuses on several topics which have to do with organizing and implementing church-related mental health programs. One issue is that of interprofessional cooperation, a difficult but essential aspect of church–mental health partnerships. Understanding and being able to draw on governmental resources in mental health is another practical dimension of effective church involvement. These topics are illuminated by two of the papers (Pattison and Ozarin) in this section. Another chapter (Vayhinger) deals with the need for research in the area of the churches and mental health. The last chapter (Joensuu) opens a window on the world, as it discusses the family life education challenge around the globe as this relates to mental health. A brief concluding chapter by the editor makes some suggestions for moving into action.

25.
TRAINING CHURCH LAYMEN AS COMMUNITY MENTAL HEALTH WORKERS

Charles W. Stewart, B.D., Ph.D.
Professor of Pastoral Theology and Supervised Ministries, Wesley Theological Seminary, Washington, D. C.

While I was serving as a parish pastor and mental hospital chaplain, a man came to the church office to see me. He told me of hearing voices and having some feelings of their religious significance. He was on the verge of a psychotic breakdown. That man went to a mental hospital, and I visited him there. He was deathly afraid of being there, for one of his brothers had died in such a place. He was afraid of what his neighbors would think of him when he returned and he was insecure about his wife and family when he was there. Six months later he returned to the community, and he came to church for the first time in years. How he was welcomed made a big difference in how he felt about himself. Fortunately there were some people who worked at that hospital and had prepared the others for his return. He was invited to the men's club work night at the church. His family was made to feel welcome after their long absence from the church. That laymen's group did many of the right things to help the returnee from the hospital. But they could just as easily have turned a cold shoulder to this man and his family. If he encounters such rejection a mental patient may not make it outside the protecting walls of the hospital.

TRAINING CHURCH LAYMEN

Health, Salvation, and Community: The church is one of the institutions in our society manned mainly by volunteers, volunteers who have a working faith about health and community. They should be on the forefront of community mental health efforts. Unfortunately, parochial endeavors, lack of concern, and insufficient training have militated against laymen getting involved in this most important work. What I propose to do here is to set down the working faith which the Christian tradition has about health and community; to list some of the pioneer areas where church-related community mental health programs are operating; to outline one such project in order to illustrate the design and plan of such training; and finally to suggest action steps and resources for those interested in going further.

"The specific character of the Christian understanding of healing and health arises from its place in the whole Christian belief about God's plan of salvation for mankind," wrote the draftsmen of the Tübingen conference on the Healing Church. Health is not the absence of illness or the simple adjustment of the individual to the pressures of his society; rather, health is the presence of new being—physical, emotional, and spiritual—which enables the individual to become the self his creator intended him to be. This is revealed in the "mature manhood" of Jesus Christ (his life, death, and resurrection), since he overcame the confusion, anxiety, and division within man's nature. The Kingdom of God is the community of those whose wholeness is found in Jesus Christ and who as his servants seek to bind up the brokenness of mankind.

Health is found in community, therefore, and the Christian community is the central agent of pastoral care with a specific healing ministry. It has certain characteristics which fit it for its role in Christian healing, says John Wilkinson. First of all, the congregation is the *fellowship of love* where mutual concern and interest are expressions of love of the brethren. This can lead to great incentive to recovery from sickness. Second, the congregation is a *fellowship of worship*. Here is an emphasis on the reality and presence of God, the physician of his people. Through the ministry of word and sacrament we are brought

195

into healing contact with God. Third, it is a *fellowship of reconciliation*. Those who find forgiveness are restored to that fellowship with God and find the aim and completion of all Christian healing. Such reconciliation has a tremendous therapeutic force. Finally, the congregation is a *fellowship of prayer*. Prayer is one of the most potent forces in the world. Even if the congregation can do nothing else for the sick, it can pray for them.

Opportunities for Laymen: With such a dynamic understanding of health, salvation, and community, what may laymen do to move into the forefront of the community mental health revolution? The professionalizing of the pastoral counselor may cause some ministers to feel that this is their business and laymen had best remain behind to do the housework of running the parish. Laymen may have been intimidated by psychiatrists and mental health workers because of their frightening jargon, diagnostic skill, and therapeutic know-how. However, the new insights into mental illness, as recorded in this volume, show us that patients get well in the community and among the people they know best—their family, co-workers, and friends. And it is this lay group which must provide the climate and the therapeutic milieu in which the restorative, and more importantly the preventative, work goes on. The community mental health effort is, therefore, a lay effort and requires committed Christian laymen at the center of the movement.

There are certain lay-led efforts which point the direction the church must take. Of longest duration are the groups organized in England for at least two decades—the Marriage Guidance Council[1] and the Samaritans. The Samaritans, organized by Chad Varah in 1953, began as a suicide prevention center in the heart of London at St. Stephen's church. It has spread to over ninety centers in England, Europe, Africa, and Asia. The organization begins with a telephone answering center manned for twenty-four hours a day, seven days a week. There are laymen who undergo certain basic training in guidance of potentially suicidal persons. Their work is one of befriending,

[1] For a description of the Marriage Guidance Council, see Chapter 35.

196

walking with this person in his time of deepest depression and severest temptation to take his life. The group has a quasi-military setup with rigorous discipline and ultimate authority resting in the hands of the leaders.

In the United States the lay-led groups have the nature of therapeutic groups. Alcoholics Anonymous with its parallel organizations for mates and children, Alanon and Alateen; Parents Without Partners, the group for single parents; Recovery, the group for returned mental patients; and similar organizations which offer support and help for those who have specific problems are widely known. The impact of the human relations laboratory movement upon the church in encouraging the development of sharing group efforts to make the church more supportive has succeeded to a degree. People going through marital trouble, sickness, or vocational readjustment have found healing in discovery or personal enrichment groups. (First Community Church, Columbus, Ohio, and Church of the Saviour, Washington, D.C., are examples.) *What has been lacking has been some concerted effort to train laymen in the pastoral care of souls, to enlist them in the mental health movement on a par with the clergy, and to use the church effectively as an arm of the community.*

A Layman's Training Program: Let me report on a layman's training program which was instigated and researched by John W. Ackerman at St. Elizabeth's Hospital in Washington, D.C., in the fall of 1965. I believe it points out some of the values and the pitfalls of such training. St. Elizabeth's conducts a course in the fall and spring in clinical experience for students at Wesley Seminary and for parish pastors. Ackerman and his supervisors, Dr. Bruder and Dr. Ward, decided that laymen should not have a different course but should be included in the same course and given all the training pastors receive. Sixteen laymen were recruited from the metropolitan Washington area, and divided for research purposes into two groups. Group I was given the lectures only; Group II was given the lectures and asked to make ward visits, submit written reports, and undergo group supervision. The research design—to determine what changes took place as a result of clinical experience—included pre-testing and post-testing and evaluation by trainer and supervisor at the end of the course.

The four orienting lectures were with psychiatrists who interviewed patients with certain mental illnesses, and also with chaplains who spoke on a panel about their knowledge of the patient and their particular ministry with them. Ward visits were made from the second session on, and the laymen were expected to write up their impressions of the visits and submit them for comments by the supervisor weekly. These written reports were discussed in group supervisory sessions at the end of the day, along with other impressions and feelings which emerged within the group. These groups remained on the supervisory level, however, and did not have a therapeutic goal. Ackerman reported that the laymen changed their perspective on mental illness through the twelve-week course. "The general dynamics of the group seemed to be movement from an original period where patients were seen as being 'just like us' through a period where the students identified with the helplessness and despair of the patients, to a final period where they began to find for themselves some individual methods of relating to the patients."

One student's report of his change through the course is significant for our topic. He said, "The most significant information gleaned during the course has been the vital importance of the role of the church and religion in the community and the urgent need of the individual patient for spiritual food and better human relationships." Ackerman found his research results inconclusive, i.e., his pre-testing and post-testing did not turn up significant changes in the experimental group. His clinical hunches were, however, that the group which did the visiting did increase their skills in listening and their understanding of the mental patient. He writes that the laymen reported increased honesty with patients; increased ability to listen to the patients; increased ability to notice nonverbal behavior; lessening of the savior role; increased ability to help the patient face the facts as they are, and a lessening of the temptation to give false assurance; and finally, further realization that their being with another person was a tangible expression of God's concern.

The weakness of the course was its lack of follow-through to the churches and the communities of the laymen involved. By being hospital based, it did not begin with the local community and the Christian congregation and return there. It had the strength, however, of tapping highly qualified professionals for the training, and of training laymen alongside clergymen for the work of hospital visitation and mental health aid.

Action Steps: One needs to develop with the responsible church body (official board, commission on Christian education) a workable plan for the total congregation in its responsibility for community mental health. One might well begin with a study group. The "Local Church Mental Health Study-Action Project," using Howard Clinebell's *Mental Health Through Christian Community* and the Leader's Guide by Paul E. Johnson, is a resource for such groups. The pastor may not be the one to lead this activity, although if he has training he may be the leader. A psychiatrist or social worker in the congregation may find this his particular stewardship. From the course there may be a selection and commissioning of pastoral aides. These persons should consider their visitation in a hospital, prison, or mental hospital a part of their training and should gather in groups to report their work and to discuss not only their growth in understanding of persons in distress, but the Christian resources available to these persons.

Those who show proficiency in such visitation might be asked to continue their training with a second course, like the one described above, in which they visited those with particular problems: the potential suicide, the alcoholic, the couple with marriage problems, the youth who has trouble with his parents, the lonely, and the aging person. Effective befriending of persons of this sort requires supervision—and here the pastor or the committee chairman might draw on the professionals in his congregation who have supervisory skills to meet with the persons doing this more difficult work. The danger of going deeper into this kind of counseling work is that it arouses personal anxieties and the supervisor needs to be there to help. Referral of those who require professional help needs to be taught and the layman shown where the limits of his competence are.

Some laymen may do a job of befriending by taking certain people in trouble into their homes—the unwed mother, the youth who is away from home and in need of certain boundaries, the mental hospital returnee. The homes need to be selected carefully, and the persons doing this kind of work should be mature enough to take the ups and downs of the emotionally distressed. I know instances, however, where providing a Christian home to persons of this sort has made the difference between life and death.

Finally those laymen who are in positions of power may work with community groups and agencies to do something about the disease-producing forces: poor housing, insufficient education, unemployment, lack of child care. It is one thing to work on the city council to shut down bars or to prosecute drug addicts or prostitutes; it is another to remove pathological conditions in which mental breakdown occurs. The church may have left an inner-city area, and so need to return to a storefront or support a Negro church in order to alleviate in a total push the kind of conditions which cause mental illness. Laymen who are concerned can do this. Such laymen are working at this in New York, Chicago, Los Angeles, and other large urban areas.

Laymen are not only capable of becoming mental health aides; they can serve as volunteers and do the housekeeping chores, so that their pastor might receive clinical training and become more professionally qualified. The challenge of our day, however, is for the *pastor to see his job as enabler and to begin to train laymen for the more challenging task of community mental health workers*. If the congregation sees its task as the pastoral care of its people, then health and wholeness can move out into the community, which will then become a leaven for the whole loaf.

26.
CONTINUING EDUCATION TO RELEASE THE MENTAL HEALTH CAPABILITIES OF CLERGYMEN

Reuel L. Howe, B.D., S.T.D.

Director, Institute for Advanced Pastoral Studies, Bloomfield Hills, Michigan

A Christian minister is an agent in individual and corporate human relations. What he is as a person is indispensable to the performance of his functions. He needs emotional and intellectual maturity to maintain and sustain himself in the work of the ministry.

1. *The Situation.* What is the prevailing state of the clergy's capabilities in mental health? Some diagnosis should precede prescription. Generalizations are not safe, but the data permit some guarded generalization.

The Institute for Advanced Pastoral Studies (hereafter in this article referred to as IAPS) during eleven years has had a teaching relationship with three thousand clergy from more than forty churches and from many parts of the world. Prior to attendance, each one completed and sent back a questionnaire designed to describe the respondent's needs and areas of interest. The study of these returns correlated with the insights about these same people during the conferences. They revealed the following:

A. They lack clarity about their own self-identity. Many clergy feel conflict between being a man and being a minister which confuses and blocks their personal and professional relationship.

B. They do not know how to deal with the hostility in themselves and others.

C. They feel a sense of loneliness, based on their fear of others and their fear of themselves, that makes them cautious and servants of the *status quo.*

D. A sense of personal inadequacy is strong among ministers. They lack discipline in the organization of their activities

201

and study. Impatience and psychological impotence often make a joint appearance.

E. The conditions just described naturally cause conflict between ministerial duties and family relations.

F. A sense of apprehension about a rapidly changing society with little knowledge and understanding of the dynamics, structures, and uses of power in that society produce in clergy a crippling anxiety.

G. Many of them have not been helped to make a working correlation between "secular" and "theological" insights. The knowledge and technological explosion makes demands on their theological understanding and interpretations that they cannot meet.

H. They lack training in educational and program design whereby the church might address community issues and problems creatively.

These conditions drain the mental health of ministers and decrease their usefulness as leaders, teachers, and priests. Systems of defense develop that stand between them and the people they serve. They become closed to feedback from those whom they serve. In turn, this tends to make them more and more monological, increases their defensiveness, and causes a growing narrowness and rigidity of outlook and operation.

The situation of thousands of ministers at this time is desperate. For many other thousands the situation is not so bad. Their problem is that they are not beginning to live up to their potential. They could have more peak experiences of living and ministry.

Here is the challenge to continuing theological education. Before discussing what continuing education can do to release the mental health potentialities of ministers, we should look at the process of theological education. For generations theological education was associated with the three years of seminary training or its equivalent. We now have a much more comprehensive view of the process.

2. *Three Phases of Theological Education of Ministers That Could Promote Their Mental Capabilities.* We now see that theo-

logical education is a lifelong process that has several phases: indigenous theological learning; seminary or pre-ordination education; and post-ordination education. The whole process should be called continuing theological education in which there are three phases or punctuating periods.

The first phase, indigenous theological learning, occurs mostly before seminary training begins. It is acquired from parents, church, and church school, from friends and companions, formal education and reading. It is made up of precepts, insights, superstitions, hunches, fears, and defensiveness. These learnings are indelible, hard to change, and tend to stay with a person all his life. An insightful wag referred to it as "bastard" theology because it was of doubtful parentage. Its most outstanding characteristics are moralism and the dependence of the individual on self-justification. The effect of indigenous theological learning on mental health is dubious at best.

The second phase of continuing theological education is experienced usually in the disciplines of a seminary career. The emphasis in this phase is apt to be more on the subject matter of theological learning. It customarily ignores the powerful indigenous learnings the students bring to their formal studies, so that they are neither assimilated nor corrected. The students themselves may be ignored in favor of the academic objectives of the institution which is not concerned with them as whole persons. Students, consequently, learn to cerebrate the gospel and derogate themselves because their senses and feelings and convictions are not educated with their intellects. Many products of formal theological education learn to substitute being a *minister* for *being,* with the result that they are frustrated in all their professional functions and in their personal relations.

Acknowledging without reservation that substantive learning is an indispensable part of theological education, I must nevertheless raise the question here about the effect of theological education on the total person. The educational methods and processes too frequently do not relate the subject to the meanings the students bring to their learning experience.

The third phase of continuing theological education is post-ordination training. Some continuing education enterprises tend to preserve the academic stereotype of seminary training. Other programs are working experimentally with the training of ministers. Need for experimentation is great, because the needs of ministers are distressing and acute.

One thing has become clear. Post-ordination education needs to be partly based on previous learning, and especially on ministers' experience in their work in order that they may discover how to learn from their experience, and to correlate these learnings with their more academically centered knowledge.

Several miscellaneous things need to be said at this point about post-ordination education. It must always expect to be re-education, no matter how adequate the preceding phases of education are. It must be designed to promote in students capacities for new experience and for learning from new experience. And it should promote in students capacities for realized wholeness and achievement of mental health for themselves and others in the context of a society that is complex, changing, and always in conflict.

3. *Contributions of Post-ordination Continuing Education to the Mental Health Capacities of Clergy.* An evaluation of conditions found in the lives of clergy, discussed earlier in this chapter, produces three areas for focus that are relevant for the promotion of mental health.

First, post-ordination education should focus on the *relational* needs of ministers, because their capacities for personal and interpersonal relationships are indispensable to their ministry.

Second, post-ordination training should focus on the *technical* needs of ministers. Clergy are often frustrated because they do not know how to communicate, to educate, and to design resources to meet situations.

A third area of focus for continuing education is therefore *topical* or subject matter competence. This area of need has much to do with the mental health of clergy. They need to know what they are supposed to know, and have the ability to correlate their theological training with other fields of human knowledge. The technological explosion has compounded this problem.

These three focuses in post-ordination continuing education—the relational, the technical, the topical—would meet the needs of clergy in contemporary society and contribute therefore to their mental health potential.

I will now discuss each focus and try to illustrate it from the program and experiences of IAPS.

Relational. As stated earlier, the questionnaire returns and the responses of the conferees indicate clearly strong relational needs—personal, interpersonal, individual, and societal—involving all the structures of life and society. A part of our program, therefore, is focused on the area of the relational.

When a group convenes on the first evening, it is made up of twenty men and a few women who are usually strangers to each other; who come from different parts of the country or even of the world; who represent the doctrine and tradition of from eight to twelve different churches, Protestant and Catholic; and who are engaged in different kinds of ministries—education, local church, seminary leaders, denominational executives, and others. These individuals bring all kinds of personal identity and meaning to this gathering. There is present fear for oneself and fear of others, fear of change and the pain of it. Each person comes with his own defensive system which he uses at home and which he will employ in the conference as it gets underway. What happens among the members of the group is significant. It will reveal the patterns of behavior at home and will therefore constitute a part of the curriculum for the conference. They also bring to the conference their respective personal educational and experiential resources which they may contribute or be helped to contribute to the process and purpose of the enterprise. Actually, many of them are unaware of their resources and often do not know how to use them. A part of the leader's responsibility is to help the conferees become aware of their resources and learn how to use them so that they may return to their home situations with a sense of liberation and new powers that are essential to mental health.

The conferees come also out of an education that seeks to educate their minds but generally ignores their feelings, with the result that they tend to intellectualize problems that have an emotional base. They need, literally, to come to their senses and then to achieve an integration and correlation of feeling and intellect, a condition essential to mental health.

Recognizing all these conditionings and needs, the progam begins with introductions that are focused on *being* rather than doing. Instead of introducing themselves in terms of the position they hold and some suggestion of their achievements, they begin by saying, "I am who I am and my name is _____. And I feel _____." (They state whatever they feel—fear, friendliness, excitement, eagerness, etc.) After each statement a leader of the conference steps forward and says to the person: "Your name is _____, and what you are gives meaning to your name. We all here hope to find and know the meaning that you are." Each person in his turn also repeats the names of all the people who preceded him, and at the end of the introductions they all know one another by name.

The next stage of introduction and organization is also focused on the personal and interpersonal, and the establishment of relationships. Each of the twenty-four persons chooses another person to be his partner. After reflection on why they chose each other, each pair sets up a criterion by which they will choose two other couples. After negotiation, four groups are formed of six people each who now have become fairly well acquainted. Each group reflects on the process of its formation and on what the members have learned about one another. These four groups now choose another group of six and, after negotiations, two groups of twelve people each are formed. Thus, the two working seminars are created through a process of communication, verbal and nonverbal, that promotes personal introduction and knowledge and understanding of one another. During the first evening, in the space of two or three hours, the group learns one another's names and acquires a considerable understanding of the persons behind the names.

Much of the anxiety with which many of them began the evening has gone. Everyone has participated and discovered that he is essential to the conference and to the formation of the community. Here is an experience that begins the transformations necessary to the achievement of mental health.

The next day after a period of Bible study and an introductory session on the nature of communication, its difficulties, and its principles of breakthrough, the two groups of twelve meet in what is called a *decathon*—a continuous seminar from 2:00 P.M. to midnight. The purpose of the decathon is to provide the conferees with a structure for encounter with one another at some depth. Here a concerted effort is made to deal helpfully with the relational concerns of the conferees. This is done early in the conference in order that they may experience release from relational preoccupations and be freed to address themselves to the task concerns of the ministry. Obviously, dealing with the relational cannot be completed even during the decathon, so that there is reconsideration of it whenever the issues of the conference require it. This capacity to deal with the meanings and feelings of what happens while men work and play together is a major contribution to mental health. During the decathon the members of the group become more honest with one another and develop a sense of trust.

Technical. A second area of focus for continuing education that is relevant for the achievement of mental health is technical concern that is necessary to the work of the ministry. Many ministers are frustrated, hostile, resentful, depressed, and uncreative because they do not know how to be ministers.

Basic to this technological incompetence is a naïveté about communication itself. Understanding and use of the dynamics of communication underlies all the functions of ministry and is indispensable to the initiation and maintenance of human relations. Training in the use of the principle of dialogue in all methods of communication is provided. Application of these principles is then made to preaching, teaching, pastoral care, worship, and the relation between church and world. The switch that most conferees are able to make from monologue to dialogue in the course of the conference they will be able to apply in their practice at home, because the change becomes a part of them. The personal characteristics of the change are to be seen in a sense of liberation from old rigidities and fears, a lessening of defensiveness, more openness and courage for human relationship, and experimentation in meeting old and new situations.

They are also given opportunity to participate in the design of their own conference and to understand the rationale and techniques of the parts of the conference they did not help to design. In this way an attempt is made to give them training in designing educational resources to meet different situations, an ability that many ministers lack with frustrating and depressing effects. The mental health of ministers requires that they have a sense of potentiality for coping creatively with the problems and tasks in their areas of responsibility.

Still another need of clergy in the area of technological training is to know how to engage people who are different and whose responsibilities and disciplines are strange. The "self-image" of many clergy is so shaky that they are not secure and free enough to risk engagement with others. Furthermore, their "closeted" training for the ministry estranged them from the world outside the church. Many of them admit that they do not know how to talk to men except about church and religion, and even then only on the level of program and operation and not on the level of the meaning of the gospel for their lives. They do not know how to talk with them about their interests, purposes, and meanings. They further admit that they are timid in relation to men who wield power and influence. They confess that they feel more at home with women and children and the sick and dependent. Something needs to be done to strengthen them for dialogue with the strong, responsible, and creative people of the world.

One answer is to provide clergymen with opportunities for engagement with industrialists, labor representatives, scientists, artists, and educators. The Institute, for example, arranges such engagements for its conferees. They visit men in their offices or places of work for the purpose of asking them questions about what they are doing, what it means to them, what part, if any, their faith plays in their work. The method of the engagement makes possible full participation of everyone in the discussion. After an introductory session, the conferees meet individually or in pairs with members of the organization for a discussion of the problems and issues of the enterprise under study. As a result of these field trips the conferees discover how possible and how significant it is for them to meet with men on their own ground. Many of them return home with a new sense of self and of resourcefulness in relation to the men in their communities and churches. They also acquire a way of becoming acquainted with the life of the world outside the church as institution, with its structure, its dynamics, and its ways of operation. Such knowledge and understanding frees the clergy for a more versatile way of life and mission which, of course, has tremendous positive implications for their mental health.

Still another example of continuing education's possible contribution to the technological training of clergy is in the area of preaching with emphasis of the importance of the preacher securing feedback from the congregation to his preaching. Too much of the clergy's communication is one-way, that is, from clergy to people and very little from people to clergy. In fact, many clergy are closed to feedback. They are afraid of criticism and respond defensively to it, a symptom of immaturity and deficient mental health. Such one-way communication does not renew the clergy, and without renewal they become more rigid and ingrown.

The design of this part of the conference demonstrates how they might provide feedback in their home situation and make their communication more dialogical. Where these suggestions are carried out, clergymen develop a new sense of excitement for preaching, they experience a new sense of relationship with their congregation in which they, perhaps for the first time, become recipients of grace. The healthy effect of these changes on their attitudes toward themselves and others and toward their responsibilities is noticed by both them and their congregations.

Topical. A third area of focus for continuing education that is relevant for the achievement of mental health is concerned with the meaning of religion in relation to the meanings of the other disciplines of human thought. Such interrelation or correlation is appropriate for religion since it is concerned with ultimate meaning of everything, but for some reason a vast number of clergy are lacking in the capacities for correlation. They have their religious understanding locked up in a closet with the result that they hold and teach it rigidly and defensively. It is something they have to protect and defend. It is as if their God cannot stand alone, but must be held up by them. This means that instead of being the beneficiaries of their faith they are its saviors. What a drain this is on their well-being! Many secessions from the ministry are due to a sense of the irrelevance and ineffectiveness of religion as a viable position for creative approaches to contemporary problems.

Instead of being worried about religion and its fate in life, clergymen may be helped to a more adventuresome and dynamic understanding of religion's role in contemporary life through participation in the dialogue between questions and answers, between the meanings of the contemporary and those of tradition, and between religion and the other fields of thought. Continuing education can help clergy learn how to stand alongside men, rather than over against them, with the treasure that men have already forged out of past dialogues. The sharing and shaping of the question is as important a task for religion as is giving an "answer." Actually, the insight of religion gives a capacity for hearing men's questions more profoundly. This kind of sense of adventure and possibility is available to clergy; and continuing theological education that is responsive to both contemporary challenge and the treasures of tradition may guide them to a new life and work. A sense of relevance is indispensable for mental health and can transform the clergy's helplessness, resentfulness, and defensiveness into resourcefulness, love, and courage, for both their living and their task.

27. DEVELOPING THE CLERGYMAN'S POTENTIAL FOR MENTAL HEALTH: INDIANA PROGRAMS

Paul E. Johnson, B.D., Ph.D.

Professor Emeritus, Boston University School of Theology, Boston, Massachusetts

Mental health is everybody's business, for we live in one world open to one another. We breathe one atmosphere in which we live or die. And we are moved by the emotional waves and attitudes arising in our community life. Slowly and painfully we begin to comprehend how deeply we are involved in one another's lives. Actually no one can live unto himself or hide within himself alone, no matter what defenses he may hold up to ward off the social currents sweeping through our common humanity. If one is mentally ill the whole family is caught up in the distress. And if one person is sound he may radiate healthy attitudes to bless many people around him.

Whatever we think of him as an individual person, the clergyman is an influential member of his community, who affects the emotional health of many persons for good or ill. A nationwide survey revealed that 42 percent of persons seeking help with emotional problems had gone first to a clergyman.[1] When they were asked why they chose a clergyman, they said, "Because we know and trust him." Consequently there is reason to be concerned for the mental health of the clergy, and how they prepare to assist persons who are wrestling, as we all do at one time or another, with emotional problems.

In Indiana several programs converge on developing the mental health potential of the clergy. In 1957 The Methodist Church, led by Bishop Richard C. Raines, began a program of pastoral care and counseling with a twofold aim: (1) to provide counseling for ministers and laymen, and (2) to offer pastors continuing education in this crucial ministry of pastoral care. District committees were formed, training institutes were held for one or more days in every part of the state, and pastoral counseling centers were opened in eight cities by the collaboration

[1] See Chapter 16 for a fuller description of this survey.

211

of pastors with several other professions. The Rev. James E. Doty, Ph.D., was the first area director, and after nine years he was succeeded by the Rev. Foster J. Williams, Ph.D., who is expanding these opportunities for pastors.

In 1965, the Indianapolis Pastoral Counseling Center[2] at North United Methodist Church received from the Lilly Endowment a three-year grant, which has been renewed for two additional years, to expand the education of pastors in pastoral care and counseling. This center has become ecumenical in the religious affiliations of the advisory board, the funding of the program, the pastors who serve as counselors, and the persons who come for counseling or education.

In 1967, 13 pastoral counselors provided 1,237 hours of counseling for 309 persons from 23 denominations. The counselors received individual supervision each week from 5 pastoral supervisors and group supervision in case conferences each week in which 18 consultants participated from medicine, psychiatry, psychology, and social work. Problems presented for counseling were: marital, 129; personality, 55; depression, 34; family, 34; divorce, 15; vocation, 14; sex, 8; religious, 5; juvenile, 4; psychotic, 4; finance, 3; premarital, 2; addiction, 1; and personal identity, 1.

This Pastoral Counseling Center was accredited by the American Association of Pastoral Counselors, provisionally in 1966 and fully in 1967. The first Director, from 1958, was the Rev. Kenneth E. Reed, Ph.D., who is Director of Chaplaincy Services at the Methodist Hopital of Indiana. There he has developed a program of clinical pastoral education, accredited by the American Association of Clinical Pastoral Education.

Clinical pastoral education brings another significant dimension to the education of the pastor for his vocation, and particularly his ministry to the emotional needs of persons. Here the pastor learns to be sensitive to feelings, to be aware of signals of stress, and to understand the motivations and responses of human behavior. With intensive supervision from a chaplain

[2] The more than 200 pastoral counseling centers in the U.S.A. and Canada represent significant new mental health treatment and training resources.

supervisor he learns how a pastor may minister to persons in face-to-face relationships with the potential resources of religious faith, hope, and love.

In 1959, the Rev. John A. Whitesel, Ph.D., came to the Indiana University Medical Center to develop a service to patients, faculty, and students; and to initiate a program of clinical pastoral education which is accredited by the Association of Clinical Pastoral Education. Other such programs have since been accredited at the Central State Hospital, the Larue Carter Memorial Hospital of Indianapolis, and the United States Penitentiary, Terre Haute, Indiana.

From 1964 to 1967, a demonstration program of continuing education for clergy and related professions in mental health was directed by John Whitesel, sponsored by the National Institute of Mental Health and the Lilly Endowment. During this program seventy-eight clergymen from twenty-three urban and rural communities participated with eighteen persons from medicine, psychiatry, social work, and psychology as co-participants. Six cities were selected as training centers where community resources were explored, clergymen and other professionals were enrolled, a local committee was formed to plan the curriculum, and a group organized for continuing education.

These persons came in the fall to the Indiana University Medical Center for one week of full-time clinical pastoral experience, and again in the spring. Before coming to the Medical Center and the related hospitals, each group had three orientation seminars with the supervisory staff. Following the first and second clinical weeks a series of tri-weekly seminars of four hours each was held in each city where case studies, theoretical concepts, and community resources were studied. The inductive method of learning was followed with a concluding evaluation to assess each person's experience and growth.

Specific objectives were (1) to promote acceptance of the mentally ill in the community, (2) to develop inquiring and collaborative attitudes in the clergy, (3) to sustain a working relationship among clergy and the mental health professions, (4) to apply the theory and methods of clinical pastoral education to a community service program, and (5) to explore instruments for assessment and educational needs.

In 1958, the Rev. Lowell G. Colston, Ph.D., was called to be Professor of Pastoral Care at Christian Theological Seminary in Indianapolis where he has developed a graduate program. Through affiliations with the above centers of clinical pastoral education and the Indianapolis Pastoral Counseling Center, the opportunities for continuing education of pastors have been notably enriched. The new curriculum is emphasizing concurrent field engagement in the community where eventually the pastor will serve persons under the varied conditions of the secular society.

There is general recognition of the urgent need for continuing education of the pastor, if he is to keep abreast of the demands and expectations confronting him. The National Institute of Mental Health in 1968 awarded a five-year grant to Christian Theological Seminary for the continuing education of the clergy in reference to mental health needs and services. This grant acknowledges the potential resources of this community for designing a broadly based program of many dimensions for pastors in mental health.

To coordinate the expanding programs of continuing education for the pastor, the Indiana Pastoral Institute is being incorporated as an association of religious bodies and educational centers who desire to cooperate in stimulating and sharing potential resources for more effective education. Ministers, priests, and rabbis who receive the benefits of this continuing education will return to their communities to serve the emotional, social, and spiritual needs of their people with deepening understanding and responsiveness.

Forms of Continuing Education

The education of pastors is moving into action along these strategic lines representing opportunities to keep growing in the ability to serve human needs:

(1) Graduate studies in the various ministries of pastoral

care are being enriched in a cluster of theological seminaries[3] and universities, with academic credit leading to master's and doctor's degrees.

(2) Clinical pastoral education is available full-time for six or twelve weeks, or part-time four days a week, in accredited centers where pastors serve on a team with other professionals to meet the crucial needs of patients. Chaplain residencies are available for one or more years of full-time intensive training.

(3) Counselor education is offered pastors who may choose a parish setting, a seminary, or a hospital as the base for this supervised intensive learning in teamwork, referral, and consultation with other professions.

(4) Parish education is available in several formats, such as:

(a) One day a week for thirty weeks including didactic and practicum sessions with case conferences, interpersonal groups, and supervised practice.

(b) Training laboratories for ten or twelve days full-time in a parish which serves as the laboratory for supervised practice and evaluation.

(c) Parish residencies where the pastor in training serves as a member of the church staff, engaging in a variety of ministries coordinated with intensive study, supervision, case conferences, training in group dynamics, pastoral counseling, and evaluations of his growth.

(5) Inner-city urban ministry either as a one-year resident or one day a week for thirty weeks to mingle with the people wherever they are, to engage the power structure of the community, to explore the economic and political strategies of community planning, to discover the potentialities for a ministry to total needs of persons who are deprived or in stress.

(6) Interagency participation to serve persons in special need, and staff the agencies of the community which seek to cope with crisis and despair, education and vocation, neighborhood associations and community organization. These services in Indianapolis may include the Community Mental Health

---

[3] The Catholic Seminary Foundation will draw together a cluster of Catholic seminaries adjacent to Christian Theological Seminary.

Center, the family courts, the juvenile courts, the Suicide Prevention Center, child guidance centers, senior citizens programs, rehabilitative workshops such as the Goodwill Industries, schools for the blind or deaf, recreation and tutoring, housing and employment projects.

For additional reading

Accredited Training Centers and Member Seminaries 1968. Association for Clinical Pastoral Education, Room 450, 475 Riverside Drive, New York, N.Y. 10027.

The Journal of Pastoral Care, a quarterly publication. Association for Clinical Pastoral Education.

Manual and Directory 1966-1968. The American Association of Pastoral Counselors, Inc., 201 East 19th Street, New York, N.Y. 10003.

Ministry Studies, a quarterly publication. Ministry Studies Board, 1717 Massachusetts Avenue, N.W., Washington. D.C. 20236.

Pastoral Psychology, a monthly publication. 400 Community Drive, Manhasset, N.Y. 11030.

Theological Education, a quarterly publication. The American Association of Theological Schools, 534 Third National Building, Dayton, Ohio 45402. See esp. Vol. IV, Spring and Summer, 1968.

28.
PARISH CLERGYMEN AND MENTAL HEALTH: THE KOKOMO AND LaGRANGE PROJECTS

Granger E. Westberg, B.D.
Professor, Hamma School of Theology, Wittenberg University, Springfield, Ohio

Over a period of four years two groups of clergymen, in two separate cities, were given intensive, brief courses on how to deal with people under stress. The pattern for the approximately twenty clergy from Kokomo, Indiana, consisted of one intensive week at the University of Chicago, followed by six monthly meetings after which the men returned for a second intensive week of instruction at the University. This was to have been the end of the project, but the clergymen continued to meet on a monthly basis, often with key groups of doctors, lawyers, nurses, and others in the town of Kokomo.

The clergy of the second community, La Grange, Illinois, following their one-week intensive program at the University, agreed to meet once each week for case conferences based on their own parish problems. After three months they returned to the University for a second intensive week and then continued to meet in La Grange on a weekly basis at the community hospital with one or more doctors present. Usually, the case presented was the patient of one of the doctors in attendance.

Both the Kokomo and La Grange projects grew out of one of the University of Chicago's regular two-week seminars for parish pastors on the subject of pastoral counseling and the relation of ministers and doctors in their cooperative ministry to the sick. These seminars had been conducted each summer since 1945. Normally they drew clergymen from a variety of denominations who live in cities and towns in widely separate parts of the country.

At the conclusion of each seminar the students would attend an evaluation session where they were asked to comment on the course and offer ways to improve it. During the evaluation session in the summer of 1957, one of the students, a pastor from Kokomo, said, "This seminar has been tremendously helpful to me. I believe it will significantly change my perception of my responsibilities and opportunities of service to my people. But if I am to follow through on some of these necessary changes in myself, I will need the daily encouragement of fellow pastors who also feel as I do. As long as I have been surrounded by these men in the seminar, I have been doing quite well in my resolution to change. But when I get back to Kokomo, my enthusiasm will probably be dampened by the fact that I will have no one to talk to about these matters." He concluded by saying, "I wish that all you fellows were from Kokomo."

COMMUNITY MENTAL HEALTH

The pastor from Kokomo touched off an animated discussion. Every man present said approximately the same thing. Courses like this would have cumulative value if the students were all from the same community, for they could work together in implementing these newer concepts of clinical theology. During the next few months, we at the University did a good deal of thinking and planning of the possible development of such a project. With the help of the Lilly Endowment we finally decided to go to Kokomo and invite all full-time clergymen to attend such a seminar. We gave it the general title of "The Role of the Clergymen in Mental Health." Through the help of various groups in Kokomo, and particularly the *Kokomo Tribune,* we were able to explain the nature of the project to this community of some forty thousand people. There were approximately thirty-five full-time clergymen in Kokomo and surrounding Howard County. Of this number twenty-three responded to the invitation.

The Kokomo project was jointly sponsored by the Department of Religion and Health of the University of Chicago with the assistance of the Department of Psychiatry. Dr. Edgar Draper, a psychiatrist, gave full time to the project during each of the one-week sessions. The late Chaplain Carl E. Wenner, of the University of Chicago Clinics, and I acted as directors of the project.

It was not long after the arrival on our campus of the twenty-three Kokomo pastors that we were convinced of the value of inviting all the clergymen of a particular community to study the force of joint clergy action in the area of pastoral care and mental health. The Kokomo group consisted of a cross section of the major Protestant denominations as well as some less known denominations like Bible Baptist, Independent, and Mennonite. A Roman Catholic priest was in the group but there was no rabbi, for Kokomo had no resident rabbi at the time. We were fortunate that Dr. John Hoigt, a newly arrived psychiatrist in Kokomo, was able to participate in the entire project. He lived with the clergymen in the dormitory on the campus. This was his first experience in such a setting, and he said it afforded him an unusual opportunity to get to know the men informally.

By the end of about the third day, many of the clergymen began talking freely about their reactions to this experiment. Some of them admitted that they had not wanted to come to this seminar, but were practically forced to attend by members of their churches who, upon reading the newspaper articles, had insisted they take advantage of this unusual opportunity. These men had tried to beg off, pleading too much work, but their parishioners won out. They admitted that during the first day they had resisted becoming involved in the small group discussions of actual case situations. They said that as they gradually realized that the teachers held parish pastors in high regard they had found themselves more willing to enter into the discussions.

Then these pastors described bull sessions lasting far into the night in which they began to explore possible ways they might utilize some of the new insights for the good of Howard County. As they learned to appreciate one another in the neutral setting of the University campus, away from the arena of competition, they vowed no longer to compete against one another. These men were kept very busy from early morning until late at night, in large groups, in small groups, and in individual consultation. An attempt was made to cover certain areas and subjects which they could use as background for their clinical work in Kokomo during the six months before they would return to the campus for the second week of intensive study. Each pastor spent approximately two hours a day on the wards of the hospital seeing patients and writing up one of the interviews. These case write-ups became the meat of the seminars and forced each man to open himself up to his colleagues concerning his ways of dealing with people under stress.

In the teaching sessions considerable time was spent in describing the process of personality development and how pastors might detect early signs of mental illness. Also discussed were the family and ways in which the clergyman might assist in getting families off to a good start, particularly since he assumes this responsibility in agreeing to marry couples. The importance of the pastor's conversation with his people was stressed. In the Kokomo group, as in previous groups, it was found that pastors felt very ineffective as counselors. All of them said that although increasing numbers of people were coming to them with their problems they felt there was little they could do for them. One of the aims of the first week of the course was to give these students a new appreciation of how helpful a pastor can be to people by carefully listening to them.

After one year the Kokomo project was technically over, except for the results of the psychological tests which over a period of two years sought to determine whether any changes were observable in the pastors who participated in this project. The results of testing seventeen out of twenty-three men from Kokomo caused the psychologist on the project, Dr. Andrew Mathis, to describe his findings in this way:

> The Kokomo project seems to have accomplished something significant. . . . The sense of isolation from which many of them seem to have moved should begin to show in their parish contacts. . . . From pre- to post-testing there was an increased tendency to be more accepting of emotionality. In terms of behavior it would indicate that these men have moved toward being more capable of accepting an emotional stimulus for what it is without having to alter it immediately to suit their own terms. . . . There was along with this increased acceptance of emotionality a decrease in the introduction of fight and flight. This is an impressive change. It suggests a greater tolerance for a broad range of emotional relatedness and a decreasing tendency to alter defensively the emotional climate of an interaction either by directly opposing it or withdrawing from it. The extent to which these responses reflect a real change in their behavior should contribute toward increased effectiveness with a wider group of people.

Before the year was over the ministers of Kokomo began an interesting experiment in education for marraige. Most of them asked couples who wished to be married by them to participate in a course conducted several times each year on an all-county inter-church basis. Church bulletins carried an announcement that couples desiring to be married in the church were expected to get in touch with the pastor at least one month prior to the date of the wedding, so that he might get to know each couple personally. As a result of this tightening up of standards for Christian marriages, couples began calling the pastor as much as six months prior to the date of the ceremony to arrange for counseling and instruction.

The Kokomo project continued with some enthusiasm for a year or so, and then gradually the interest declined as men who were leaders in the project moved from Kokomo to other cities.

The La Grange project was similar to the Kokomo project except that the pastors came from a suburban community made up primarily of executives and junior executives. Several of the pastors in the group were now serving top churches in their denomination and had therefore reached the pinnacle of their professional mobility.

One of the most significant differences between the two projects was that a serious attempt was made to incorporate physicians, especially psychiatrists, into the La Grange project. It was one of the concerns of the leaders to get professional level conversations started between doctors and ministers. It was felt that some frame of reference needed to be developed so that each discipline could speak to and be understood by the other —a need for a common language to bring about meaningful communication.

When the La Grange area pastors met for the first week at the University of Chicago, they had opportunities to meet perhaps a dozen different doctors in a variety of situations including lectures, ward rounds, and small discussion groups. Every effort was made to encourage the clergymen to talk with as many physicians as they could while they were there, so that they might learn to discuss constructively common problems concerning patients. While most of the pastors were reluctant to "bother" the doctors a few said they had more professional level conversations with doctors during that week than they had experienced in their entire ministry.

When the clergymen from La Grange completed their first week at the university and returned home to their local churches, they had some glowing hopes of more effective professional interchange with their local doctors on the staff of Community Memorial Hospital in La Grange. It was not long, however, before they discovered that these physicians were not prepared for this kind of conversation with clergy. This difficulty in communication showed up one of the weaknesses in the planning of the La Grange project. While a few doctors in the La Grange area were aware of the purpose of this special study of the role of the clergymen in community health, the majority of doctors had not been brought in on the early planning in any real way, and as a result they hesitated to enter into a project which to them had dubious value. In an attempt to explain to these doctors just what the La Grange project was, a committee of pastors sent the following letter to approximately one hundred physicians who were on the staff.

Dear Doctor:

As you probably know, clergymen of the various denominations who serve churches in the west suburban area have been providing chaplaincy services for the patients of Community Memorial Hospital. In our desire to improve our care of the increasing number of patients who ask to speak to a minister, a number of us have taken a post-graduate course at the University of Chicago in ministering to the sick.

We have now been meeting once a week for about two months to discuss actual cases of parishioners who are ill or on the brink of illness. We feel we could be much more helpful to these parishioners, who in some cases are your patients, if the physicians in the community would join us from time to time with these weekly discussions. We think that there is no better time than the present for us to try to discover ways in which our two professions might together better serve the patient.

PARISH CLERGYMEN AND MENTAL HEALTH

As a result of this invitation to physicians about a dozen different doctors sat in on two or more meetings over the two year period, four doctors sat in on more than ten meetings and two on more than twenty. In addition to the physicians, two clinical psychologists attended eight meetings each, a psychiatric social worker who is director of the Southwest Suburban Mental Health Clinic in La Grange attended many sessions, and a lawyer who participated in both weeks with the clergymen at the university attended faithfully.

The theme which perhaps recurred more often than any other was that of the difficulty of communication between ministers and doctors. This came out in many different ways. The following is an excerpt from a tape recording of one of the sessions. (All sessions were taped.)

Pastor A: "Oh I don't have any trouble talking to the nurses about patients. Most of them belong to my church. It's the doctors I don't feel comfortable with because they haven't asked for us as the nurses have."

Physician: "We don't ask for you because we don't know yet what you do. That's why I'm coming to these meetings so that I can find out. But if, as Pastor B says, you ministers don't know what it is you are trying to accomplish with a sick person, then I think probably you'll want to back up and begin to define for yourselves what you think you can do for people."

We found then that modern clergy are generally uncertain of their ministry with respect to sickness. It was also clear that in their own theological education they had seldom been forced to relate their theological stance to a particular clinical situation. The method of these weekly seminars was to start with a clinical situation confronting the pastor. He would usually take fifteen to thirty minutes to make his presentation. Then for the next hour the group dealt with why this pastor responded in the particular ways he did to this person's needs. His response was usually predicated on his particular religious stance, so his colleagues, and particularly the physicians and psychiatrists present, would ask him to spell out how this was related to his theological position. The case study method meant coming at the minister's task in quite the reverse order from that to which he had been accustomed in his theological preparation.

This reverse approach to the examination of one's doctrinal position was upsetting to some of the men, and one or two clergymen dropped out of the weekly seminars shortly after presenting cases on which they were questioned about their work with people. But those of us who led the group and who are accustomed to this clinical approach felt that there was more than the usual amount of kindness and charity demonstrated among the participants throughout the two years of weekly sessions. In fact we felt that there was never quite enough open criticism of one another. They treated each other with gloves on, perhaps, in part, because their own theological training had been conducted in dignified classroom settings. Most of them had *never* before had their own clinical work examined with any degree of candor and criticism.

The La Grange clergymen were quite open to frank criticism, provided it did not take the form of personal attack. While there was a good deal more self-searching than any of them had ever been subjected to before it did not go as deep as it might have.

As we worked with the men of these two projects we found ourselves listing ten goals toward which we were striving. We had to a degree—

1. Introduced parish clergy to the idea that they can take brief one- or two-week seminars which deal with subjects immediately applicable to their parish situation.

2. Succeeded in getting a medical school to offer a course for clergy in what might be called "clinical theology."

3. Helped clarify the minister's role and responsibility in the search for underlying causes of mental illness.

4. Helped prepare parish clergy to recognize emotional problems which had their roots in religious conflict.

5. Demonstrated the importance of a cooperative attack on

mental illness by fellowship and exchange among all the members of the clergy in a particular community.

6. Introduced clergymen to other professional people working in the area of health.

7. Encouraged pastors to promote an ongoing educational program in their own churches related to mental and spiritual health.

8. Gave impetus to an organized program of continuing postgraduate education for the parish pastor in a variety of subjects.

9. Discovered how a cross section of American clergy with traditional courses in theology would respond to a radically different manner of teaching.

10. Helped ministers obtain new insights for their own personal mental health.

29.
SEMINARY TRAINING IN MENTAL HEALTH FOR PARISH CLERGYMEN

Wayne E. Oates, B.D., Th.D.
Professor of Pastoral Care, Southern Baptist Seminary, Louisville, Kentucky

Theological seminaries began in the 1930s to involve both students and faculties in the actual life situations of the mentally ill as a way of educating clergymen in the ministry to the mentally ill and the prevention of mental illness. This was no new fad nor a departure from the basic claims of the Christian faith. The concern of the prophets and the Lord Jesus Christ for the epileptic, the demoniac, the anxious, and the fear-ridden provided both model and motivation for this effort to teach ministers about the contemporary ministry to people in mental illness. The anointing of rabbis and ministers to "heal the broken-hearted" in the tradition of Isaiah and Jesus is involved here. The minister or rabbi actualizes his own unique destiny as a minister or rabbi when he does this.

World War II threw clergymen of all faiths into the maelstrom of a world-wide catastrophe. Clergymen learned to work with other clergymen of all faiths. The lines between the other helping professions of medicine, psychiatry, social work, and psychology ceased to be walls. They became moving lines of creative collaboration between the clergy and men of other faiths and men of other professions. The training of clergy in mental health, which began after World War II, was an ecumenical and interprofessional endeavor. Human suffering knows no barrier, nor does the love of God. The work of the clergy is to communicate the love of God to people in times of developmental and emergency crises. Here they must not indulge in racial, denominational, national, and creedal conflicts. They are concerned with matters of life and death of persons, regardless of these differences.

Some specific guidelines for churches and temples in their efforts to train clergymen in mental health are as follows: first, intensive workshops in suicide prevention, the convalescent care of mental patients, mental retardation, personality disorders in children, and so forth, could be financed and provided by the church or synagogue. I recall being a part of such brief three-day workshops for clergymen of all faiths provided by the First Baptist Church of Greenville, South Carolina. Second, the churches and synagogues can participate together in the development of chapels and chaplaincies in public institutions. Sick people with "all manner of diseases" are cut off from the natural community. In our city, for example, the large charity hospital has a fine chaplaincy program, but worship is held in the medical school amphitheater or in a medical school classroom. The churches and synagogues have yet to do something about building a chapel, although they do supply the whole salary of two chaplains. Training the clergy in hospitals is made more distinctly pastoral if a chapel is available. Third, a synagogue or church can re-think what its youth needs. Our most common assumption is that the church should provide them with recreation and parties. The generation gap could be closed some-what if the people over thirty would enter a planned collabora-tion with middle and late teen-agers in their interest in cars, in driver education, earning money for themselves, and in "con-sumer education." When a church asks a young theological student to be an assistant minister, a young rabbi to participate in the leadership of young people, these activities could be part of his assignments rather than "leading recreation."

The unique contributions of the theological schools and churches to the training of clergymen in mental health is reflected in the kinds of things we expect the minister, priest, or rabbi to know and to be able to do in this area. First, we expect him to know the basic evidences of psychopathology as it appears in religious garb. To do this, at our seminary we have an in-tensive twenty-four-hour-a-week course in psychiatric informa-tion for ministers and religious workers taught in another hospi-tal where the students function as ministers alongside the chap-lains. They are trained to deal with the specific distortions of religion that appear among the mentally ill. They are taught to collaborate with a psychiatrist in the care of the mentally ill in the hospital. They are taught what the convalescent mental patient needs from his parish clergymen and fellow parishioners when he returns home from the hospital. They are taught the principles of preventive psychiatry.

Another important contribution of the theological school to the training of the clergy in mental health is direct experience in small groups. Students themselves are being taught the dy-namics of small groups by being members of small groups with one another. They are taught how to become effective leaders of groups of lay persons. More emphasis needs to be placed upon the difference between the function of the purely voluntary group, such as one finds in a church, and the controlled and not so voluntary group found in the classes of a theological school. For example, the motives of a theological student in a required course in school are very different from those of a person not being rewarded with professional status and a way of earning a living for participating in the group—that is a lay person.

COMMUNITY MENTAL HEALTH

One of the most significant forms of education in mental health the minister, priest, or rabbi of today receives is in participating as a clergyman with mental health professionals. This involves the clergymen in seeing their own work as being both a profession and more than a profession. They are professionals in that (1) they are trained for their work, (2) they operate according to basic principles and not merely according to the ad hoc expectations of disturbed and anxious people, (3) they follow a specific and defined code of ethics in relation to other ministers, rabbis, or priests, as well as in relation to their communicants and to other professional persons, (4) they have a specific body of data or information in which they are informed authorities—i.e., biblical knowledge; knowledge of the history of the churches and synagogues; knowledge of ethical and moral teachings; knowledge of theological beliefs in their variety, similarity, and unique contribution to mental health and well-being, and (5) they have a specific symbolic meaning to people *as ministers,* as representing God.

In theological school, the task of education is to enable the students to lay hold of the resources of the just-described professional identity and to overcome any major impediments that prevent them from assuming this identity with courage and dignity. Learning about mental health alongside other professionals in training has a way of helping to sharpen and clarify their own identity. The student is steadily pushed into a decision to function or not to function as a minister. In a hackneyed phrase attributed to Harry Truman, he is expected to get out of the kitchen if he can't stand the heat. In a much less blunt statement, which nevertheless is not so clear, the student is encouraged to find the kind of profession to which he can give himself wholeheartedly from internal and not external motivation.

This points to probably the most important work going on in the training of the theological student in mental health. Real attention is being given in theological school to improving the student's own mental health as a part of his education. This is being done through several different channels. For example, the Theological Student Inventory developed by the American Association of Theological Schools and the Educational Testing Service is being used more and more to enable students to assess and reappraise their *motivations* for entering the ministry. If they are responding to undue expectation of parents and home community, to the more intense religious zeal of a wife (in the case of minister or rabbi), or to the opportunity for evasion of the military draft, these motives are being surfaced and dealt with positively more often now than formerly because of the teaching of mental health values in the curriculum. If the student himself has brought with him specific pathologies, a more therapeutic and less moralistic approach to them has been developed in the modern theological school. If the student simply comes to the conclusion that he is in the wrong calling, he can do so now with somewhat less social pressure, rejection, and isolation. He is more often encouraged to find the thing that he *is* "with" and that *does* have durable meaning for him.

Another example of the way in which the mental health of the minister is being fostered in theological school is the way in which Protestant seminaries are at last giving some ordered attention to the education and care of wife and children of the theological student. Prior to World War II, the theological student was ordinarily—eight out of ten times—a single man. The ratio now is just reversed. By the time they graduate, theological students are more often than not married, and many of them are parents of children. On our campus, for example, we began by starting an effective nursery-kindergarten program for the children of students. We moved toward a second objective of providing a "mini-curriculum" for the working wife. Thus she could become acquainted with a telescoped version of her husband's education and meet personally some of the persons who teach him. We continued by developing pre-marital and post-marital counseling and guidance on a group basis for the husbands and wives together. At this time we are exerting an influence to encourage as many wives as possible to participate in the classes with their husbands at whatever level their own preparation and obligations permit. We are convinced that the best way to communicate mental health is through contagion. If these people whom we graduate are relatively healthy people, then maybe health, and not disease, will be "catching."

The most important thing we have discovered, however, was in a research project we conducted with a group of twenty-two students who were in a clinical pastoral education program. We learned many things about these students' life situations that will enable us to help the succeeding student generations to be more effective ministers and to function as creative agents of mental health. Through intensive psychological testing, careful interviews, the writing of personal autobiographies, the use of interpersonal interaction groups, and other ways of getting to know them better, we discovered that the students tended to think in a continuum on a power-person scale. Some of them did their work on the predominant motivation of the political influence—power, prestige, and so forth—which would accrue to them. This was not their exclusive or conscious motivation. Others moved more in terms of *personal* values in relation to their involvement with the people to whom they ministered as persons. Like the other group, this was not their exclusive or conscious motivation. All twenty-two were strung out along this continuum.

We were not so concerned with this continuum as we were with *where* and *how* the men became this way. We discovered the key to this was that the persons who had first influenced them to think about entering the ministry had much to do with their concept of the ministry. Also, the persons with whom they continued to identify and like whom they most surely wanted to become were sources of these patterns of motivation. Consequently, the valuable thing here to suggest to synagogues and churches is that each synagogue or church should give systematic, ordered, and careful attention to persons planning to enter the clergy. These persons should be led by person-centered, not power-oriented, leaders. Projects could be developed in the preparation of candidates for ordination and in maintaining a durable and lasting relationship to the aspirant for the ministry throughout his education.

But the main thing we discovered about this group of students was a sort of built-in timidity and inarticulateness about their own religious life. The issues of effective prayer, creative religious fellowship as such, expression of religious concern, and implementation of religious resources—these were available strengths and assets the student was reluctant to use. The most important function of theological education, then, would be to encourage and effectively reinforce the student's confidence in the "gift of God" that is within him. As Goethe said, the truth that is his must be made his own.

30.
ADVANCED TRAINING FOR PASTORAL COUNSELORS

Carroll A. Wise, B.D., Th.D.
Professor of Pastoral Psychology and Counseling, Garrett Theological Seminary, Evanston, Illinois

Advanced training is the training of clergymen to be specialists in pastoral counseling. These are men or women who have completed their college degrees, and who have also graduated from an accredited theological school with a Master of Divinity degree or its equivalent. This means a total of at least seven years of previous preparation. In college they may have had work in psychology, sociology, and anthropology. In the theological school they will have had some work in psychology, sociology, and counseling, along with the standard theological courses. The work described here leads to a Ph.D. or a Th.D. degree upon completion. This requires at least three years, usually longer. The average student entering advanced training is around thirty years of age, has had a period of clinical pastoral training in an accredited institution, and three years or more in a parish. Most are married and have a family.

Advanced training in pastoral counseling has three major aspects. They are, first, the development of the student's emotional, intellectual, social, and professional life; second, knowledge and understanding of human behavior in breadth and depth; and third, the ability to relate to others therapeutically through an understanding of psychotherapeutic approaches and processes.

Most directors of such programs would consider the first of these goals as the most important, though they would also give full significance to the others. We believe it is more important to develop persons who can be therapeutic, in the broad sense of the term, than it is to develop some kind of pastoral technicians. This conviction is grounded both in our religious faith and in our understanding of the processes by which persons grow, become distorted, and find their way back to wholeness. We are concerned to help each student develop his own potentials and uniqueness, to become, as much as possible, a full human being, and to avoid creating some kind of stereotype of a pastoral counselor.

This concern is manifest in all aspects of the advanced training of pastoral counselors. One is in making it clear to the student that his own personal therapy is a requisite for training on this level. The student's personal therapy is his responsibility and is obtained independently of the school, from psychotherapists in the community. The following statement in the requirements for accreditation by the American Association of Pastoral Counselors is taken as a guideline for this experience:

> It is required that a candidate for membership in this category (category III) shall have undergone sufficient personal psychotherapeutic investigation of his intrapsychic and interpersonal processes that he is able to protect the counselee from his (the counselor's) own problems, and to deploy himself to the maximum benefit of the counselee.

A second expression of this concern for the growth of the student as a person is in the teaching methods. There are few lecture courses in such a program. Most classes are based on the seminar-discussion method, and many revolve around actual case material presented by a student from his profession experience. The teaching staff is composed of men who are both practitioners and teachers, men who are concerned with both theory and practice. Most courses are team-taught by a pastoral counselor and a psychiatrist or a clinical psychologist, sharing in the teaching-learning process. Thus the clinical and theoretical material is integrated; psychological and theological understanding is related; and the student is helped to think critically about his own work, to benefit from the insights of his peers as well as those of his teachers, and to honestly face the problems involved in his relationships with others. These sessions often verge on a therapeutic experience for the student, and frequently provide material which he works through in his personal therapy. The educational process is intensified and deepened through supervision in counseling.

Supervision as a form of teaching is conducted both individually and in groups. It is supervision of individual and group counseling, including marriage counseling. The counseling takes place in a number of different settings, such as parish churches, schools, hospitals, and pastoral counseling centers. The supervision is given by consulting psychiatrists, psychologists, social workers, or pastoral counselors. The pastoral counselors doing supervision are accredited for membership in the American Association of Pastoral Counselors, Category III. By the time a student has completed the program he should have approximately four hundred hours of supervision.

The fulfillment of the second and third goals is achieved, not only through the educational methods, but also through the content of the curriculum. For a detailed description of the curriculum the reader is referred to the catalogue of any school offering such a program, and also to the statement of standards for membership in the American Association of Pastoral Counselors.

At Garrett the qualifying examination which the student takes about the beginning of his third year (and which requires the equivalent of five days of writing, plus an oral examination) covers five major areas. These are: (1) theories of personality development in health and illness, including psychopathology, (2) theories of counseling and psychotherapy and their application in practice, (3) the psychology of religious experience, (4) the relationship between the theological and psychological understanding of man, and (5) research theory and practice. Included in the above would be such topics as marriage and family processes and counseling, group processes and group therapy, an understanding of the viewpoints and work of the other helping professions. For further elaboration, the reader is referred to the "Standards for Membership" of the American Association of Pastoral Counselors, which deals with requirements for education for clinical work under supervision, and for personal therapeutic experience.

Obviously such a program must be under the direction of a trained and experienced pastoral counselor, one who qualifies for the highest level of membership in the American Association of Pastoral Counselors. Depending on the size of the program he needs one or more associates who also are highly qualified pastoral counselors. Beyond this an interprofessional faculty is a necessity. This means teachers or supervisors who are psychoanalysts, psychiatrists, specialists in marriage therapy, clinical psychologists, research psychologists, social workers, and others.[1] Thus the relationship between the pastoral counselor and other helping professions is a matter of continuing discussion. Through the interprofessional faculty, other disciplines make a very valuable contribution to the training of the pastoral counselor. In addition the entire faculty of the school is utilized in the program, as the student is expected to understand the relationship of his discipline to cognate disciplines. Where there is affiliation with a university, this faculty is also utilized. For example, in the combined Garrett–Northwestern University program, the student receives excellent training in modern research design and methodology through the psychology depart-

---

[1] Community resources such as psychiatrists, psychoanalysts, clinical psychologists, and social workers are used on a part-time basic as teachers and supervisors. In some instances they are given faculty appointments as "Adjunct Professors."

ment of the University, and also guidance in adapting modern research methods to religious data.

There is a great deal in such a program which would also be found in the training programs of other helping professions. But there is a unique aspect to the training of pastoral counselors, and that is the pastoral or religious orientation. All the men accepted into such a program are committed to the religious ministry and are ordained by some faith group. Such student groups are ecumenical; Catholic priests and Jewish rabbis as well as Protestants of all theological persuasions are accepted. The goal of such training is to equip a man or woman for the work of counseling as a pastor or as a teacher in the field, and also as a competent research person in the field.

There is a continuing emphasis on the integration of scientific and philosophical material with the religious and theological point of view of the student. There is no attempt to indoctrinate the student in any particular theological point of view. Each student is helped to relate what he is learning to his own background and faith group. He is encouraged to examine his personal religious experiences and beliefs and to understand the purposes they serve in his life and ministry. This includes looking at the negative aspects of his religion as well as the positive. Students are encouraged to an understanding in depth of the personal, social, and historical-cultural processes in religion. Aesthetic, symbolic, and ritualistic aspects are studied. The ecumenical nature of the student group and faculty helps to broaden the understanding of the student. Religious issues which emerge in actual counseling experiences are discussed in individual and group supervision. Thus the religious dimension of such experiences as guilt and anxiety, love and hate, faith and fear, hope and despair, autonomy or control, insight or defensiveness—to mention only a few—receive attention. It is this concern to bring an understanding of the religious dimension to the therapeutic process which distinguishes pastoral counseling from other helping professions.

Perhaps this is the place to mention some of the unique contributions of pastoral counseling to community mental health.

First, pastoral counseling maintains and develops the long tradition of the religious ministry in the care and cure of souls. Pastoral counseling is thus an essential part of total pastoral care and fulfills a necessary function in the total work of the pastor. Cooperation with members of other helping professions is both possible and necessary for the welfare of persons in a manner not possible in previous periods of human history.

Second, pastoral counseling provides the opportunity desired by many in our culture to receive personal help through the religious community and the pastor. Pastoral counseling thus becomes an extension of the basic pastoral relationship and expectancy, and is related to the other functions of the clergyman and of the religious community. Within the religious community there are resources of profound value to mental health, but they need to be used with skill and understanding. These resources may play a significant role in the mental health of the total community.

A third contribution lies in the unique meaning of the pastor and the pastoral relationship. To the various dimensions to be found in any therapeutic relationship there is the added religious symbolic meaning. The pastor represents, in addition to the religious community, the realities of his personal faith, culminating in the image of the God to whom he is devoted. The deeper meaning of the faith of the pastor is reflected unwittingly in his relationships, and becomes a source of identification within the religious dimension.

Fourth, because of his specialized training in religion, the pastor is able to understand and deal with religious elements within the intrapsychic, cultural, or relational aspects of the experience of the counselee. This means distinguishing between healthy and unhealthy aspects of a person's religion; recognizing both the existential and pathological sources of anxiety, the significance of religious defenses, regression, and growth; and giving whatever encouragement he feels is indicated to positive religious directions. Many secular counselors are justifiably uncomfortable in dealing with religious aspects of a counselee's experience.

In conclusion then, we would restate our main goal in this training as assisting the student to move toward the fulfillment of himself as a human being, with the additional understanding of those disciplines and the appropriation of those skills which are necessary to the pastor in the counseling process. We ask of our students a high level of excellence both academically and professionally. We seek to offer an educational and religious environment which encourages the development of breadth, depth, and wholeness within the student. We expect the student to develop the kind of religious understanding which quietly bears witness to its value and reality and hence does not have to be compulsively sold to others. To the extent that we succeed in this, the student then becomes the kind of pastor who can help others find a religious faith which is viable for them.

31.
TRAINING CLERGYMEN IN MENTAL HEALTH

George Christian Anderson, T.S.B., D.D.
Founder and Honorary President, Academy of Religion and Mental Health

There is one overriding problem in training clergymen in mental health. Simply put, it is that no one has yet defined mental health in terms that will suit everyone. The fault lies in traditional concepts of mental health. People attempted to make these concepts too specific. They confined mental health to the health of the mind. But what is and where is the mind?

To the ancient Hindus and Chinese, the mind was seated mainly in the organs of the chest or abdomen. Aristotle conjectured that the heart and blood vessels were sources of thought. It was not until the time of Galen in the second century A.D. that the function of the mind was believed to be seated in the head. But why must the function of the mind be limited to the brain?

COMMUNITY MENTAL HEALTH

The late Harold G. Wolff, one of our most distinguished neurologists, pointed out that the function of nerve cells was not confined to the function of the brain. All the nerve cells of the body connect with one another. Furthermore, nerve cells have a relationship to all other types of living cells in the body. Dr. Wolff called attention to the fact that, in a sense, the "mind" resides in every cell of the body. Sinnott stated that mind is present in all of life. The term "mental health" has little meaning if it implies that mental health is something apart from other types of health and not related to the total health of the human organism. The psyche and the soma of the human being are not separate entities, but are inexorably interwoven.

Attempts to deal with mental health or to plan training programs in mental health without recognizing the interconnection between the mind and the body not only give a limited view of health and illness, but can hinder efforts of clergymen who counsel individuals with behavioral problems. For instance, we all know the influence of body chemistry on behavior. A sufficient amount of ingested alcohol can make a person act like a lunatic. Infection which creates high fevers also distorts behavior. Deterioration of nerve cells such as we see in advanced senility also has an effect on conduct. Trauma, such as in a concussion of the brain, can have a significant impact on the way we act. It is impossible to think of the function of the mind without recognizing these mind-body relationships. Those who would be specialists in mental health need to have an adequate understanding of all the body functions and activities that influence behavior. The interaction of psyche and soma is what makes human beings live and die.

Many courses offered to clergymen in pastoral counseling ignore this mind-body relationship. The psychoanalytic theories of Freud, Jung, and others who have laid the foundation for modern psychiatry provide merely one approach to the understanding of human behavior. Theories of psychoanalysis and training in psychoanalytic or counseling techniques provide only partial information for those who must deal with the behavioral problems of those they are counseling.

This is not to say, however, that clergymen who wish to become involved in the field of mental health must first be trained as physicians. It would be preferable if they had this training, but then the clergyman would be a clergyman-physician. It is important, however, that in training clergymen in mental health, opportunities be provided for some discussion of the physiological factors that enter into psychological behavior. I have known instances where a clergyman has attempted to counsel an individual with a behavioral problem using the insight and techniques of psychoanalysis, when what was really indicated was a physical checkup, since the behavioral pattern of the individual was being distorted by physiological factors. Clergymen who attempt to deal with deep-seated emotional problems in individuals should always make certain that such individuals have had a thorough physical checkup as part of the counseling process and program.

A serious problem, however, confronts most clergymen who desire to obtain sufficient knowledge of the physiological factors that influence behavior. Until recently, few medical schools permitted others than those pursuing a medical degree to attend their classes. At times I have heard psychiatrists condemn the pastoral counseling movement because pastoral counselors had inadequate knowledge of the various functions of the body. My reply to such criticism was: how could one expect clergymen to acquire this knowledge if medical schools were unwilling to open their classes to clergymen seeking this kind of information? Today, however, more opportunities are being provided in medical schools (particularly in the departments of psychiatry) for clergymen who are pursuing courses in pastoral counseling to participate in some of the courses offered to medical students.

For instance, the medical school of the University of Pennsylvania has an arrangement with the Marriage Council of Philadelphia whereby clergymen being trained in counseling under the auspices of the Marriage Council are permitted to attend classes in the medical school. This is a pioneering effort. More medical schools should make courses available for clergymen who are seeking training in mental health.

COMMUNITY MENTAL HEALTH

A few years ago a series of lectures and discussions was given in a pilot course in Psychotherapy in General Practice at the University of Minnesota. Some of the goals of the pilot course could well serve as a model for the objectives of mental health training for pastoral counselors. In retrospect, specific goals were defined as follows: (1) to give the doctor a feeling of dynamic qualities in the value of doctor-patient relationship, (2) to introduce him to broad patterns of human motivation and to the common causes of emotional disturbance, (3) to lead him to think in terms of the relation between emotional disturbance and illness, (4) to teach him easily understandable methods of therapy so that he can treat a share of such illness, (5) to give him some knowledge of more malignant conditions so that he may refer them to specialists.

If we were to substitute the term "pastoral counselor" for "doctor" in these goals, they would also serve as excellent guidelines on which courses in mental health for clergymen could be built. Obviously, it would not be possible to give such training in the limited time that clergymen can give to it. But at least these guidelines provide a broad outline and objectives for designing curricula in mental health.

One must always keep in mind that there is a significant difference in the treatment of the mentally ill between that provided by a physician and that offered by pastoral counselors. In the first place, the physician has a vast battery of diagnostic skills not available to clergymen. Secondly, in therapy he can prescribe drugs or even surgery. The limitations of the goal of psychotherapy as seen by the physician and the pastoral counselor are indeed different, as has been pointed out time and again by those involved in the field of pastoral counseling. Clergymen who attempt to manage severe emotional illness in individuals who come to them for help can be as guilty of malpractice as though they attempted to perform an operation or prescribe drugs. Yet there are many parallel goals of clergymen and others who engage in counseling. The important thing is to recognize one's area of competency and not to attempt to invade a field of special knowledge without having been adequately trained in that particular field. Courses in health for clergymen must stress the limitations of the clerical role.

Most courses in counseling for clergymen are primarily confined to healing. This is all to the good. But I strongly believe that the primary function of the clergy in the health field is that of prevention. The opportunities are enormous. In the United States there are over 240,000 clergymen who are active in parish or synagogue work and dealing directly with congregations. This vast army of clergymen could make an effective contribution to the emotional health of the 125,000,000 Americans who are members of organized religions. We know that among many of the emotionally disturbed there is a crisis of morals, contradictory attitudes toward behavior, an uncertainty concerning a way of life, and often an unrealistic drive toward perfectionism. Organized religions have helped to keep moral values high, to provide high goals of living, to create dissatisfaction with anything less than almost a perfect human being. But many individuals cannot achieve this high level of behavior. In the attempt, many are plunged into emotional distress by excessive guilt and lack of self-esteem.

Some of this excessive guilt is nourished in religious groups. Many moral values become part of an individual's ideals or style of life in early childhood. It is pertinent to note that over 55,000,000 children are exposed to moral training provided by religion and their clergymen. Because morals involve guilt, emotions are also involved. Clergymen with adequate knowledge of personality development could avoid those things that are likely to create difficulties for individuals as they grow up. For instance, most of the crises in adolescence, particularly in juvenile delinquency, are the result of inner conflicts between ideal behavior and those urges, many of them primitive, which the adolescent seeks to enjoy. Religion can lead an individual to mental health, but the wrong kind of religion can also help make an individual mentally ill.

It seems almost ridiculous for seminaries to train future clergymen to guide and influence people without giving them adequate knowledge concerning the factors that enter into human development and personality. Until recently, the vast majority of clergymen in the United States had little or no adequate training concerning these factors. Most of them were well versed in Scriptures, religious history, liturgy, church law, and other tools of their trade, but they knew very little about the human beings with whom they had to deal. It is only recently that courses in pastoral psychology have been introduced into the curricula of most forward-looking seminaries in this country.

A major contribution of organized religion is to enable clergymen to develop healthy emotional attitudes among those they serve. This is preventive mental health. But before this can happen, clergymen must understand much more than they do about all the ingredients that enter into the making of a human being. There are constitutional factors (both physiological and psychological), environmental factors, sociological factors. Actually the training of clergymen in health concepts must begin much earlier than seminary days. Their college preparation must include more than the liberal arts. They need to know something about the medical, behavioral, and social sciences. Some training in clinical psychology is a must for anyone who hopes to lead individuals to the internalization of moral and spiritual values. Clergymen must understand that not all individuals can achieve total spiritual health—there will be cripples, some with distorted behavioral patterns, who must be accepted without hope of change. How to deal with such individuals is an important responsibility of clergymen. With adequate training, they can provide the kind of support that will prevent such an individual from being plunged into deeper despair. The preventive role of the clergyman in dealing with emotional health is an essential one.

Today, we are living in a new era in which the majority of physicians and others dealing with health seek the collaboration of clergymen. However, physicians, especially psychiatrists, rightly insist that the price of collaboration is the ability of the clergyman to function as an effective member of the healing team. Yet the collaboration must work well on both sides. Physicians and others must recognize that clergymen have a unique function and that religious resources can be valid. There are two sides of the coin of clergy-physician collaboration. On the one hand, the physician has his unique and specific resources. On the other hand, physicians should respect the unique and particular resources that are available for those with deep spiritual conviction and beliefs. There are rich resources in the treasure chest of religion; they must be made known to physicians and others who seek collaboration with clergymen.

Despite the fact that there is a growing desire for further collaboration between psychiatrists and clergymen, there is still a significant number of psychiatrists and other behavioral scientists who take a dim view of the invasion of the clergy into the health field. However, I have noticed as a result of my own experience with psychiatrists here and abroad that most of those who object to the involvement of clergy in the health field do so because of their own personal conflicts or ignorance about religion and its teachings. Many of them have little knowledge of the enormous changes that have taken place among theologians and clergymen over the past decade.

Generally speaking, today's clergyman is a much different person from those of two decades ago. The modern preacher lives under a big umbrella; he is more liberal, more aware of contemporary life and its problems. This new-fashioned clergyman has helped to improve collaboration between the clergy and the physician. Today, the climate is right for medico-religio-psychological collaboration. The question still remains whether or not all those engaged in health and behavior realize how much they need one another.

32.
PROBLEMS AND POSSIBILITIES OF INTERPROFESSIONAL COOPERATION

E. Mansell Pattison, M.D.

Associate Professor-in-Residence, Department of Psychiatry and Human Behavior, University of California at Irvine, California

The development of community mental health programs is predicated upon the development of interdependent working relationships between direct mental health treatment services and agencies, institutions, groups, and people in the community. Since the clergy and the churches are a major segment of the community there has been considerable interest in the development of effective working relationships between mental health professionals and the professional clergy.

During the 1940s and 1950s there was considerable interest in the so-called rapprochement of psychiatry and religion. During that time most of the problems of interprofessional cooperation centered around conceptual issues. By and large mental health professionals and clergy had their own domains of professional concern which did not significantly overlap. Both had concerns for the welfare and healing of distressed persons, but their respective approaches rarely crossed paths. During those two postwar decades there was an exploration of the conceptual issues that had seemed to loom so large in the debates of the earlier decades. The success of these conceptual explorations seemed to some a "fait accompli" after a time; for areas of agreement were reached by some, others felt that they had explored the ideas of the other professional group and finding them wanting had discarded them, while still others "bought" a psychological line or a spiritual line, so to speak. Thus the seeming conceptual rapprochement may have turned out to be an uneasy truce, without a clear exploration of the differences in points of view of mental health professionals and clergymen. Such conceptual issues included: naturalism vs. supernaturalism;

monism vs. dualism; free will vs. determinism; whether man is morally good, bad, or neutral; how to eradicate mental distress and social problems; the values of the concept of unconscious motivation; absolute vs. relative moral codes; and the desirability of examining one's religious beliefs.

Up until 1960, this pattern of relationship worked fairly well, for neither group of professionals had any great necessity to work intimately with the other. However the development of sophisticated chaplaincy training programs and pastoral counseling training among the clergy, and the development of community mental health programs by the mental health professionals, brought the two groups of professionals into a number of areas of professional overlap or mutual concern. This introduced problems of professional role conflict that were added to still unresolved, but more hidden, conceptual conflicts.

Although this chapter is concerned primarily with issues related to interprofessional cooperation in community mental health services, these cannot be discussed without calling attention to the fact that behind the issues of professional role allocation still lie conceptual disagreements that often play a major role in preventing effective collaboration and the working out of mutually satisfying professional roles. As we shall see, most problems in interprofessional relations involve combinations of both conceptual and role conflicts.

Cooperation in Referral. One of the major areas of community mental health where collaboration is most necessary is in the area of referral. Clergy are most frequently the first professionals in the community to whom people in emotional distress turn. Thus, community mental health services were planned to establish liaison with the clergy so that the emotionally ill could be quickly and effectively referred to the appropriate mental health services. Likewise the pastor, beset by many troubled persons, was looking for mental health resources to assist him. Theoretically the situation appeared ideal for mutual collaboration where both professional groups would profit.

However, after some five years' experience with community mental health programs, it appears that such collaboration has not developed. It is estimated that over one-third of clergymen's clients suffer from severe mental illness. Yet the clergy refer only 33 percent of such severe cases to mental health facilities, whereas general practitioners refer 88 percent of such clients. In terms of total case-contact, several recent surveys demonstrate that clergy refer *less than 1 percent* of their contacts to mental health resources. To look at the problem from the other side, data from community mental health services reveal that only *from 1 to 8 percent* of their referrals come from the clergy. Even in model community mental health centers, including several which are church-sponsored, the figures are minimal—for example: 2 percent, 1 percent, 4 percent, "few."

These findings have stimulated a number of research studies to determine why the clergy–community mental health center referral network has not developed as was envisioned. Several major reasons have been demonstrated.

First, there is a marked discrepancy between the role definitions and role functions of the clergy as defined by mental health professionals and as defined by the clergy. Mental health professionals tend to restrict and confine the role of the clergyman and even may voice grave warnings about the clergy assuming professional functions or encroaching on mental health domains. Hence the message is transmitted overtly or covertly to the clergy that liaison and referral is acceptable only within certain limited boundaries. Disagreement over those boundaries may lead both the mental health professionals and the clergy to withdraw from contact and collaboration as the easiest way to resolve the conflict.

Second, other studies have shown that mental health professionals engage in an asymetric relationship with professional clergy. That is, while mental health professionals usually acknowledge referrals from social agencies and physicians and will in turn refer patients back, with clergy referrals the referral is not acknowledged, nor is referral back to the clergyman made.

Third, some community mental health centers have established referral policies which accept referrals only from medical or social agency sources and exclude clergy referrals. This has certain screening advantages, but it also is a powerful deterrent to the clergy.

Fourth, effective clergy referral has been found to correlate with education, social status, and theological attitude. Clergy with little education have low referral rates, whereas clergy with the highest education have the highest referral rates. Clergy with low social status in the community have low referral rates. They indicate that communicating with high-status mental health professionals would "show them up" or "expose their inferiority." On the other hand, high-status clergy have high referral rates. Finally, several studies have revealed that clergy of the more conservative theologies tend to refer less, but also try to cope with the most severe problems. These clergymen tend to define all emotional problems as spiritual ones, and consequently deal with all problems in a spiritual manner with the least psychological sophistication. On the other hand, it has been shown that clergy of more liberal theology are apt to have exceedingly high rates of referral of all types of problems. They tend to define all problems as psychological and eschew any spiritual approach to human problems.

Fifth, many of the clergy trained in the decade of the 1960s have received basic, and at times advanced, training in pastoral care skills. Such pastors have redefined their role in relation to those seeking help in distress. These clergy consider that they have the knowledge, skill, and responsibility for the care of many of the problems they see. Thus these clergy have a lower referral rate because they elect not to refer as a professional decision.

Sixth, many clergy have not had the opportunity to acquire skills in pastoral care that will equip them to handle skillfully referrals, or to communicate easily and knowledgeably with mental health professionals.

Seventh, at least a few years ago many mental health professionals did not define the role of the pastor as including primary care, and only suggested that pastors refer all emotional problems. This was unrealistic, and many pastors have had no guidelines as to which type of problems might best be handled by the pastor, and which problems might best be referred to mental health services.

In summary, the area of referral illustrates both the conceptual and role problems that have interfered with successful development of referral cooperation. Yet this is an area in which both groups of professionals may indeed profit from establishing a working liaison with each other.

Cooperation in Consultation. As the churches have become involved in mental health activities there has been increasing need for consultative services with mental health professionals. Such consultation may occur at many levels: consultation to pastors concerning problem clients with whom they are working; consultation to a pastor and the church administration regarding human relation problems in the congregation; consultation to groups or programs in a congregation that are designed to assist people in the church; consultation to a local, regional, or denominational administration in regard to evaluation of religious candidates, human relations problems in the administration, or denominational programming related to mental health issues; consultation to a group of churches who sponsor a joint community program. Such joint consultation will benefit the mental health professionals in that it will foster the contributions of the churches, while it will benefit the clergy and churches in providing assistance in the achievement of their tasks.

There are several problems that may arise in such joint enterprises. First, there is the problem of *reductionism*. By this I mean the tendency to translate the concepts and ideas of the other professional into one's own frame of reference. Thus the psychiatrist may reduce all the concerns of the clergy to psychological problems, or the clergy may reduce all the concerns of the psychiatrist to spiritual issues. A corollary to this is to implicitly or explicitly use the other professional for purposes other than what has been contracted in the consultation. For example, a psychiatrist may use a consultation to prove himself superior to the clergyman or expose the neuroticism of religion; or the clergyman may use a consultation either to seek a covert means of therapy or perhaps to gain power and prestige for an administrative maneuver. It is incumbent for effective consultation that both professionals have respect for their own professional discipline and role, and seek to use the help from the other for the purposes contracted, while avoiding aggrandizement of the other.

Another problem in consultation is that of *syncretism,* that is, conducting consultation in such a way that disagreement is avoided at all costs and the parties must stick together regardless of the means used or the goals set. If effective consultation is to occur both parties must feel free to see issues from their own point of view, yet respect other viewpoints that may suggest modifications. Frequently mental health professionals feel they cannot be of much assistance to clergy with whom they do not agree philosophically, while clergy may feel that a psychiatrist who shares no common theology cannot possibly be of value. It may prove fruitful to spell out carefully areas of disagreement in consultation so that differences can be respected and not interfere with the mutually agreed upon goals of consultation.

A final problem in consultation may be that of *competition.* Here either party may wish to win out and gain power over the other. This may be an intellectual competition, such as a psychiatrist proving that the clergyman is dead wrong in his entire approach, or vice versa. Or the competition may be administrative or political, in terms of responsibility and power to make decisions or direct actions. Usually, openly competitive consultations quickly abort; however, subtle competitions may develop which can effectively sidetrack the consultation work from its intended goals. The end result, however, is a hollow victory.

In summary, there are many levels at which consultation may be part of the community mental health program. This is one of the potentially most fruitful areas of cooperation, for the benefits may accrue long after the completion of a consultation project. To be successful, however, consultation must be a collaborative enterprise between two professional who bring their own unique skills, knowledge, and concerns to the task at hand.

Cooperation in Treatment. Here we may consider opportunities for collaboration in the care of a patient who is receiving mental health treatment, either on an outpatient basis or on an inpatient basis.

In terms of outpatient care, patients in various types of psychotherapy were traditionally treated alone, and the problems were dealt with solely by the psychotherapist. More recently it has been found that the emotionally ill profoundly influence those around them and are influenced in return. Thus we have seen the development of joint treatment of married couples, family therapy, and treatment programs that enlist the aid and cooperation of relatives and friends. In instances where the pastor has a close and ongoing relationship with a parishioner who enters therapy, the pastor may play a role complementary to that of the psychotherapist. The therapist may inquire, question, observe, probe, interpret, and restructure in terms of the patient's emotional dynamics; while the pastor may continue to provide support, guidance, and a continuing reality of the life of the congregation and the patient's religious faith and practice. Some therapists have compared this to the needs of the child for both correction and instruction on the one hand, and love and nurture on the other hand.

In terms of inpatient care, we come more directly to specialized pastoral roles, in most instances a chaplaincy role. A number of recent studies indicate that there is considerable strain at the present time in the function of the chaplain. Mental health professionals tend to define the chaplain's role solely in terms of traditional religious functions such as conducting worship services and administering the sacraments. However, chaplains with clinical training tend to define the bulk of their work in nontraditional areas such as pastoral visitation to patients, counseling patients, teaching in in-service programs, developing liaison with the community, conducting clergy training, performing administrative work, teaching religious classes, participating in research, working with volunteers, counseling employees, and doing religious group work. This list suggests many opportunities for vital contributions to a community mental health center program, but also represents unresolved role conflicts.

Other areas of cooperation include joint enterprises in community education projects such as those concerned with alcoholism, drug abuse, sex education, parent-child relations, marital relations, race relations, problems of poverty. Both groups of professionals may bring particular insights, knowledge, and skills to such educational programs.

Finally, mental health professionals and professional clergy may join forces in developing programs of social action in the community. Here they will probably work with other professionals and disciplines in the community who also have concern for social problems. In such programs both groups of professionals may be only part of larger community programs under the leadership of other citizens.

To sum up this chapter, it should be pointed out that there are many areas of joint concern to both groups of professionals. There are areas of conflict regarding conceptual issues and professional roles. These problems cannot be ignored. However, the fact that problems exist does not mean that inter-professional cooperation cannot be developed successfully. Indeed, the honest facing of areas of conflict may be an avenue toward the development of successful collaboration.

Action programs aimed at increasing interprofessional cooperation should focus on these needs:

1. The need for locally based in-service training programs for parish pastors. Such training should be geared not toward developing specialists, but toward enhancing and enlarging their pastoral care skills and providing them with skills and knowledge to collaborate with mental health professionals.

2. The need for education of mental health professionals in the structure, function, and role of the clergy and church institutions, and how to collaborate with them.

3. The need for establishing clear communication between local community mental health services and the clergy of the community, so that effective means of referral collaboration can be established.

For additional reading

Clinebell, H. J., Jr. *Basic Types of Pastoral Counseling*. Nashville: Abingdon Press, 1966.

Halmos, Paul. *The Faith of the Counsellors*. New York: Schocken Books, 1966.

Hofmann, H., ed. *The Ministry and Mental Health*. New York: Association Press, 1960.

Klausner, S. Z. *Psychiatry and Religion: A Sociological Study of the New Alliance of Ministers and Psychiatrists*. New York: Free Press, 1964.

Linn, L, and Schwarz, L. W. *Psychiatry and Religious Experience*. New York: Random House, 1958.

Oglesby, W. B. *Referral in Pastoral Counseling*. Englewood Cliffs, N.J.: Prentice-Hall, 1968.

Pattison, E. M., ed. *Clinical Psychiatry and Religion*. Boston: Little, Brown, 1969.

Westberg, G. E., and Draper, E. *Community Psychiatry and the Clergyman*. Springfield, Ill.: C. C. Thomas, 1966.

33.
UNDERSTANDING GOVERNMENTAL STRUCTURES FOR MENTAL HEALTH

Lucy D. Ozarin, M.D., M.P.H.
Division of Mental Health Service Program, N.I.M.H., Chevy Chase, Maryland

Planning and delivery of mental health services are both a public and a private responsibility. Federal, state, and local public agencies have statutory authority and public funds to carry out their tasks. Private groups and individuals participate through their agencies, organizations, and through philanthropy. Coordination and cooperation of effort between the public and private sectors are necessary for optimal functioning of the mental health care system. This chapter outlines the governmental structure for mental health which also provides for participation of private groups and individuals through various types of advisory councils.

UNDERSTANDING GOVERNMENTAL STRUCTURES

Federal Level

The National Institute of Mental Health, part of the Public Health Service in the Department of Health, Education and Welfare, is the federal agency with major responsibility for development of mental health services, mental health research, training, and continuing education for all types of professional and subprofessional manpower. Federal funds are also granted to state public health programs ($66,000,000 in the fiscal year 1969). Community mental health receives a minimum of 15 percent of each state's allotment, and 70 percent of the grant is available to support services in communities for which both public and private nonprofit groups may apply. Other federal programs also provide funds for mental health–related purposes including Medicare, Medicaid, Vocational Rehabilitation, Office of Economic Opportunity, Office of Aging, and Office of Education. Recent legislation provides support for construction of community mental health centers and initial operation of new services in them.

A mental health staff is located in each of the nine regional DHEW offices to administer the NIMH program and to consult with public and private groups who desire assistance. (See list at the end of this chapter.)

State Level

Each state has designated a state-level agency called the Mental Health Authority to administer the federal community mental health grant. This Authority may be the same agency which administers the state mental hospitals. More than thirty states have passed community mental health service acts or other legislation which makes funds available on a continuing basis to match local public or private nonprofit expenditures for mental health services.

Local Level

State community mental health acts usually require that a local mental health board be established on a county or multicounty basis to serve as an administrative or policy-making board or as an advisory body. The board, usually appointed by the local government, in turn appoints an administrator of the local program.

Involvement by Clergymen

Clergymen and congregants have been involved in mental health programs for many years, the former usually in the role of pastoral counselor and therapist and the latter as volunteers in a variety of mental health and mental health–related settings. Both serve as members of boards operating mental health facilities.

Each mental hospital, clinic, or other facility uses clergymen and volunteers in keeping with the philosophy and practice of the facility and staff. The newer community mental health programs are developing broad community-based programs which are expanding the traditional roles of pastors and citizens.

In the Far West, a mental health center has established a panel of fifty qualified community professionals who accept patients for individual and group psychotherapy after screening and evaluation at the mental health center The center pays a small fee to the panel members and retains responsibility for the patient's total treatment program. Several qualified clergy are on the panel of therapists.

In a Midwestern city of 50,000, a marriage counseling center begun by a group of clergymen and based in a local general hospital which furnished secretarial service, is to be incorporated into the new mental health center established in the community. The clergymen will continue to provide counseling as part of the center's activity.

An innovative school program carried out at a mental health center in New York uses parent-tutors to assist in remedial reading, which often is needed by children showing maladaptive behavior. The parent-tutors receive three preliminary training sessions in a special reading method followed by group supervision on a weekly basis. About seventy-five parents from public and parochial schools are involved.

In a ghetto of New York, an Interfaith Counseling Service has been organized with a membership of more than one hundred local clergymen who refer their troubled parishioners to the center for help for a broad variety of problems in living. The Council holds workshops for parents, couples, single people, and young people; helps to develop local community leaders; provides training in counseling for ministers and qualified laymen; and serves in an advisory capacity to the neighborhood educational system. The agency's brochure states, "Our plans are geared toward providing alternatives to the use of destructive means to cope with feelings of frustration, isolation or helplessness. We aim to place appropriate responsibility on residents to create the kind of community atmosphere in which they will choose to live." The service, directed by a clergyman, employs two trained social workers, and a nearby mental health center provides part-time services of a psychiatrist to consult, teach, and supervise.

The Prairie View Mental Health Center in Newton, Kansas, whose roots were in a small mental hospital established under the sponsorship of the Mennonite Mental Health Service, has an administrator who is an ordained clergyman. This center won the top Mental Hospital Achievement Award of the American Psychiatric Association in 1968.

New roles for clergy and congregants in community organization and consumer participation are also developing. The establishment and maintenance of a community mental health program requires planning, organization, funding, interpretation to and support by the public, support by legislative bodies, and an ongoing dialogue between the provider (sources of funding and professional staff) and the consumer (user of therapeutic and preventive services).

Clergy have filled prominent roles as officers and board members of mental health agencies and associations; most boards include one or more clergymen. Their skills in community organization have been put to good use. They are also in key positions to channel information from the public into the mental health agency and vice versa. They are strong molders of public opinion. Congregants also are represented on boards and are in a position to provide a link between the agency and the community.

Recent federal legislation has given a prominent role to the consumer or user of health services. P.L. 89-749, Comprehensive Health Planning and Public Health Services Amendments of 1966, requires that a state health-planning council be established and that a majority of the membership shall consist of representatives of consumers of health services. Other health-related legislation also provides for consumer advisory representation and participation in shaping the services to be made available to individuals and their communities. Members of various governmental advisory councils are usually appointed by governing officials or bodies. Advisory councils are also often established to assist regional and local planning and service agencies.

Through membership on planning and other types of public and private councils and boards, clergy and congregants can fill key roles in shaping and furthering community mental health programs.

NIMH Regional Offices Mental Health Programs

Region I, Boston, Mass.
  John F. Kennedy Fed. Bldg.
  Boston, Mass. 02203
  Phone: Code 617, 223-6824
  Office Hours: 8:30-5:00
  States
  Conn., Maine, Mass., N.H.,
  R.I., Vermont

Region II, New York, N.Y.
  26 Federal Plaza
  New York, N.Y. 10007
  Phone: Code 212, 264-2567
  Office Hours: 8:30-5:00
  States
  Del., N.J., N.Y., Pa.

Region III, Charlottesville, Va.
220 7th Street, N.E.
Charlottesville, Va. 22001
Phone: Code 703, 296-5171
Office Hours: 8:00-4:30
States
D.C., Ky., Md., Puerto Rico,
N.C., Virgin Is., Va., W. Va.

Region V, Chicago, Ill.
New P.O. Bldg.
433 W. Van Buren Street
Chicago, Ill. 60607
Phone: Code 312, 353-5226
Office Hours: 8:15-4:45
States
Ind., Ill., Mich., Ohio, Wis.

Region VII, Dallas, Texas
1114 Commerce Street
Dallas, Texas 75202
Phone: Code 214, RI 9-3426
Office Hours: 8:15-4:45
States
Ark., La., N.M., Okla., Texas

Region IX, San Francisco, Calif.
Federal Office Building
50 Fulton Street
San Francisco, Calif. 94102
Phone: Code 415, 556-2215
Office Hours: 8:00-4:30
States
Alaska, Ariz., Calif., Guam, Hawaii, Nev.,
Oreg., Wash., Am. Samoa, Wake Island

Region IV, Atlanta, Ga.
50 7th St., N.E.
Atlanta, Ga. 30323
Phone: Code 404, 526-5231
Office Hours: 8:00-4:30
States
Ala., Fla., Ga., Miss., S.C.,
Tenn.

Region VI, Kansas City, Mo.
601 East 12th Street
Kansas City, Mo. 64106
Phone: Code 816, FR 4-3791
Office Hours: 8:00-4:45
States
Iowa, Minn., Kansas, Mo.,
Neb., N. Dak., S. Dak.

Region VIII, Denver, Colo.
Federal Off. Building
19th and Stout Streets
Denver, Colorado 80202
Phone: Code 303, 297-3177
Office Hours: 8:00-4:30
States
Colorado, Idaho, Montana,
Utah, Wyoming

34.
RESEARCH ON THE CHURCHES AND MENTAL HEALTH

John M. Vayhinger, B.D., Ph.D.

Professor of Psychology and Pastoral Care, Anderson School of Theology, Anderson, Indiana

The goal of research is to discover information through the application of scientific procedures. [1] Research begins with a problem or a question, to which techniques of observation or experimentation may be applied. The question may be either *intellectual* (simply the desire to know) or *practical* (for the sake of being able to do something better or more efficiently). Both would seem appropriate reasons for research on the churches and mental health.

Research into the role of the churches in community mental health may take two directions: (1) statistical studies, empirically designed, as to the effect of religious beliefs, membership in, and activities of, members of churches and synagogues, and (2) the effects of training in mental health principles and skills of clergymen and laymen in improving their effectiveness in religious behavior.

Since research in confined to "empirical" data mainly, any person carrying out research in this area of experience should keep in mind that scientific research "can tell us nothing about the truth, validity or usefulness of religious phenomena" though it may be very enlightening and useful when it furnishes "information about the conditions under which people become religious . . . the influence of religion itself on other dimensions of behavior: . . . and the empirical laws governing religious behavior may help in understanding phenomena which are the causes of undue concern." [2]

Gordon W. Allport reinforces this concept when he writes that "neither religion nor mental health . . . (is) a discrete, measurable thing. Each has many factors and aspects, and one

---

[1] Claire Selltiz, *et al., Research Methods in Social Relations* (New York: Henry Holt, 1959), pp. 1-5.

[2] Michael Argyle, *Religious Behavior* (London: Routledge & Kegan Paul, 1958), p. 3.

must . . . talk about things that are related to essential trust or things related to constructiveness of personality or other concepts into which one might be able to break down religion and mental health." [3]

The goals of research on mental health and the churches are, necessarily, at this point vague and indistinct, mainly because of problems of definition and instrumentation. Many studies (some to be referred to later) have relative and situational validity, but few useful instruments or techniques have as yet been developed.

One report summarizes general goals which are usable for direction:

> The objectives are stated as: (a) increasing the awareness of mental health professionals and the clergy of their common interest in helping people, (b) exploring the ways in which these groups could assist each other in dealing with mental health problems in the community, and (c) stimulating the development of a framework and atmosphere of cooperation which would lead to an ongoing program of education and communication.[4]

A major research direction, then, might well develop a design for research in which pastors would develop psychological skills in aiding parishioners in the development of wholesome (as part of "holy"), mature personalities, and in assisting persons in developing meaning and purpose in their lives, as well as dealing therapeutically with specific emotional problems which cripple their functioning. The design would include pastors' application of psychological insights in the total range of pastoral activities and relationships, with training presented through classroom teaching; clinical supervised involvement; and personal counseling and/or psychotherapy to prepare them better to use their theology, the formal rituals of the church,

---

[3] Academy of Religion and Mental Health, *Research in Religion and Health,* 1961 (Bronx: Fordham University Press, 1963), p. 32.

[4] J. Levy and R. K. McNickle, eds., *A Clinical Approach to the Problems of Pastoral Care* (Boulder, Colo.: Western Interstate Commission for Higher Education, 1964), VII, 250.

and the religious faith they transmit in living relationship with their people.

In the definition of any goals, the theologian and clergyman must have first priority in formulation. The psychiatrist's preoccupation, arising out of his professional training, with the causes and treatment of mental illness;[5] the preoccupation of the psychologist with purely human behavior, its description, and development; the preoccupation of the sociologist and cultural anthropologist with the forms and development of society, make these mental health professionals unable to define the function of the churchman, though their professions may well be of immense importance in providing information when the clergyman thinks through his unique and necessary role as pastor to persons.

Practically, psychologists, statisticians, and the rest of the research teams must be involved in these research designs, but the hidden goals and preconceptions of both clergymen and psychologically trained professionals must be articulated before the designs are firmed up. In designing studies, for instance, which would seek information on how the religious community could produce a "healing fellowship" for the emotionally disturbed and a healthy atmosphere for developing children, the scientist and the religious leader must both keep in mind that "that which frees man from moral evil is not mental health but God's grace." [6]

This section will select individual research designs which seem productive of further research implementation. Selected studies are suggestive of the general field and not representative of all potential research.

1. The National Institute of Mental Health, Religion and Mental Health Project

Three related projects were funded by the NIMH in 1956 to construct extended programs for training seminarians in mental health skills. The programs were designed to bring

[5] Richard V. McCann, *The Churches and Mental Health* (New York: Basic Books, 1962), pp. 133-34.

[6] Robert G. Gassert, S.J., and Bernard H. Hall, *Psychiatry and Religious Faith* (New York: Viking Press, 1964), p. 43.

together professionals and materials in psychiatry, psychology, anthropology, medicine, and sociology and to relate mental health information to the theology of the three major religious traditions.[7] The Academy of Religion and Mental Health, under the direction of the Rev. George Christian Anderson, as well as the churches involved, encouraged this research in improving their pastors' and rabbis' mental health skills. The curriculum developed from this project is available to other seminaries.

A. Loyola University of Chicago was chosen to develop a curriculum for Roman Catholic priests. Under Father Vincent Herr's direction, materials were prepared to cover (1) the psychodynamics of normal personality and religious development; (2) "small group" dynamics, particularly of the family; (3) problems of personality maladjustments; and (4) interviewing and counseling techniques. At the time of the first report by Kobler, *et al.*,[8] some 740 seminarians and priests from five seminaries had participated.

B. Rabbi I. Fred Hollander of Yeshiva University directed the development of training courses for rabbis. Not simply to enlarge the clergyman's store of secular knowledge, he declared, and not to train him to be a professional psychotherapist, the project was rather "to prepare him for the practical task of fulfilling his pastoral responsibilities more effectively"[9] and to increase his ability to help people who turn to him *as rabbi* in their time of need. This ability is an integral part of his function as a minister of religion. While religion's importance to people transcends its healing value, Rabbi Hollander reports, its primary value lies in defining every phase of man's existence—describing his condition, his place in the universe, and his role in the shape of things.

C. Hans Hofmann at Harvard Divinity School probed the literature of the world for instances of "religious behavior."

[7] Vincent Herr, S.J.: "Mental Health Training in Catholic Seminaries," *Journal of Religion and Health,* January 1962, p. 127.

[8] F. J. Kobler, *et al.,* "Loyola University NIMH Project on Religion and Mental Health," *Pastoral Psychology,* Feb., 1959, pp. 44-46.

[9] I. F. Hollander, "Mental Health Teaching Materials for the Clergy," *Journal of Religion and Health,* April, 1962, p. 273.

Believing that "the rigidity inherent in orthodox theories has fostered mere shadow boxing between ministers and psychiatrists," [10] he deliberately sought human experiences which (1) in their complexity were "true to life," (2) that touched directly on problems of religion and mental health, and (3) that encouraged free and independent thinking. He encouraged experimentation with pastoral counseling which went beyond an exclusively supportive conception of counseling, because he believed that "within the Christian tradition in which we believe [is] the power of the Holy Spirit to regenerate people through merciful judgment and a loving challenge to grow through suffering into a stronger and deeper faith." [11] So he suggests that studying historical expressions of religious awareness should suggest challenging hypotheses which may well find that mental health in the Western "Christian" civilization cannot be achieved without the confrontation of the religious aspects of culture.

2. Institutional Experiments in the Churches and Mental Health.

A. *The Church of the Savior, Washington, D.C.*

In addition to orthodox research design composed of experimental controls and statistical analyses of the data, an experiment set in a parish began when the Rev. Gordon Cosby returned from military service to involve a small band of persons (seventy) in total commitment to a disciples' way of existence. Intense training prepares the members for "ministry" in a mission group, each strengthened by spiritual discipline. "Dayspring" is a 175-acre farm in Maryland within which a retreat was built as a renewal center for the emotionally and spiritually disturbed. The Rev. Joseph W. Knowles describes the goals of the Renewal Center Mission as (1) developing the Life Renewal Center through small "groups," (2) giving attention to the use of present structures to focus the whole life of the church as a healing community, (3) developing a program of supervised clinical pastoral education for theological students, and (4) maintaining a Residential Center halfway house for twenty men

[10] Hans Hofmann, *Religion and Mental Health* (New York: Harper, 1961, p. xv.

[11] *Ibid.*, p. 15.

and women who have been previously hospitalized for mental illness.[12] Continuous therapy groups are carried on as well as individual counseling and Adult Intereducational Mission Groups, which combine sensitivity training and the development of skills in writing devotional materials. Research with such churches as this will clarify the general role of religious institutions in developing the mental health of involved persons.

B. *The American Foundation of Religion and Psychiatry.*

This center for the training of clergymen in counseling was founded in 1937 as the Religio-Psychiatric Clinic in Marble Collegiate Church in New York City. Its purpose, as described by Paul E. Johnson is to enable persons to "come for psychiatric help where ethical and religious values will not be overlooked and religion thus aids in the acceptance of psychiatry." In this center, clergymen and psychiatrists are joined in treating psychiatric patients and in carrying on research on healing on cooperative levels by the two professions.[13]

C. *Pastoral Counselors Serving in Psychiatric Settings.*

In 1964, the federal government, in developing comprehensive community mental health centers, insisted that:

> equally important is the fact that in addition to family physicians, the clergymen of the community, . . . and the other guardians of mental health can consult with the center's professional staff to aid in serving individual patients about whom they share concern, as well as to add to their own knowledge of mental health and mental illness through formal and informal classes and meetings presented by the center's staff.[14]

Centers already involving clergymen are as widespread as Fort Logan Mental Health Center in Denver, Colorado, where ministers serve as therapists in the Division of Alcoholism, and the Oaklawn Psychiatric Center, Elkhart, Indiana, and San

[12] Elizabeth O'Connor, *Call to Commitment* (New York: Harper, 1963), pp. 135-44. Also, personal communications with the Rev. Joseph W. Knowles, 70CT68.

[13] Samuel Z. Klausner, *Psychology and Religion* (New York: Free Press, 1964), pp. 197-255.

[14] Comprehensive Community Mental Health Centers, U.S. Dept of Health, Education and Welfare. Service Publ. No. 1137. April, 1964 p. 6.

Mateo County Mental Health Center in the San Francisco area which employ pastoral counselors.

D. *Cooperation Among Psychiatric Personnel and Clergymen in Referral and Training.*

While Becker probably overstates the case when he claims that the unity of aim of religion and psychology has brought clergymen and psychiatrists "into a contiguity and interlacing of work where it is no longer possible to distinguish neatly the psychologist from his religious colleague," [15] it certainly seems accurate to say that cooperation is increasing, and many persons turn to clergymen for help in emotional disorders. One study revealed that in a representative sample of 2,460 Americans, persons with more education were more likely to seek out a clergyman, and regular church members were also quicker to call on their pastor (54 percent among Protestants and 52 percent among Catholics). [16] The same study indicated that church attenders were somewhat happier and had less worry, and infrequent church-goers and non-goers had a more negative evaluation of their overall adjustment. In short, "low church attendance is associated with a somewhat higher level of distress in the general adjustment measures, a more negative self-percept, less happiness on the job, and strikingly less marital happiness." [17]

E. *Influence of Religious Observance in the Home.*

Fein reports that home observance of religious customs contributes to the mental health of persons involved,

> Normal adult samples can be distinguished from mentally and emotionally sick adult samples better than 99 out of 100 times on the basis of the degree of religious observance in the childhood home . . . the degree of religious observance in the childhood home plays an important role in the maintenance of mental health. [18]

[15] Russell J. Becker, "Links Between Psychology and Religion," *American Psychologist,* 1958, 13, pp. 566-68.

[16] Gerald Gurin, *Americans View Their Mental Health,* p. 335.

[17] *Ibid.,* p. 245.

[18] Leah G. Fein, "Religious Observance and Mental Health," a note, *Journal of Pastoral Care,* 1958, 12, p. 101.

RESEARCH ON THE CHURCHES AND MENTAL HEALTH

3. Suggestions for Research.

Here follows a necessarily limited set of suggestions for further study:

A. *Training of clergymen and laity in mental health skills:*
Seminary training in special psychological skills for pastoral counseling, leader-trainer roles in groups

Identification of pastoral and psychological roles of hospital chaplains

In comprehensive community mental health centers, the role of the staff pastoral counselor, and his acceptance by staff colleagues and the community

Referral patterns among clergymen to and from psychiatric clinics

Changing attitudes toward the clergyman's role and image, by clergymen and laymen

B. *Pastoral situations, effects of congregational structures on persons:*
Effects of denominational environment on mental health of constituents, including administrative structure and religious beliefs of the group

The place of the church as a therapeutic and redemptive community (a) on the mental health of the members, (b) as a referral source for post-treatment patients, (c) for persons under situational stress—e.g. vocational, family, bereavement, etc.

Effects of "group belongingness" in religious experiences in worship services. Therapeutic and disruptive effects of small groups, study, Bible, prayer, etc.

"Binding" and "supporting" effects of congregational sharing in times of grief, life decisions, depressions, etc.

C. *Types of individual religious experiences:*
Ernest Bruder: "the distinctive contribution of religion is to present God adequately to the patient, using the basic, common resources of religion";[19] compare this with simple psychological counseling care of patients.

[19] Quoted in O. Hobart Mowrer, *Morality and Mental Health* (Chicago: Rand-McNally, 1967), p. 351.

COMMUNITY MENTAL HEALTH

The effects of the Judeo-Christian faith, as expressed through church and synagogue, as a moderating factor in the competitiveness of American culture

Effects of individual religious sacred acts—e.g. confession and penance, conversation, communion in times of crisis, etc.

The "integrating effects" of personal religious experience, especially in adolescent years

Theoretically, there should be no competition between professionals trained in religion and those trained in psychotherapy, for "the hitherto existing chasm between religion and psychology is somewhat unusual because . . . both concern themselves with human nature and behavior."[20] But there is a vital need for valid research into the effects of religious belief and behavior on individual and group mental health.

Much needed is research beyond that already completed which will develop guidelines for improving the church's many roles in community health—from meeting the existential crises of being human and belonging to social groups and facing anxiety and dread, to providing more efficiently the "learning atmosphere" for a religious style-of-life. The assumption is made in most congregations that these things do happen. Now we have the tools for investigating and improving these mental health functions of churches.

Even though we recognize and accept the fact that some of the most crucial problems of man and his existence (e.g., death, destiny, and divinity) are all but unresearchable by science's tools, it is still true that well conceived and developed research designs are useful in the area of mental health and religion. They will sharpen the expectations by mental health professionals of the church's proper role in community mental health, and they will increase the church's and synagogue's already considerable functional role in the mental health of the community.

[20] Herman Feifel in "Symposium on Relationships between Religion and Mental Health: Introductory Remarks," *American Psychologist,* 1958, 13: 565, 566.

RESEARCH ON THE CHURCHES AND MENTAL HEALTH

For additional reading

Academy of Religion and Mental Health. *Religion in the Developing Personality*. New York: New York University Press, 1960.

―――― *Religion, Science and Mental Health*. New York University Press, 1959.

―――― *Research in Religion and Health*. Bronx: Fordham University Press, 1963.

Argyle, Michael. *Religious Behavior*. New York. Free Press, 1959.

Eister, Allan W. "Empirical Research on Religion and Society," *Review of Religious Research,* Spring, 1965, pp. 125-30.

Godin, A., S.J. "Belonging to a Church: What does It Mean Psychologically?" *Scientific Study of Religion,* Spring, 1964.

Gurin, Gerald, Veroff, Joseph, and Feld, Sheli. *Americans View Their Mental Health: A Nationwide Interview Survey*. New York: Basic Books, 1960.

Herr, Vincent V., S.J. "The Loyola National Institute of Mental Health Seminary Project: A Progress Report," *American Catholic Sociological Review,* Winter, 1960, pp. 331-36.

Hofmann, Hans., ed. *The Ministry and Mental Health*. New York: Association Press, 1960.

Hollander, I. Fred: "Mental Health Teaching Materials for the Clergy," *Journal of Religion and Health,* April, 1962, pp. 273-82.

Klausner, Samuel Z. *Psychiatry and Religion*. New York: Free Press, 1964.

Kobler, F. J.; Webb, N. J.; Herr, V. V.; Devlin, W. J. "Loyola University NIMH Project on Religion and Mental Health, Report on Research Procedures," *Pastoral Psychology,* Feb., 1959, pp. 44-46.

Lenski, Gerhard: *The Religious Factor*. Garden City, N.Y.: Doubleday, 1961.

Lowe, C. Marshall and Braaten, Roger O. "Differences in Religious Attitudes in Mental Illness," *Journal of Scientific Study of Religion,* Fall, 1966 5(3), pp. 433-45.

McCann, Richard V. *The Churches and Mental Health*. New York: Basic Books, 1962.

Menges, Robert J. and Dittes, James E. *Psychological Studies of Clergymen, Abstracts of Research*. Camden, N.J.: Thomas Nelson, 1965.

Srole, Leo; Langner, Thomas S.; Michael, Stanley T.; Opler, Marvin K.; Rennie, Thomas A. C. *Mental Health in the Metropolis: The Midtown Manhattan Study*. New York: McGraw-Hill, 1962.

35.
THE CHURCHES AND FAMILY COUNSELING AROUND THE WORLD

Matti Joensuu, B.D., D.D.
Executive Secretary, Board of Family Questions, The Lutheran Church of Finland, Helsinki, Finland[*]

It is not necessary here to stress the important role played by relationships in the family; these affect the mental health of every member of the family unit, and especially that of the children and adolescents in their development into adulthood.

When reading the Old and New Testament, one finds that right from the start, both in Judaism and early Christianity, family relationships were considered extremely important, and this is also seen in the work of the churches throughout the centuries. But looking at church history from this aspect, we also find things which have not caused a mentally healthy development. There have been—and still exist—rigid religious movements with such strict rules that they provoke neuroses in human development. We also have examples of how missionaries have taken along with them the Western family pattern, identifying it with Christianity, and treating people living in polygamous societies mainly with church discipline. However, without a doubt, we can affirm that much wisdom about healthy family life, based on the experience of generations, has been taught by the churches.

A new development in the work of the churches started with the emphasis on family counseling. Some pioneering efforts were made before the first World War. Professor David Mace has been the most well-known and creative person in this field. After World War II, in the forties and early fifties, some churches in Europe set up specialized family counseling services, especially in England, Finland, Germany, and Switzerland.

*Former Secretary of the Department of Cooperation of Men and Women in Church, Family, and Society of the World Council of Churches.

FAMILY COUNSELING AROUND THE WORLD

Now such services exist in many countries, and they have developed according to various patterns.

In England there is the National Marriage Guidance Council, a secular organization, in which the church and church workers are playing an important role; this means that the work is in fact on an ecumenical basis. In England there is also a parallel Roman Catholic Advisory Council. Both of these organizations use lay workers to do marriage guidance. The basic idea is that there are many people who are mentally mature and have genuine personal gifts which can be used in helping people who have difficulties in their family life. The decisive thing is to find the right kind of persons to work as volunteers. The Marriage Guidance Council in England has developed a thorough system of selection of candidates for this kind of work. The selecting process lasts several days, and includes personal interviews, psychological tests, and observations of how the candidates behave in group situations. The volunteers accepted for the work receive continuous training for two years from professional people. They usually work under the continuing supervision of professional family counselors, and a number of psychiatrists, psychologists, and lawyers are available as consultants.

This same pattern has been developed in Australia and New Zealand. To give some examples, there are at present 117 local family counseling centers functioning in Great Britain, conducting 61,000 interviews a year. In Australia in 1967, 41 marriage guidance centers were functioning; they conducted 33,000 interviews.

Quite a different pattern has developed in Germany, where the churches sponsor family counseling services staffed mainly by physicians and psychologists. At present there are 60 family counseling centers run by the Protestant churches, and 37 of them include child-guidance clinics. The Roman Catholic Church in Germany has 80 counseling centers; it has a plan to recruit a great number of volunteers to serve in this field.

In Finland, the family counseling work was started by clergymen, but from the beginning was in cooperation with psychiatrists and lawyers. All the workers are professional people. Approximately one half of them are clergymen and the others psychologists or social workers. All of them undergo at least one year's clinical training in family counseling before becoming accredited counselors. Each center also has a consultant psychiatrist and lawyer. There are 10 family counseling centers in Finland, with full-time workers (total population, 4,700,000). In 1966 approximately 12,000 interviews were conducted in these clinics.

The churches which have been active in family counseling have produced family education programs on a large scale; often these are based on clinical experience obtained in the counseling centers, thus relating to real problems in the lives of people. Clinicians are continuously being used on radio and television, in journals and newspapers, as resource people dealing with family problems.

The World Council of Churches, in Geneva, has a special secretariat dealing with family questions. This secretariat has concentrated on helping the churches in the developing countries in the field of family counseling and family education. As industrialization spreads to these countries the structures of society undergo rapid change, and the pattern of the extended family system breaks up, causing much greater confusion in family life than occurred in societies in the West, where industrialization developed over a much longer period.

During the last few years, the World Council of Churches has gained wide experience in leadership-training seminars of four weeks' duration, usually called Basic Training Seminars. The program of these seminars has been directed by qualified persons able to win support and cooperation from the religious and secular leaders of the region concerned. The Caribbean area is an outstanding example of this kind of program. In 1964, Professor and Mrs. David Mace conducted the first seminar in Antigua Island. Since then there have been three seminars of four weeks in this region every year.

These four-week seminars constitute a kind of "demonstration," at which participants can experience what kind of contribution modern family counseling and family education can make. It is very often a strong and positive personal experience for the participants. It is a process in which the local persons, together with the foreign experts, try to understand what the real problems in their region are. The experts probably have less insight but more objective understanding. During the four weeks they try to develop in the seminar participants as much understanding as possible, based on scientific knowledge.

These seminars seem to cause a rethinking process in the societies concerned and bring about pioneering actions—especially in the field of family education. It is necessary to emphasize that these seminars do not produce experts, but some of the participants at these Basic Training Seminars decide to continue and obtain further supervised training afterwards.

A similar process has begun in Africa, where, by the end of 1968, four regional Basic Training Seminars had taken place. A plan has been evolved whereby four further regional seminars per year will be held during the next five years. In 1969, a seminar of the same kind will be held in the South Pacific, which again will probably be followed by a long-term plan.

But the Basic Training Seminars are not the only means of action adopted. It is planned to find at least a few well-chosen persons from the regions concerned for training as experts in family life. This training entails proper clinical training in counseling. At present, three persons from the Caribbean area and two from Africa are undergoing clinical training in the United States. When these people go back to their home region in the near future, the aim is for them to begin working full-time and, little by little, they will train other persons in the necessary counseling skills. My personal conviction is that these people must have a chance to create a clinical setting and work personally with individual cases, although, in a pioneering situation they must, in addition, do educational work and act as organizers.

One very difficult problem in international work is the lack of deep understanding of cultural differences. Family life in Africa or Asia is very different from what it is in the West.

If Western specialists, however well trained and clever they may be, go to the other continents and give family education, there is a big danger that they may advocate Western ideas, with all their mistakes. Their teaching is not well received, because it is not relevant and helpful in quite different circumstances. It is true that when societies become industralized and the ties of the extended family break down, there are certain common problems everywhere. The personal relationship of husband and wife plays an increasingly important role in all cultures. At this point the understanding and contribution of Western experts are relevant everywhere. But, in spite of that, there are many differences which it really takes years for a Westerner to learn to know and understand.

If, however, we have a counseling center with skilled personnel of the same culture, the possibilities are much more favorable. The counselor does not teach; he investigates, together with his clients, and tries to understand what the problems really are. The counseling center is like a laboratory, in which people are learning intensively year after year and gaining a deeper understanding of the problems of the people and their family life in that particular culture. The counseling center can also train new counselors and influence the attitude of the whole clergy and others dealing with the people, so that an ordinary pastor in the congregation is better able to understand the problems of the people and to help them. It is possible to observe this kind of development already in some countries.

There are many problems to solve when we are sending persons for clinical training overseas, in a cultural situation different from the one they come from and to which they should return. But in many cases this is the only possibility. However, there are some training centers functioning in developing countries. Three years ago, the Rev. Albert Dalton, an Episcopal minister from the United States, fully qualified as a chaplain supervisor, began to work at an Episcopal hospital in Manila, Philippines, giving one year's clinical training to the local pastors. In 1966 in Singapore, Dr. Gunnar Theilman, also from the United States, created the Churches' Counselling Centre, which has already been very influential for short-term training. Now it is giving long-term clinical training to local persons. At Ibadan, Nigeria, negotiations are proceeding to build up a clinical training system in family counseling in relation with the University of Ibadan. It also seems possible that in the near future such training may begin in French-speaking West Africa. In some years' time, it appears possible that there will also be a center able to give clinical training in Tanzania, East Africa. Thus, the policy of the World Council of Churches is to try to help the churches in developing countries to acquire their own experts as soon as possible and become independent of foreign experts. I am sure that, after some years, these people will have a deep understanding which will prove of value to the West.

It is impossible to describe the vast and many-sided family educational work that the churches are carrying on around the world. Many denominations have their own experts preparing programs and helping the local congregations in family education. A rather new and widespread lay movement is the Christian Family Movement of the Roman Catholic Church, a group movement which has recently become increasingly ecumenical, including members from other churches. It has rapidly spread to all the continents.

It seems that the churches everywhere are now eager to start special services in the field of family counseling and family education. I would like to emphasize that the most important thing in starting such work is to have at least *one* well-trained person to lead the work. Many are interested in the use of volunteers and lay people. But it will be successful only if the volunteers are led and supervised by well-trained professional people. Training may cost money, but experiments made without thorough consideration of what has already been learned are much too costly in human terms.

In this short article, I have not referred at all to developments in North America. But I would like to mention that many qualified experts from America have given significant help in various kinds of training programs all around the world. The small secretariat of the World Council of Churches can do something only in cooperation with skilled people around the world, who kindly offer their time, energy, and financial help to this worldwide task.

Most of the specialized functions in the field of family counseling and family education have been organized on an ecumenical basis, especially in the developing countries. Experience has shown that it is relevant and natural for the churches to work together in this field. Whatever the doctrinal differences of the churches may be, the need to help people and families is a common concern. Practical experience in this work also builds up a common basis and increases mutual understanding. Even in some regions where there does not yet exist an official ecumenical body, the churches work together effectively in this field, and this naturally increases ecumenical cooperation as a whole. The Roman Catholic Church and the Protestant churches increasingly are working together on family problems. It has been recognized on both sides that in the near future common arrangements will be necessary, especially in the regional training programs. But cooperation does not exist just between the churches; in every place where there are developed counseling services, these work in close contact with the social, medical, and mental health agencies of the district concerned.

For additional reading

Report on the All-Africa Seminar on the Christian Home and Family Life. Geneva: World Council of Churches, 1963.

Sex, Love and Marriage in the Caribbean. Geneva: World Council of Churches, 1965.

For the Family, Report of a World Consultation, St. Cergue, Switzerland, 1967. Geneva, World Council of Churches, 1968.

CONCLUSION: INTO ACTION

Howard J. Clinebell, Jr., B.D., Ph.D.

A pastor asks, "How can I get *my* congregation involved in the community mental health action in our town?" A priest muses to himself, "The new mental health program in this area is good for making referrals; it helps make my work more effective. But, what should my people and I be doing to help *it*? How do we get started?" Or a rabbi poses this problem, "With all the other things I have to do, how can I guide my congregation to gear into local mental health strategy?" These are the kinds of practical questions which some clergymen are raising. Those who are not raising them, should be!

Effective involvement of churches and temples in community mental health requires *strategies* for moving into action. This concluding statement will suggest some key aspects of such strategies, designed for leaders of local congregations, denominational and ecumenical leaders, those in the mental health field, and seminary teachers and administrators. Each of these groups has a significant role in releasing the untapped mental health potentialities of religious organizations.

A Strategy for the Local Church or Temple

Those congregations which have come alive to their mental health mission typically seem to have gone through certain general stages:[1]

1. *Someone who is a "self-starter" and is concerned about mental health took the initiative.* In some cases this was the minister; in others, a layman. Frequently the layman was in a mental health profession. In other cases, the person who took the initiative was one who had had painful personal or family problems and who knew firsthand the crucial importance of mental health work. Experience shows that if a layman takes

[1] These strategy steps are adapted from "An Alcoholism Strategy for the Congregation" in H. J. Clinebell, Jr.'s *Understanding and Counseling the Alcoholic* (Nashville: Abingdon Press, rev. ed., 1968).

the initiative, it is essential for him to discuss the matter with his clergyman and get his support. Most ministers are pleased when a lay person shows an interest in helping to begin a mental health emphasis. The main point here is that in most successful projects, *one or two concerned persons* started the ball rolling.

2. *A mental health action team (or task force) was recruited and trained.* In some congregations, an existing committee was used. In others, an ad hoc action team was established to be responsible for only this one area. In such cases, it has proved to be important to keep the lines of communication open between the mental health action team and related committees— e.g., social action, education, and pastoral care committees. The main point here is that *some one group* should have particular responsibility for developing a congregation's mental health ministry. Otherwise, this issue often falls between various groups in the church.

The mental health task force should include mental health professionals from within the congregation; if none are available in the membership, they can be recruited from the community as advisors to the group. Other members should be drawn from the youth and adults in the congregation who are both relatively mentally healthy and socially concerned. It is essential that they care about people.

The training of the task force should include experiences which will awaken a lively interest in making their church relevant to the community mental health movement. Helping them catch the excitement of this social revolution and the challenging of the opportunity with which it confronts the churches, serve to enliven and motivate a task force. It is useful to have them read chapters from a book such as this one (see the list at the end of this statement), and then discuss it in the group. The theological nature of the mental and spiritual health ministry should be emphasized in terms of the particular beliefs and traditions of the group. Mental health should be seen as a *central* concern for the servant church in the last third of the twentieth century.

CONCLUSION: INTO ACTION

3. *The unmet needs of the local situation were discovered and priorities established.* Before the task force decides on a course of action, it should explore the unmet mental health needs in these areas within the congregation and in the community: (a) To what extent are persons of all ages finding "life . . . in all its fullness" within the groups of the church? (b) What are the *needs* in the community for better treatment and more effective prevention? (c) What *resources* in the church and community can be developed or mobilized to meet these needs? If a task force is perceptive, they will discover a sea of unmet needs and unrealized human potential, both in the church and in the community at large.

Two priority lists should be drawn up—one of unmet mental health needs within the church and the other of unmet needs in the community. The final decision about what is needed most should be made by the entire task force. By so doing they are determining the starting point of the action project(s) in which they will then be more likely to participate with enthusiasm. If a small clique chooses the goals, it should not be surprising that involvement by the other members will be less than wholehearted. By using the democratic process in decision-making, the mental health task force practices principles of good mental health in its own operations. Ideally, two projects should be chosen as a starting point for action—one focusing within the church and one in the community. It is important to maintain this inreach and outreach balance in mental health action projects.

4. *Plans were formulated by the task force concerning procedures in the project or projects that have been chosen.* Plans should be cleared with the responsible parties and boards within the church administration. Brainstorming can be useful in drawing out the creative ideas of all group members. Alternatives approaches should be discussed and compared by the task force and a decision reached concerning realistic implementation of the projects chosen.

5. *Action was initiated involving the task force and others whom they recruited and trained.* After work is begun, it is

helpful to have regular evaluation and feedback sessions which may lead to scrapping the particular project or revising it radically.

It is desirable to maintain a four-pronged perspective in planning action for mental health, as represented by this diagram:

	Prevention	*Treatment*
Within the Church:	A. Releasing the growth potentialities of persons through the church program.	B. Ministering to the troubled through pastoral care and counseling.
In the Community:	C. Social action to help make a more person-fulfilling society. Mental health education in community organizations.	D. Working with other groups for better treatment facilities in the community and encouraging the participation of clergymen and laymen in their programs.

In order to convey a clearer picture of the many kinds of mental health action projects which churches can initiate, here are some examples in these four areas.

A. The following are some ways in which churches can *develop preventive projects within their own programs.* (Many of these have been implemented by congregations.) Churches can—

Develop a child-study group for parents to help them meet the needs of their children and themselves more fully.

Set up growth groups for persons in particular age categories most vulnerable to stress.

Develop a church school teachers training series in methods of creating a positive climate in the classroom.

Establish a marital enrichment group for the recently married.

Encourage the worship committee to examine the weekly

worship service to find innovative ways of making them more need-satisfying.

Train leaders of ongoing groups in leadership methods which increase the self-esteem and involvement of group members.

Organize a couples' retreat on the theme, "Deepening Your Marriage."

Change the church school curriculum to increase an emphasis on factors which make for good interpersonal relationships.

B. *The therapeutic or healing aspect of the church's mental health role within its own fellowship* has to do with the topics discussed in Part II of this book. Here are some illustrative projects from local churches which suggest the wide range of possibilities. A church can—

Recruit and train a pastoral care team of sensitive laymen to work with the clergyman in supporting persons going through difficulties in living.

Encourage their minister to take clinical training or obtain in-service consultation regarding his counseling to sharpen his tools in helping the burdened.

Employ a minister of "pastoral care and group life" to give special leadership to the growth/healing needs of the congregation.

Set up a systematic program to acquaint the congregation with available church and community resources for helping persons with problems in living. This includes speakers from A.A. and the local mental health clinic, and a regular statement in the church's newsletter regarding the availability of counseling by the minister.

Form a group for alienated youth or school drop-outs, co-led by a social worker, for example, or the minister and one of the youth.

Organize a counseling group for couples with troubled marriages, led, for instance, by a clinically trained chaplain from the community hospital.

Organize a group for parents of handicapped children, perhaps led by a psychologist or other qualified member of the congregation.

C. *Fostering primary, secondary, and tertiary prevention in the community is a major responsibility of a congregation* that aims at being a creative leaven in society. Churches can participate in prevention through—

A social action project to encourage businessmen in the congregation and community to employ recovered alcoholics, ex-prisoners, and former mental patients (tertiary prevention).

A similar program to encourage employment of ghetto-trapped youth (primary prevention).

A church-sponsored halfway house which is available to recovering psychiatric patients, alcoholics, or ex-prisoners (tertiary prevention).

A project aimed at improving teachers' salaries in ghetto schools (primary prevention).

Cooperating with a community project to encourage recognition and early treatment of alcoholism and other emotional problems (secondary prevention).

A systematic effort to encourage church members to become involved in the activities of the local Mental Health Association, a citizens group which engages in educational and preventive programs on all three levels.

The leaders of a church giving recognition to National Mental Health Week in its newspaper publicity, indicating the stake of the church in the mental health of its community.

A social action project aimed at mobilizing congregational support of legislation to provide more opportunities for job training for the poor (primary prevention).

A project aimed at increasing the role of governmental agencies in disseminating family planning information in the United States, and in developing countries through the U.N. (primary prevention). Interrupting the population "time bomb" is tremendously important for the mental health of our planet! The same is true of the efforts to protect the physical environment from pollution.

CONCLUSION: INTO ACTION

A project aimed at reducing international threats and conflict, with special emphasis on the effective control of nuclear and biological weapons (primary prevention).

Prevention in the community is a broad goal. The above are only suggestive of hundreds of projects which contribute to the three levels of prevention.

D. Here are some illustrations of how churches can cooperate with other groups in working for *more adequate treatment resources in their communities, states, nation, and the world.* Churches can—

Encourage the minister and laymen to become involved in citizens advisory committees of community mental health services (such services are beamed toward both prevention and treatment).

Become familiar with the state's master plan for community mental health development and help both to publicize and to encourage moral support of its implementation.

Cooperate in providing volunteers for working in mental hospitals, hospitals for the mentally retarded, and in community mental health programs.

Work through the council of churches or denominational headquarters to establish a religiously oriented counseling center serving the community.

Encourage the appointment of clinically trained pastoral specialists to the staff of the community mental health service in their catchment area.

Work for the involvement of clinically trained clergymen at the state planning and programming level in the mental health program.

Convene regular meetings of interested social workers, psychologists, psychiatrists, and pastoral counselors to discuss the spiritual dimension of mental health, and cooperation between clergymen and mental health professionals.

Write, telegraph, phone, and make personal calls on legislators and governmental officials (national, state, and local) encouraging them to support legislation designed to provide humane treatment for alcoholics, drug addicts, the mentally ill, and the mentally retarded.

Work to replace the inferior mental health treatment now available to the poor, with effective programs of therapy.

Organize a service to help families of those in prison.

Cooperate with other churches and temples in working to attract competent psychotherapists to the community and to set up community-sponsored outpatient services, alcoholic treatment programs, psychiatric wards in general hospitals, day hospitals, night hospitals, halfway facilities, and crisis clinics.

Organize the congregation to provide foster family care for recovering psychiatric patients.

Sponsor homeless alcoholics and released prisoners, much as churches sponsor refugees from war-devastated countries.

Provide a telephone referral service if none exists in the community, or a crisis counseling phone service staffed by trained laymen backed up by professionals.

Back research into the most effective treatment methods for different types of psychological and sociological pathology.

Sponsor research into the spiritual component in the causation and treatment of personality problems and emotional illnesses.

Give moral support and encourage government support of mental health activities around the world, through the World Health Organization of the United Nations. As an island of affluence in a widespread sea of crippling poverty (in many nations), our country should share its resources and mental health personnel.

A part of the job of a church or temple is to develop its own strategy for reaching out redemptively into the community, using its own unique style of mental health ministry. In all four areas of mental health opportunity, a local church needs to develop *its own* master plan and strategy, to make *its own* unique contribution to the meeting of human needs. In developing their own thrust, churches should emphasize the *spiritual* dimension of mental health—the role of values, meanings, ultimate commitments, and relationship with God. This is the *unique* contribution of churches and temples! Thus churches become the "salt of the earth," distributing their constructive influence through the lifestream of society to lift the quality of relationships and of the total human environment.

A Strategy for Denominational and Ecumenical Leaders

Leaders of denominations and of councils of churches are in a strategic position to encourage local churches to join the mental health revolution. Such leaders can set the tone of involvement in this vital social movement. Furthermore, they can develop pilot projects and cooperative counseling programs representing the united witness of a group of churches or denominations. Each denomination should develop its own mental health *master plan,* including objectives toward which it desires to move, ways of implementing the plan, and a timetable of target dates for achieving certain goals. By top-level planning and strategy, denominations and ecumenical bodies can exert a significant influence on the mental health movement and on the involvement of their churches.

Rather than discuss the matter in the abstract, let me report or some relevant developments:

The National Council of Churches has taken the initiative in establishing an Inter-faith Task Force on the Churches and Mental Health charged with responsibility for stimulating interest in this field among the denominational and faith groups.

In several parts of the country, the United Methodist denomination has established programs employing pastoral counseling specialists to counsel with clergymen and their families, and to provide in-service training for parish ministers.

The National Council of Churches now has a staff person whose responsibilities include the churches and mental health thrust.

The American Baptists in Southern California, as a denomination, sponsor a pastoral counseling service.

The council of churches in one California city sponsors a pastoral counseling center, open to the community.

Several denominations have programs through which they encourage their clergymen to engage in continuing education, including clinical training and study in the area of counseling.

One denomination has a program for encouraging local congregations and groups of churches to establish telephone crisis counseling centers.

Several interfaith professional groups have collaborated in setting unified standards for clergymen who serve on the staffs of community mental health centers. (See Kempson's second paper.)

Most denominational and ecumenical groups have only scratched the surface of their opportunity in the area of community mental health. Of particular importance is their opportunity to exert constructive influence on the state and federal levels of mental health planning, with respect to matters such as the inclusion of qualified clergymen on mental health center teams. The more broadly representative and interfaith a group is, the more influence it will have on those responsible for mental health decision-making on state and national levels. Denominational curriculum writers, editors, and policy makers are in a strategic position to increase the emphasis on positive mental health in their teaching materials.

A Strategy for Mental Health Leaders

Leaders of local, state, and federal mental health programs need a strategy for releasing the untapped mental health potential in the churches and temples of their areas of responsibility. Such a strategy should be formulated in close collaboration with an interfaith advisory committee composed of clergymen representing the major denominations.

Here are some of the things which mental health leaders have been instrumental in doing to mobilize the resources of organized religion for mental health:

In at least three states, they have included clergy specialists on the state level of mental health programming.

In numerous places, they have involved clergymen in advisory and planning committees.

As reported in Hathorne's paper, a number of community mental health programs are using clergymen in part-time staff positions.

Consultation for clergymen and various continuing education programs in pastoral counseling are being made available through staff members of community mental health services.

Community mental health centers have provided psychiatric consultants for several pastoral counseling services.

Mental health professionals in various places have served as resource persons and trainers of pastoral care teams in their churches. Others have taken the initiative in arousing their clergymen and congregations to involvement in the mental health movement.

Leaders in mental health face two areas in which a great deal needs to be done in relation to churches. One is in helping churches utilize more fully their broad educational programs and their contacts with parents of young, impressionable children. The other is that of assisting clergymen and mental health services in making more referrals to each other, particularly of persons who are in the early stages of the need for help.

A Strategy for Seminary Teachers and Administrators

Seminary teachers and leaders are responsible for training tomorrow's ministers, priests, and rabbis. As such they are in *the* most strategic position to influence the long-range mental health effectiveness of churches and temples. To utilize this opportunity, seminary teachers themselves need clinical training and growth group experiences to release *their* potential as creative teachers.

Here are some of the things that seminaries could do to increase their mental health impact:

The curriculum should be evaluated and revised in terms of its effectiveness in preparing the students to become facilitators of growth and healing, and of the development of therapeutic-redemptive communities in the churches.

Every student should be strongly encouraged, if not required, to take at least one quarter of clinical pastoral training and another in an urban internship; the first would help equip him to be a change agent in individual relationship, and the second would help equip him to be a change agent in organizations, structures, and social systems.

Pastoral and prophetic skills (using educational, counseling, and political models of change) should be taught in an integrated or at least interrelated way.

Field education should be offered in *lively* churches (which have a mental health program) where small groups of students are supervised by experienced clergymen (with faculty status) who are themselves instruments of growth and healing.

Seminary education should include supervised opportunities to learn how to work with other professions in serving troubled persons.

Throughout their seminary years, students and their wives should be members of growth groups led by qualified persons and designed to accelerate their personal, marital, and professional maturation.

The emphasis through the entire seminary experience should be on integrating traditional theological and contemporary psychosocial insights about man and society, and applying them to the needs of the present situation.

The skills of effective *communication* and *relating* should be at the center of the entire process of theological education, since these skills make it possible to bring the riches of a religious tradition to life in the experience of persons.

Financial plans should be developed to allow theological students who need personal or marital therapy to obtain as much of this as is required to release their potential for ministry.

Adequate support of student aid programs in seminaries would remove the exhausting pressure on many students to earn a living and support a family, often at considerable sacrifice of significant learning.

Seminary faculties could contribute to the mental health of students, and through them to the mental health ministries of the churches, by enhancing their own ministry to students, creating a climate of healing concern in the seminary community, and resolving devisive in-fighting that, when it exists, reduces the seminary's effectiveness in producing mentally healthy and spiritually mature ministers.

The other teachers who are making a major contribution to educating person-centered ministers are the *chaplain supervisors* staffing the two hundred and fifty plus clinical pastoral education centers (accredited by the Association of Clinical Pastoral Education). Clinical training is, by far, the most important single learning experience available to a seminary student or minister. Nothing in theological education can equal the opportunities in clinical training for becoming open to self, for confrontation with human needs, for intensive supervision, peer teaching, and interprofessional experience. The mental health effectiveness of religious organizations could be increased dramatically in a generation if all seminarians were required to have this experience.

Throughout this volume, there has been repeated evidence of the enthusiasm of the authors for the church's many and significant roles in the community mental health movement. Few qualities are more vital than *enlightened* enthusiasm in those who plan to move into effective action. This is a quality which is particularly relevant to the involvement of religiously dedicated persons in mental health programs, for the root of "enthusiasm" is two Greek words meaning "in" and "God." When a man of religious awarenesses pours his life into the person-serving work of mental health, he experiences enthusiasm in this profound sense. He discovers that he is in God and that God is in the relationships by which persons grow, are healed, and find life in all its fullness.

For additional reading

(The editor is indebted to E. Mansell Pattison for this list.)

Clinebell, H. J., Jr. *Mental Health Through Christian Community*. Nashville: Abingdon Press, 1965.

Dittes, J. E. *The Church in the Way*. New York: Scribner's, 1967.

Knight, J. A. and Davis, W.E. *Manual for the Comprehensive Community Mental Health Clinic*. Springfield, Ill.: C. C. Thomas, 1964.

McCann, R. V. *The Churches and Mental Health*. New York: Basic Books, 1962.

Maves, P. B., ed. *The Church and Mental Health*. New York: Scribner's, 1953.

Pattison, E. M., ed. *Clinical Psychiatry and Religion*. Boston: Little Brown, 1969.

Seifert, Harvey and Clinebell, H. J., Jr. *Personal Growth and Social Change*. Philadelphia: Westminster Press, 1969.

Westberg, G. E. and Draper, E. *Community Psychiatry and the Clergyman*. Springfield, Ill.: C. C. Thomas, 1966.

PB 07624
5-07

RENEWALS: 691-4574

DATE DUE

DEC 0 5			
APR 19			
NOV 0 8			
DEC 4			
SEP 20			
OCT 0 5			

Demco, Inc. 38-293